Basic Floral Design

Basic Floral Design

BY
REDBOOK FLORIST SERVICES
EDUCATIONAL ADVISORY COMMITTEE

Paragould, Arkansas

Basic Floral Design

© 1991 by
Redbook Florist Services
Paragould, Arkansas

All Rights Reserved.

No portion of this book may be
reproduced without the written
consent of the publisher.

The brand names listed in this manual were selected by the Redbook Florist Services Educational Advisory Committee as examples which are suitable for the uses described. However, it is recognized that there are other brands of similar products available which may be equal to or better than the brand names included in the text, depending upon the designer's specific manner of use and personal preference.

Library of Congress Catalog Card Number: 91-61275

Printed by:
Printers and Publishers, Inc.
Leachville, Arkansas

Acknowledgments

*R*edbook Florist Services gives special thanks to each committee member who participated in the creation and development of this comprehensive floral training manual.

Frances Porterfield	Topeka, Kansas
Terry Lanker, M.Ed., RMC	Wooster, OH
Christy Holstead-Klink, M.S.	Nazareth, PA
Carl Lemanski, AIFD, RMC	Berkeley Heights, NJ
Pamela Linder, AIFD, RMC	Harbor City, CA
Harvey Pope, AIFD	Toronto, Ontario, Canada
Frankie Shelton, AAF, AIFD, PFCI, RMC	Houston, TX
Janice Stutters, AIFD, RMC	Littleton, CO
Gary Wells, AIFD, RMC	Kentwood, MI

Contents

Acknowledgments	v
Preface	xi
List of Illustrations	xiii
List of Tables	xxiii
Introduction	1
Chapter 1 - Elements and Principles of Floral Design	**5**
Evolution of Floral Design	5
Principles of Floral Design	6
Elements of Floral Design	11
Chapter 2 - Supplies and Containers	**23**
Basic Supplies	23
Containers	34
Chapter 3 - Design Mechanics	**41**
Fresh Flower Arrangement Mechanics	41
Silk Flower Arrangement Mechanics	51
Corsage Mechanics	53
How to Make a Bow	65
Paint and Dye Techniques	69
Special Decoration Mechanics	72
Chapter 4 - Fresh Flower Care and Handling	**79**
Flower Structures, Classifications, and Names	79
Basic Flower Needs	82

Basic Floral Design

Chapter 5 - Flowers to Wear	109
Conditioning	109
Boutonnieres	110
Corsages	113
Prom and Party Flowers to Wear and Carry	123
Hair Flowers	129
Stem Finishes	132
Accessories and Accents for Flowers to Wear	134
Finishing Dips and Sprays	135
Packaging	135
Wearing Flowers Appropriately	136
Chapter 6 - Designing Basic Arrangements	141
Pre-design Considerations	142
Constructing Line-mass Designs	145
Designing Profitably	162
Chapter 7 - Novelty Designs	171
Kitten	172
Poodle	174
Treasure Chest	176
Ice Cream Soda	177
Birthday Cake	178
Love Bug	179
Clown	180
Rabbit	181
Bird	183
Chapter 8 - Designing with Permanent Flowers	189
Types of Silk Flowers	189
Care and Handling of Silk Flowers	191
Preparing Silk Flowers	193
Types of Dried and Preserved Flowers	194
Care and Handling of Preserved Flowers	197
Glossary	217
Appendices	
Care and Handling Charts and Checklists	229
Dried and Preserved Materials	237
Bibliography	249
Index	253

Preface

Basic Floral Design has been prepared for the person who seeks knowledge and professionalism as a floral designer.

Flower shops sell balloons, gourmet foods, greeting cards, and plant maintenance contracts and often combine services with related or neighboring businesses. Still, the majority of business does not come from the sale of unique products and services, but from the sale of basic floral arrangements. Therefore, it is imperative that professional floral designers be skilled in all areas of design. Thus, basic design styles must be mastered first.

Basic Floral Design is intended to provide retail florists with a comprehensive pool of information regarding basic floral design. The essential tasks of conditioning flowers and preparing floral mechanics are discussed in detail. Principles and elements of design are explained and fundamental guidelines for creating floral arrangements of all kinds are provided. Step-by-step instructions for constructing basic arrangements, as well as, novelty designs, silk and dried arrangements, and flowers to wear are also included.

Many of the methods and ideas discussed in this book were drawn from the combined experiences of a select group of retail florists and floral industry professionals. Any information drawn from other sources has been noted.

Basic Floral Design was written for use as a reference and training manual and will prove beneficial to floral designers at all levels of expertise. The concise text contains step-by-step instructions for creating basic floral designs, and illustrations reinforce the design techniques described.

List of Illustrations

Figure			Page
1.1	Proportioning Stem Length to Container Size		
	1.1a		9
	1.1b		9
1.2	The Five Lines of Floral Design		
	1.2a	Vertical	11
	1.2b	Horizontal	11
	1.2c	Curvilinear	12
	1.2d	Zigzag	12
	1.2e	Diagonal	12
1.3	Geometric Forms of Western Style Design		
	1.3a	Symmetrical Triangle	13
	1.3b	Asymmetrical Triangle	13
	1.3c	Crescent	13
	1.3d	Vertical	13
	1.3e	Horizontal	14
	1.3f	Oval	14
	1.3g	Hogarth Curve	14
2.1	Cylinders		
	2.1a	Cylinder Vase	35
	2.1b	Tall Vase	35
2.2	Bowls and Trays		
	2.2a	Low Bowl	35
	2.2b	Oblong Suiban	35
2.3	Urns		
	2.3a	Urn	35
	2.3b	Classic Low Urn	35
2.4	Miscellaneous Containers		
	2.4a	Shallow Compote	36
	2.4b	Weed Pot	36

List of Illustrations

3.1	Waterproof Tape Application		
	3.1a	Side View Step 2	43
	3.1b	Top View Step 2	43
	3.1c	Side View Step 4	43
	3.1d	Top View Step 4	43
3.2	Pan Melt Gluing		
	3.2a	Step 1	44
	3.2b	Step 2	44
3.3	Anchor Pin		
	3.3a		45
	3.3b	Step 1	45
	3.3c	Step 2	45
	3.3d	Step 3	45
3.4	Securing a Foam Filled Liner in a Basket		
	3.4a	Step 2	46
	3.4b	Step 3	46
	3.4c	Step 4	46
3.5	Raising a Liner in a Basket		
	3.5a	Step 3	46
	3.5b	Step 4	46
3.6	Mylar Lining		
	3.6a	Step 1	47
	3.6b	Step 1	47
	3.6c	Step 2	47
	3.6d	Step 3	47
3.7	Tape Grid		
	3.7a	Top View Step 2	49
	3.7b	Side View Step 2	49
3.8	Lacing Greens for a Grid		
	3.8a	Step 1	49
	3.8b	Step 2	50
	3.8c	Step 3	50
	3.8d	Steps 4 - 7	50
	3.8e	Step 8	50
3.9	Basic Parts of the Flower		55
3.10	Pierce Wiring Method		
	3.10a	Step 2	55
	3.10b	Steps 3 & 4	55
3.11	Insertion Wiring Method		55
3.12	Hook Wiring Method		
	3.12a	Steps 2 & 3	56
	3.12b	Step 4	56
3.13	Wrap-around (Clutch) Wiring Method		56
3.14	Stitch Wiring Method		
	3.14a	Step 2	56
	3.14b	Step 4	57

List of Illustrations

3.15	Hairpin Wiring Method		
	3.15a	Step 2	57
	3.15b	Step 4	57
3.16	Splinting Wiring Method		57
3.17	Taping a Wired Stem		
	3.17a	Step 1	58
	3.17b	Step 2	58
	3.17c	Step 3	58
3.18	Wiring Cattleya, Cymbidium, and Japhet Orchids		
	3.18a	Step 2	59
	3.18b	Step 3	59
3.19	Wiring Dendrobium and Cypripedium (Lady Slipper) Orchids		
	3.19a	Step 1	60
	3.19b	Step 2	60
3.20	Wiring Phalaenopsis Orchids		
	3.20a	Step 3	60
	3.20b	Step 6	60
3.21	Wiring Gardenias		
	3.21a	Step 2	61
	3.21b	Step 3	61
	3.21c	Step 4	61
3.22	Creating a Gardenia Collar		
	3.22a	Step 2	61
	3.22b	Step 3	62
	3.22c	Step 3	62
3.23	Wiring Camellias		
	3.23a	Step 1	62
	3.23b	Step 2	62
3.24	Gluing Delicate Blossoms		
	3.24a	Step 2	63
	3.24b	Step 3	63
3.25	Feathering Carnations		
	3.25a	Step 1	63
	3.25b	Step 1	63
	3.25c	Step 2	64
	3.25d	Step 2	64
	3.25e	Step 2	64
	3.25f	Step 3	64
	3.25g	Step 4	64
	3.25h	Step 5	65
	3.25i	Step 6	65
3.26	Wiring Silks		
	3.26a	Wiring Silk Flowers	65
	3.26b	Wiring Silk Foliage	65

List of Illustrations

3.27	Making a Bow with a Center Loop	
	3.27a Step 1	66
	3.27b Step 1	66
	3.27c Step 2	66
	3.27d Step 3	66
	3.27e Step 4	66
	3.27f Step 5	66
	3.27g Step 5	67
	3.27h Step 6	67
3.28	Making a Bow without a Center Loop	
	3.28a Step 1	67
	3.28b Step 2	67
	3.28c Step 3	67
	3.28d Step 4	68
	3.28e Step 5	68
3.29	Making Tail Tuck-ins	
	3.29a Angle Cut	69
	3.29b *W* Cut	69
3.30	Anchoring Balloons	
	3.30a Step 3	72
	3.30b Step 3	72
3.31	Plush Animals	
	3.31a Protecting Plush Animals with Cellophane	73
	3.31b Anchoring Plush Animals with Hyacinth Sticks	73
3.32	Candles	
	3.32a Tapered Candles	75
	3.32b Cutting Tapered Candles	75
3.33	Securing Pillar Candles	75
4.1	Basic Anatomy of a Complete Flower	80
4.2	Arrangement of Structural Parts of a Hybrid Lily	80
4.3	Arrangement of Structural Parts of an Anthurium	80
5.1	Single Flower Boutonniere	111
5.2	Constructing a Three Flower Boutonniere	
	5.2a Step 2	111
	5.2b Step 3	111
	5.2c Step 4	111
	5.2d Step 6	112
5.3	Constructing a Garden Style Boutonniere	
	5.3a Steps 2 & 3	112
	5.3b Step 4	112
5.4	Single Flower Corsage	114

List of Illustrations

5.5		Constructing a Double Flower Corsage	
	5.5a	Step 2	114
	5.5b	Step 3	115
	5.5c	Step 5	115
5.6		Constructing a Triangular Corsage	
	5.6a	Step 2	116
	5.6b	Step 3	116
	5.6c	Step 5	116
	5.6d	Step 6	116
	5.6e	Step 8	116
5.7		Constructing a Crescent Corsage	
	5.7a	Step 3	117
	5.7b	Step 4	117
	5.7c	Step 5	117
	5.7d	Step 6	117
5.8		Creating a Glamellia	
	5.8a	Step 1	118
	5.8b	Step 1	118
	5.8c	Step 1	118
	5.8d	Step 1	118
	5.8e	Step 1	118
	5.8f	Steps 6 - 9	120
	5.8g	Step 10	120
	5.8h	Step 12	120
5.9		Creating a Larger Glamellia	
	5.9a	Step 2	121
	5.9b	Step 4	121
	5.9c	Step 4	121
	5.9d	Step 5	121
	5.9e	Step 7	121
5.10		Creating a Nestled Boutonniere	123
5.11		Constructing a Wristlet	
	5.11a	Step 2	124
	5.11b	Step 3	125
5.12		Football Mum Corsage	127
5.13		Making a Football Mum Collar with Foliage	
	5.13a	Step 1	128
	5.13b	Step 3	128
5.14		Constructing a Barrette Hairpiece	
	5.14a	Step 1	130
	5.14b	Step 2	130
	5.14c	Step 5	130
5.15		Haircomb	130
5.16		Floral Wreath	131
5.17		Floral Headband	131
5.18		Profile Hairpiece	131
5.19		Curled Stem Finish	132

xvii

List of Illustrations

5.20	Garden Stem Finish	132
5.21	Creating a Ribbon-wrapped Stem Finish	
	5.21a Step 1	133
	5.21b Step 2	133
	5.21c Step 3	133
5.22	Corsage Placement	136
5.23	Boutonniere Placement	136
6.1	Placement, Proportion, and Scoring	
	6.1a Free-standing Arrangement	145
	6.1b Asymmetrical Triangle	145
	6.1c Symmetrical Triangle	146
6.2	Constructing a Small Symmetrical Triangle	
	6.2a Steps 3 & 4	147
	6.2b Steps 3 & 5	147
	6.2c Steps 6 & 7	147
	6.2d Step 8	147
6.3	Constructing a Medium Symmetrical Triangle	
	6.3a Steps 3 & 4	148
	6.3b Step 6	148
	6.3c Step 7	148
6.4	Constructing a Large Symmetrical Triangle	
	6.4a Step 2	150
	6.4b Steps 5 - 8	150
	6.4c Step 17	151
	6.4d Step 18	151
	6.4e Fan Shape	151
6.5	Symmetrical Balance	152
6.6	Symmetrical Imbalance	152
6.7	Asymmetrical Balance	152
6.8	Constructing an Asymmetrical Triangle	
	6.8a Steps 2 & 3	153
	6.8b Step 4	153
	6.8c Steps 4 - 6	153
	6.8d Step 7	153
6.9	Constructing a Pointed Oval	
	6.9a Step 2	154
	6.9b Steps 4 & 5 Top View	154
	6.9c Steps 4 & 5 Side View	154
	6.9d Steps 6 & 7	154
6.10	Constructing a Vertical Arrangement	
	6.10a Step 2	155
	6.10b Steps 4 & 5	155
6.11	Constructing a Horizontal Arrangement	
	6.11a Step 2	156
	6.11b Step 6	157

List of Illustrations

6.12		Preparing Vases for Rose Arrangements	
	6.12a	Using Chicken Wire	157
	6.12b	Using a Grid	158
	6.12c	Using Floral Foam	158
	6.12d	Using Shredded Styrofoam	158
6.13		One Dozen Roses	159
6.14		Free-standing Oval	159
6.15		Rose Bowl	160
6.16		Bud Vase	
	6.16a	With One to Four Flowers	161
	6.16b	With Mixed Flowers	161
	6.16c	With a Rose	162
7.1		Constructing a Kitten	
	7.1a	Step 2	172
	7.1b	Step 3	172
	7.1c	Steps 4 - 6	172
	7.1d	Step 7	173
	7.1e	Step 8	173
	7.1f	Step 8	173
	7.1g	Step 9	173
	7.1h	Step 9	173
	7.1i	Step 13	174
	7.1j	Step 14	174
7.2		Constructing a Poodle	
	7.2a	Steps 1 & 2	174
	7.2b	Step 3	174
	7.2c	Steps 4 & 5	175
	7.2d	Step 6	175
	7.2e	Step 8	175
	7.2f	Steps 10 - 12	175
	7.2g	Step 14	175
	7.2h	Step 16	176
7.3		Constructing a Treasure Chest	
	7.3a	Steps 1 & 2	176
	7.3b	Step 3	176
	7.3c	Step 4	177
	7.3d	Steps 5 & 6	177
	7.3e	Step 8	177
7.4		Constructing an Ice Cream Soda	
	7.4a	Step 1	177
	7.4b	Steps 2 & 3	178
	7.4c	Steps 4 & 5	178

List of Illustrations

7.5	Constructing a Birthday Cake		
	7.5a	Step 1	178
	7.5b	Step 2	179
	7.5c	Step 3	179
	7.5d	Step 4	179
7.6	Constructing a Love Bug		
	7.6a	Step 1	180
	7.6b	Step 1	180
	7.6c	Step 3	180
	7.6d	Steps 4 - 6	180
7.7	Constructing a Clown		
	7.7a	Step 2	181
	7.7b	Step 2	181
	7.7c	Step 6	181
	7.7d	Step 7	181
7.8	Constructing a Rabbit		
	7.8a	Step 1	182
	7.8b	Step 3	182
	7.8c	Step 4	182
	7.8d	Step 6	182
	7.8e	Steps 7 - 9	183
	7.8f	Step 11	183
7.9	Constructing a Bird		
	7.9a	Step 1	183
	7.9b	Step 4	184
	7.9c	Steps 6 & 7	184
	7.9d	Steps 8 - 10	184
8.1	Positioning Silk Flowers in Natural Progression		194
8.2	Flower Types		
	8.2a	Line	199
	8.2b	Mass	199
	8.2c	Form	199
	8.2d	Filler	200
8.3	Multiple Flowering Stems		204
8.4	Flowering Silk Bush		204
8.5	Pre-formed Silk Bouquet		204
8.6	Wreaths		
	8.6a	Grapevine	205
	8.6b	Straw	206
	8.6c	Foam	206
	8.6d	Wire	206
8.7	Wreath Mechanics		
	8.7a		207
	8.7b		207
8.8	Trimming a Basket with Silk		208

List of Illustrations

8.9		Constructing a Silk Tree	
	8.9a	Steps 2 & 3	209
	8.9b	Step 4	209
	8.9c	Step 4	209
	8.9d	Steps 5 - 7	210
	8.9e	Step 8	210
8.10		Constructing a Silk Dish Garden	211

List of Tables

Table		Page
1.	Geometric Form of Western Design	12
2.	Ribbon Specifications	34
3.	Basic Flower Needs	83
4.	Causes of Early Flower Deterioration	84
5.	Hygiene Checklist	99
6.	Popular Boutonniere Flowers and Foliage	110
7.	Popular Corsage Flowers and Foliage	113

Introduction

Flowers have been used to decorate the homes of men and women from all cultures and social classes for many centuries. Artists, poets, musicians, writers, and sculptors have been inspired to create form, color, and muse by the sight and scent of flowers. The use of garlands, boughs, and cut flowers for decoration or for fragrance was, perhaps, the start of floral design.

Creating a floral design was previously seen only as an interpretation of one's inner sight. The elements and principles of Japanese ikebana and the mass of historical European designs were combined to create western design. Western design incorporates a combination of line and mass to create geometric styles of floral design.

American designers have carefully blended European and Eastern forms of floral design to create forms and shapes that are visually comfortable to consumers. The design styles most requested by consumers are the round centerpieces and the one-sided triangle. Therefore, it is not surprising that these are the design styles most often used for wire service promotions.

Floral shop product quality, mechanical stability, and adherence to the principles of design are directly related to the ability to sell and deliver an arrangement. Physical balance, along with secure mechanics, adds stability. Transitions between flower patterns create a rhythm which encourages the eye to explore the entire design. Color, texture, and a unique container add interest. The ability to effectively blend all of these points enhances one's reputation as a florist.

Purchasing long-lasting flowers is important to consumers. To make flowers last as long as possible, floral designers must practice proper care and handling before, during, and after design. Consumers must also be educated by florists so that proper care and handling of floral products continues after the sale.

Basic Floral Design

Variety is also important to consumers. Therefore, floral designers must be able to design basic styles with a creative flair. The challenge of floral design is to make every corsage, centerpiece, or silk arrangement an original. A conscious effort to make each design unique will help the designer grow artistically.

The most important factor in developing floral design skill is practice. While books and pictures provide volumes of ideas and information on how to design, one cannot become an accomplished designer quickly. It takes time to develop any talent, especially an artistic one. Dedication to the artistic craft of designing, combined with a love of flowers, is the necessary ingredient to insure success in this field.

Elements and Principles of Floral Design

Chapter 1

*F*loral design is based on fundamental principles which are applicable to all forms of art. These principles are the guidelines for constructing flower arrangements, and no floral artist can excel until he has mastered them. Floral design involves the organization of materials to fit a need or purpose. A designer can start with beautiful fresh flowers, different types of foliage, and a lovely container, but if the end result does not appear organized or appropriate for the floral need, it will not provide satisfaction to the designer or customer. The principles and elements of floral design provide a means for organizing floral materials into pleasing arrangements. Floral designers at all levels of expertise must use these guidelines routinely, whether they are creating very simple, basic styles or very detailed, contemporary bouquets. With practice, the use of these principles and elements becomes instinctive. Until then, these guidelines should be followed with a conscious effort toward applying each "rule" properly in every design created.

Evolution of Floral Design

Floral design has evolved through the centuries from two major influences, Japanese ikebana and European mass design. Ikebana is the Japanese word meaning "flower arranging." It is an ancient design style with emphasis on the artistic statement of oriental philosophies, linking the three concepts of spiritual truth, material substance, and human creativity. Ikebana arrangements are characterized by strong lines and the sparse use of floral materials.

European mass design is sometimes referred to as the continental style. Paintings and books provide a valuable record of this type of design. Seventeenth and eighteenth century

Basic Floral Design

paintings by Dutch and Flemish masters provide many examples of these large, showy arrangements composed of flowers of many varieties and colors.

The blending of ikebana and continental styles evolved into western style design. By combining the strong lines of ikebana style with the tight masses of the continental style, geometric shapes were created and labelled line-mass designs. The standard symmetrical triangle, horizontal centerpiece, and crescent arrangements are examples of this style.

Principles of Floral Design

The principles of floral design are a set of guidelines which help create pleasing and saleable designs. They assist the designer throughout the process of selecting plant material, visualizing a design, and constructing it. Each of these principles should be practiced with skill and sensitivity when designing an arrangement. Because many of the principles are interdependent, the improper use of one principle can result in the failure of the design. The principles of floral design are the foundation from which florists work to create beautiful designs. The following principles should be evident in every basic design created.

Radiation

Radiation is used in floral design to create the illusion that all of the stems are emerging from a single point in the arrangement. To understand radiation, imagine a daisy. The center of the daisy is round, and all of the flower petals radiate from the center circle. Radiation in design repeats the natural radiation of plant material as it emerges from the soil. To achieve good radiation in design, it is important not to crisscross stems. As a beginning designer, it is also helpful to begin each design with the central stem placements and work outward in all directions.

Repetition

Repetition is the repeated use of a flower or form in an arrangement. This is achieved, for example, by placing pink carnations from the perimeter to the center of a design. Repetition strengthens an arrangement and helps unify its components. Too much repetition can be boring, so it is important to incorporate variety into designs. To insure that an arrangement is interesting, use at lease three different kinds of plant material repeatedly throughout the design.

Notes

Elements and Principles of Floral Design

Notes

Balance

Because it serves a dual function, balance is one of the most vital principles of floral design. Flower arrangements must be both physically and visually balanced. Physical balance is crucial to insure the stability of an arrangement. Physical balance involves an equilibrium between two weights. Imagine a scale with a bar of gold on one side and a bar of aluminum on the other side. The scale would be imbalanced. Equal balance is achieved by placing bars of equal weight on each side. Similarly, an arrangement can be physically balanced by placing equal amounts of flowers on each side of the container. Assuming that the design is proportionate to the container, such a design will be balanced.

Visual balance is important if a design is to be pleasing to the eye. An arrangement that does not look balanced is disturbing to the eye. The effect is comparable to looking at a crooked picture on a wall. It is difficult to concentrate on the subject in the picture without straightening it first.

Floral designs may be symmetrically or asymmetrically balanced. Symmetrically-balanced designs have equal amounts of material on each side of the central vertical axis, and often one side of the arrangement is the mirror image of the other.

Asymmetrical balance is achieved through the uneven distribution of material on each side of the central vertical axis. If a long, wispy branch is extended horizontally out one side of an arrangement, a short, heavy pod might be used on the other side to provide asymmetrical balance. Additionally, the point of radiation in a design may be positioned off center to provide asymmetry.

Balance is also affected by the visual weight of materials used in a design. As a general rule, large or bulky materials should be used at the base of the design, while small or delicate materials should be used at the perimeter. Colors also appear to have different weights. Dark colors typically appear heavier than light ones. Thus, an arrangement of pink roses and red carnations should be designed with the roses at the perimeter and the carnations near the base.

Depth

To achieve a three-dimensional appearance, depth is essential in floral designs. A design with good depth is interesting and will hold the viewer's attention for an extended period of time. When positioning the preliminary lines of a design, height and width are established first. Depth is then added by extending

Basic Floral Design

flowers several inches over the front edge of the container. This helps prevent the design from having a flat appearance. Additional depth is added by positioning flowers on varying planes within the outline of the design. Short-stemmed flowers placed deep in the center of an arrangement give it maximum depth.

Rhythm

Rhythm in floral design creates the sensation of motion. A design with good rhythm keeps the eyes actively involved while viewing it. Often, the visual movement or rhythm of a design leads the eyes to the focal point. Rhythm may be repetitive or variable. Repetitive rhythm is reminiscent of the consistent beat of a drum. Flowers are placed at regular intervals from base to tip to create an obvious, strong rhythm. Variable rhythm is more subtle and may be achieved through transitions from light to dark colors, smooth to rough textures, or small to large sizes. Whichever method is used to achieve rhythm, it should be used to create a single visual movement throughout the design.

Focal Area

A focal area is the heart of most western style designs. This area, which may also be referred to as a focal point, point of interest, or emphasis, is most often located just above the lip of the container in the center of the design. The focal area has the largest flowers in the deepest colors and the greatest concentration. This gives the focal area dominance in the arrangement. When creating an area of dominance, it is important to avoid stopping the flow of rhythm. Therefore, the colors and flowers used in the focal point must blend with those at the perimeter of the design for a smooth transition. Not all flower arrangements have a focal area. The traditional round centerpiece, for example, contains equal flower placements on all sides with no single area of emphasis. Many contemporary styles of design feature several points of interest rather than a single focal area. Most traditional arrangements, however, are designed with a focal area created by an interesting accessory, exotic form flower, or striking color accent.

Transition

Transition is the gradual progression of plant material from the perimeter of the design to the focal area. Transition in floral design refers to movement from small flowers to large flowers.

Notes

Elements and Principles of Floral Design

Intermediate flowers are needed in a design to achieve transition between the mass flowers and the line flowers. Filler flowers are excellent for this purpose. A planned pattern of plant material is necessary to create a smooth transition. For example, standard chrysanthemums and miniature carnations mixed throughout an arrangement do not provide a pleasing transition. The design lacks a medium-sized flower to bridge the gap between the extreme sizes of the flowers. If two or three standard mums are used at the focal point, and snapdragons are added as an intermediate-sized flower, then the miniature carnations at the perimeter will not be dwarfed by the larger flowers. Thus, better transition is achieved.

Color transition is also important to the effectiveness of a design. An arrangement created with two competing colors and no transition color will lack a feeling of unity. For example, a Valentine's Day arrangement consisting of bright red carnations and pale pink roses would benefit from the addition of a medium pink flower to provide a color transition. Smooth transitions between flowers, colors, and areas of an arrangement help create a stronger feeling of rhythm.

Proportion

Proportion in design refers to the size of the flowers in relationship to each other, the flowers to the container, and the arrangement to its surroundings.

Rules of proportion evolved from Japanese ikebana. The length of the principal line in most Japanese arrangements is at least one and a half times the height or width of the container, whichever is greater **(see Figures 1.1a and 1.1b)**. This rule is also followed in most western style designs. Additionally, the height limitation is set at no more than two to two and a half times the height of the container. These limits should be exceeded only in some contemporary design styles or in unusual situations. This is a very important principle. Before beginning a design, consider where the arrangement is going to be placed. The size of the space should help to determine the container and arrangement size.

Once the container and arrangement size have been determined, flowers must be selected which are proportionate to the container and each other. Irises, carnations, and alstroemeria form a well-proportioned flower combination. All three of these flowers are similar in size and require approximately the same amount of space in an arrangement. In contrast, a combination of

Figure 1.1a Proportioning Stem Length to Container Size

Figure 1.1b Proportioning Stem Length to Container Size

birds of paradise and sweetheart roses is too extreme. The large birds of paradise would obviously not be proportionate to the petite roses.

Color proportion is also important in a well-designed arrangement. Since different shades and tints of a color carry different visual weights, they must be properly proportioned to maintain balance. As a general rule, the darkest color has the heaviest weight and, therefore, should be used in the smallest quantity and should be placed near the center of the design. Mid-value colors should be used in moderate amounts between the perimeter and focal point. The lightest colors should be used in the greatest quantity, primarily at the perimeter of the design. Partial blending of colors is necessary to unify an arrangement.

Harmony

Harmony in an arrangement is achieved by blending all of the elements in the design. The harmony of flowers and foliage as they are combined is of key importance. It is also important that plant materials be in harmony with the container and the chosen style of design. When contemplating harmonious flower combinations, consider the harmony of nature. The gracefully-textured leaves, beautifully curved lines, and exciting colors of individual flowers, have a natural harmony. Some flower combinations, such as tulips, daffodils, and irises, are naturally harmonious because they bloom and die together in nature.

Foliage should also be in harmony with flowers. The most harmonizing greenery is the foliage found on the flowers themselves. However, since additional foliage is often needed, a suitable type should be chosen. Foliage of different shades of green and gray can enhance a design.

Choosing the right container to maintain harmony is a matter of common sense. Garden-grown zinnias and daisies look very natural in an earthenware crock, while roses are more suited to a crystal vase. Harmony in an arrangement is not dictated by hard and fast rules. It is a process of selecting pleasing combinations of materials that are suitable for the design's intended purpose.

Unity

Unity in an arrangement is the look and feeling that the design is one singular unit. A unified arrangement is well balanced and proportioned. Its parts are harmonized to provide smooth transitions from the perimeter to the focal area. Flowers placed

Notes

Elements and Principles of Floral Design

deep within the arrangement add a strong three-dimensional effect. Repetition and radiation of flowers from a central point give the design a clear and interesting rhythm. Unity in an arrangement happens naturally when all of these principles are executed with precision.

Elements of Floral Design

Design elements are the physical characteristics of the plant materials used in a design. They are the "stones" that build the designs and determine the quality of a designer's work. There are four key elements of floral design. They are line, form, color, and texture. Regardless of how complicated a design may be, these elements will always be part of the arrangement.

Line

A line represents the visual movement between two points. Line gives an arrangement structure, shape, movement, excitement, height, width, and depth. There are five lines in western style design: vertical, horizontal, zigzag, curvilinear, and diagonal. All of these lines radiate from the point of centralization in an arrangement. Lines can be straight, curvilinear, continuous, interrupted, forceful, or passive. Lines can be achieved with linear materials or with a progression of flowers in stages from bud to full bloom or from light to dark.

Vertical Line *(Figure 1.2a)*

The vertical line is the strongest line in floral design. It is sometimes called the "masculine" line of design. Height and strength are achieved by the placement of this line. The structure of a design is established by placing the first flower (central vertical axis) into position. Repetition of this line with additional flowers placed in vertical positions creates a vertical line.

Horizontal Line *(Figure 1.2b)*

Horizontal lines, like the horizon, are very relaxed or passive and are usually near the surface of the container. This relaxed line works well in centerpieces and in designs to be placed on low tables. The horizontal centerpiece is often designed with a vertical line of opposition created by candles. This is one of the most popular design styles for Thanksgiving and Christmas.

Figure 1.2a The Five Lines of Floral Design - Vertical

Figure 1.2b The Five Lines of Floral Design - Horizontal

Curvilinear Line *(Figure 1.2c)*

The curvilinear line is the transitional line between the vertical and the horizontal lines. Materials may need to be manipulated or wired to achieve this line if flowers with strong, graceful lines are not available. The Hogarth Curve (Lazy-S design) is an example of this line.

Zigzag Line *(Figure 1.2d)*

The zigzag line is formed by placing flowers at different levels on each side of the central vertical axis. This line adds weight, visual movement, and value to the design. All of the stem placements used to create this line must be positioned so that they radiate from the central vertical axis.

Diagonal Line *(Figure 1.2e)*

Diagonal lines are used between the vertical and horizontal lines of a design and are placed at 45-degree angles. This dramatic line adds power to designs. It is also used to complete the outlines of several geometric styles of design.

Form

The three basic forms used in design are the circle, square, and triangle. These forms are either one-sided (often called flat-back designs) or free-standing (also called all-around designs). In western design the following geometric forms are used to form the outlines for one-sided and free-standing arrangements:

Figure 1.2c The Five Lines of Floral Design - Curvilinear

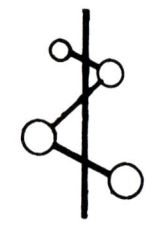

Figure 1.2d The Five Lines of Floral Design - Zigzag

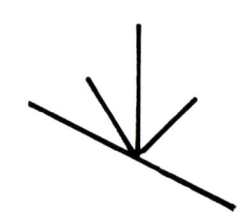

Figure 1.2e The Five Lines of Floral Design - Diagonal

TABLE 1

GEOMETRIC FORMS OF WESTERN DESIGN

	One-sided	Free-standing	Both Styles
Symmetrical triangle			X
Asymmetrical Triangle	X		
Crescent			X
Vertical	X		
Horizontal		X	
Oval			X
Hogarth Curve	X		

Elements and Principles of Floral Design

Floral design is a three-dimensional work of art. Circular, square, and triangular forms are used as the basis for design shapes. The circle or sphere can be seen everywhere in nature, and is, therefore, a very adaptable shape for floral designs. The square does not have the curves and movement needed to create visual impact; therefore, it is seldom used. The triangle, however, is used a great deal. When symmetry becomes boring or restrictive to the designer, asymmetry can be used within the same triangle form.

Symmetrical Triangle *(Figure 1.3a)*

A symmetrical triangle has flowers, branches, and greens designed in a triangular shape with equal weight on each side of the central vertical axis. This design is best suited for use in churches or other symmetrical surroundings. This design form is also popular for wire service specials because it is well accepted by the public and is easy to duplicate.

Asymmetrical Triangle *(Figure 1.3b)*

An asymmetrical triangle is designed with the central vertical axis positioned off center. This form gives the designer greater artistic freedom. It excites the eye and has good visual movement. Designers often favor this style when designing for special occasions.

Crescent *(Figure 1.3c)*

The crescent is a segment of a circle that resembles a new moon. The curved line of this arrangement gives it a graceful look, which is appealing to the eye. Although the shape of this arrangement is beautiful, the crescent is not very valuable commercially. However, when a crescent is superimposed inside another geometric form, it creates a visually-appealing line.

Vertical *(Figure 1.3d)*

The vertical arrangement is usually designed in a columnar container. It has strong vertical movement and may be quite tall. This style of design is excellent for placing in areas that require height in arrangements, but that are limited in width.

Horizontal *(Figure 1.3e on page 14)*

The horizontal form is low and near to the surface like the horizon, but with a rounded shape over the top. This prevents a

Figure 1.3a Geometric Forms of Western Style Design - Symmetrical Triangle

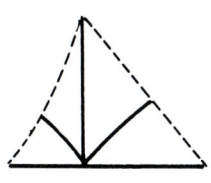

Figure 1.3b Geometric Forms of Western Style Design - Asymmetrical Triangle

Figure 1.3c Geometric Forms of Western Style Design - Crescent

Figure 1.3d Geometric Forms of Western Style Design - Vertical

dull, flat appearance. The horizontal arrangement is an ideal centerpiece or decorative arrangement for a coffee table.

Oval *(Figure 1.3f)*

The oval is one of the most popular arrangement styles in floral design. The popular "round mound" or "nosegay" is a variation of this design. These arrangements are a favorite with customers because they can be placed in a wide variety of locations, they include an abundance of flowers, and they are long lasting due to the flowers' proximity to the water line.

Hogarth Curve *(Figure 1.3g)*

William Hogarth was an English painter who loved flowers. He developed the "line of beauty" in the eighteenth century. This line has often been referred to as a lazy "S." Mr. Hogarth took two pieces of a circle, put them together, and created this graceful line. The Hogarth curve is visually appealing, and as a result, it is a popular design for public display.

Texture

Texture is the surface quality of a flower, foliage, or container. Textures include the actual physical feeling of an item, as well as, the visual feeling. Some plant materials, for example, appear soft, but are actually very prickly. Certain varieties of cactus are an example of this. Texture can be used to make an arrangement formal or casual. Texture can also be used to lend gender to a design, making it male or female. For example, a design with bright colors and lots of gypsophila accented with lace ribbon would be considered a feminine design. A woodsy design in a basket with twigs, mosses, and protea would usually be considered a masculine design.

When creating an arrangement, it is important to utilize a variety of textures. When working with plant material, it is helpful to note the textural qualities of all the parts of the plant. The texture of a leaf can be smooth and shiny, while the flower on the same stem is coarse and dull. Although textural variety is desired, utilizing too many textures or combining textures which are extremely different can weaken a design. A conservative approach to using texture as a design element should be practiced until textural combinations can be made with confidence.

Figure 1.3e Geometric Forms of Western Style Design - Horizontal

Figure 1.3f Geometric Forms of Western Style Design - Oval

Figure 1.3g Geometric Forms of Western Style Design - Hogarth Curve

Elements and Principles of Floral Design

Notes

Color

To many, color is the most important element of floral design. Sir Isaac Newton discovered the first theory of color. He recognized the colors red, orange, yellow, green, blue, and violet. By blending the spectrum into a circle, he developed the color wheel.

Color is a vital part of the world. It is seen in the sky, water, flowers, and foliage of nature. Human response to color can be happy or sad. Color affects the feelings of each individual differently.

Light is necessary to see color. Color is light. Every color in the spectrum can be found in daylight. When an object reflects all colors, we see the object as white. If the object absorbs all of the colors, we see the object as black.

The Color Wheel

To understand and achieve success in design, a florist must be familiar with the color wheel. The pigment theory divides the color wheel into warm and cool colors. The warm colors are red, orange, and yellow. The cool colors are green, blue, and violet. The warm colors are called advancing colors and require less light to be seen. These are important factors to remember when creating floral designs. A sample color wheel is provided in the back of this book for reference.

The Vocabulary of Color

To fully understand the concept of color, it is important to understand the vocabulary used to describe colors. The sample color wheel in the back of this book provides visual examples of the vocabulary of color.

Hue

Hue is a particular color, regardless of the quantity of black or white it contains. The quality of the color helps decide the family name.

Chroma

Chroma is the purity of a color, determined by its degree of freedom from white or gray. Chroma refers to the intensity, the strength, or the weakness of a color.

Tint

Tint is any color that has had white added to it. For example, adding white to red makes pink.

Tone

Tone is any color that has had gray added to it or that has been grayed by its complement.

Shade

Shade is any color that has had black added to it. For example, adding black to red makes burgundy.

Value

Value is the lightness or darkness of a color. For example, the value of red changes when white is added, and the color is lightened to a pink tint.

Intensity

Intensity is the dullness or brightness of a color.

Color Harmonies

Color harmony refers to the emotional effect of two or more colors on the viewer. The acceptance of color harmonies varies according to geographical area and educational background.

The color harmonies are created by the twelve hues on the color wheel. The following color harmonies are the ones most often used in floral design. These color harmonies are illustrated with the color wheel in the back of this book.

Monochromatic

The word mono means one, and the word chromatic means color. The monochromatic color harmony includes all the tints, tones, and shades of one color. An example of a monochromatic color harmony using the color red is the combination of pink, rose, mauve, and burgundy flowers in a design. This color harmony is one of the most popular, because it is pleasing to the eye, and in the home it unifies colorful surroundings.

Notes

Elements and Principles of Floral Design

Notes

Analogous

Analogous colors are adjacent to each other on the color wheel. Perhaps color harmony is pleasing to the eye because of its rhythmic color flow. The analogous color harmony has at least one primary color, and its scope covers at least one-fourth of the color wheel. The color harmony must have at least three hues. For example, brown, orange, gold, and yellow-green blend to create a popular color harmony for autumn arrangements.

Complementary Colors

Complementary color harmonies consist of one primary color and the secondary color directly across from it on the color wheel. The three complementary color schemes are blue and orange, red and green, and yellow and violet. These color harmonies are always dramatic. The colors become more forceful through contrast and offer a light-dark contrast that gives the design impact.

Split-complement

The split-complement harmony is achieved by combining one hue with the two colors on either side of its direct complement. For example, yellow is combined with blue-violet and red-violet. This color harmony provides a softer contrast than that achieved in the complementary harmony described above.

Triadic Color

A triadic color harmony consists of three colors equally spaced on the color wheel. The primary colors (red, yellow, blue) and the secondary colors (orange, green, and violet) are most commonly combined to create this exciting color harmony.

Psychology of Color

The psychology of color involves the study of how individuals react to color. People react differently to color, and this reaction can usually be traced to one's educational background, personality, and geographical location. Colors create moods and express personalities. In general, outgoing people are attracted to warm colors: red, orange, and yellow. Private people are usually attracted to cool colors: green, blue, and violet. Most customers

Basic Floral Design

look at color first when selecting an arrangement. Thus, a thorough knowledge of the use of color is necessary to insure customer satisfaction.

Physics of Color

Color is a pigment, but the color of the pigment is the color of the light that it reflects. Pigment has the ability to absorb certain wavelengths from the light that falls on it while reflecting other colors to the eye. Therefore, lighting is vitally important in floral design. Flowers look different when placed in dimly lit areas. Blue and mauve lose their crisp, clear color that natural light gives them and become a dull gray when placed under an electric light. Fluorescent light makes red appear to be dark brown.

These principles and elements are the foundation for all styles of floral design. They are the guidelines which are used to insure that an arrangement will be visually appealing. This is achieved when a design is balanced, well-proportioned, and unified by a harmonious combination of floral materials. A strong focal area and clear rhythm make the arrangement more interesting and visually appealing. Line and form create the outline of the design. Texture and color give it character. However, none of these principles or elements is effective when used independently. For optimum results, they must all be properly executed simultaneously. The reward for following these long-standing rules of design is a beautiful arrangement with guaranteed saleability.

Notes

Elements and Principles of Floral Design

Notes, Photographs, Sketches, etc.

Basic Floral Design

Notes, Photographs, Sketches, etc.

Elements and Principles of Floral Design

21

Notes, Photographs, Sketches, etc.

Supplies and Containers

Chapter 2

*O*btaining and maintaining the proper tools and supplies are essential to insuring success in floral design. To enhance the efficiency of flower shops, florists must utilize the correct tool or mechanical device for specific tasks. As modern technology provides updated materials for use in design, florists must adapt and incorporate them into their work. A knowledge of available supplies and their uses is mandatory before professional floral designing can begin.

Containers are also important items to stock in quantity and variety. Containers are available in a wide variety of sizes, shapes, and colors. Manufacturers create containers of elegant crystal, fine porcelain, brass, copper, ceramic, wicker, and other materials, providing florists with endless options. Florists must then choose an appropriate container for the desired design style. Plastic containers are commonly used to fill everyday flower orders. However, the choice of containers in this line is very diverse. An understanding of the types of containers available will assist florists in selecting containers that suit specific needs.

Basic Supplies

Floral designers must have access to a variety of basic supplies before quality designs can be created. The tools, adhesives, packaging supplies, stationery, and other items discussed below are essential to any well-organized floral shop.

Tools

Each designer in a flower shop is usually given his own set of tools. It is important that each set includes all of the tools needed for the various tasks involved in design. Tools should not be used

Basic Floral Design

for overlapping functions, such as using ribbon shears to cut wire. Purchasing quality tools and using them properly will, in the long run, save time, effort, and money.

Knives

Florist knives are available in a wide variety of styles. Folding pocket knives are popular with many designers. They have a quality blade that will hold its sharpness.

Knives similar to kitchen paring knives are also available. However, their blades contain less steel and tend to dull quickly. To insure a clean cut when designing with fresh flowers, a sharp blade is a must.

Plastic-handled knives are also available. These knives have a relatively short life and are designed to cut soft materials, such as foam. They are inexpensive and are not recommended for cutting fresh flowers.

Scissors

Sharp, quality scissors are a must in any design room. Ribbon scissors have a slender blade and are only used to cut ribbon and fabric.

Serrated scissors are used to cut heavier materials, such as florist wire and plastic containers. They are not used to cut ribbon. Because serrated scissors have longer blades than wire cutters, they can be used to cut wires that cannot be reached with wire cutters. Serrated scissors are available in two sizes: 8-inch, all-purpose scissors that have a long blade and may be used to cut a variety of materials, and 7 1/2-inch, utility scissors which are very strong and can be used to cut thick or heavy materials.

Wire cutters are available in different sizes and styles. A spring-action handle is most often preferred because it makes them easier to operate. Wire cutters have a short blade and are ideal for cutting wire, corsage stems, and other heavy materials.

Tapes

Several kinds of tape should be found in every design workroom: floral tape, waterproof tape, aisle runner tape, and double-faced tape.

Floral Tape

Floral tape is used to wrap floral wires, bind materials, and assemble corsages and wedding bouquets. It is a waxed crepe

Notes

Supplies and Containers

Notes

paper which sticks to itself when stretched. Floral tape is available in many colors, however, green is the most widely used.

Waterproof Tape

Waterproof tape is available in green, white, and translucent colors, and in widths of 1/4 inch and 1/2 inch. It is used to secure floral foam in containers.

Aisle Runner Tape

Aisle runner tape is designed to secure aisle runners to floors or floor coverings. It is often used in many other ways, as well. Aisle runner tape is white and approximately 3 inches in width. It is extremely sticky and is excellent for binding large elements.

Wire

Wire is a necessary item for any floral shop workroom. It is utilized in one form or another in most everyday designs. The types of wire available are 18-inch florist wire, paddle wire, and chicken wire.

Florist Wire

Florist wire is usually pre-cut in 18-inch pieces and is available in several gauges (weights) ranging from #16 gauge to #30 gauge. The heavier the wire, the lower the number. It is packaged in 12-pound boxes and is available in two colors: green (referred to as enamel) and silver (referred to as bright). A variety of gauges should be available in flower shops. This wire is used to bind materials, strengthen stems, and construct corsages and wedding bouquets.

Paddle Wire

Paddle wire is a continuous piece of florist wire that is wound on a wooden paddle. It is available in sizes from #16 gauge to #30 gauge and is used primarily to create garlands and to bind large materials.

Chicken Wire

Chicken wire is available in 12-inch and 18-inch widths in 150-foot rolls. It is placed over floral foam in large arrangements to help stabilize heavy stems. It may also be used to form topiary shapes.

Pins and Picks

Pins and picks are standard items in floral shop workrooms. They are used for connecting materials and securing items in arrangements.

Greening Pins (Philly Pins or Fern Pins)

Greening pins are U-shaped pins similar to hairpins. They are commonly used to secure moss to foam.

Dixon Pins

Dixon pins are two wooden pins attached in the center by pliable metal. The two pins are usually bent into a U-shape and inserted into foam with the ends pinched together. The ends release slightly inside the foam and lock the pin in place. The wood swells as a result of the moisture in the saturated foam and causes the pins to hold securely.

Bank Pins

Bank pins are heavy straight pins with flat heads. They are used in arrangements, such as set pieces, where the repeated pinning of flowers is required.

Corsage/Boutonniere Pins

Corsage and boutonniere pins are used to secure body flowers to garments. Corsage pins are usually 2 inches long and have a white or pearl head. Boutonniere pins are available with either white or black heads and are 1 1/2 inches long.

Wooden Picks

Green or natural wooden picks are available in lengths of 2 1/4 to 6 inches. One end tapers to a point and the other end is wrapped with fine wire. Wooden picks are used to secure bows to plants, to extend stems for clusters of dried or silk flowers, and to insert accessories into foam. Wire is wrapped around the item to be inserted into the foam. When the pick is inserted into a plant or saturated floral foam, the moisture will cause the wooden pick to swell, thus securing the pick into place. When dried/silk foam is used, pan glue may be added to the end of the wooden pick before inserting it into the foam.

Notes

Supplies and Containers

Notes

Steel Pick Machines

Pick machines are used to place a thin, steel-type pick onto the stems of silk and dried materials or to bind small materials for insertion into foam. Items to be picked are held against a steel pick at the end of the machine. A lever is then pulled, bending the clamps of the pick around the materials and securing it into place. The edges of the steel picks are razor sharp, allowing for easy insertion into styrofoam or floral foam.

Steel Picks

Steel picks are the individual picks used in a pick machine. They are available in several lengths and in bundles of one hundred or cases of two thousand.

Hyacinth Stakes

Hyacinth stakes were originally designed as a support for plants whose blooms were top-heavy. Hyacinth stakes may also be used as supports in large flower arrangements or to increase stem length in artificial designs. They are available in lengths of 12 inches, 18 inches, and 24 inches.

Chenille Stems

Chenille stems are best described as large pipe cleaners. They are available in a variety of colors and have several uses. They can be attached to a bow and placed in an arrangement or inserted into the stem of a flower to stabilize the stem for a corsage. They are also used to secure pew bows and to create faces and figures for novelty designs.

Adhesives

Several different adhesives are incorporated into effective, labor-saving floral design techniques. With many of these adhesives, experimentation is necessary to determine which ones are best for specific needs.

Pan Glue

Pan glue is available in bags of beads which are melted in an electric fry pan at about 275 degrees. The main advantage of this glue is that it holds securely, despite changes in temperature and moisture. The glue should be the consistency of molasses when properly melted. Pan glue will adhere to most clean, dry surfaces and will take paint.

Design elements can be dipped into the glue and used immediately in a design. The glue can also be applied to an item using a spoon or stick.

When not in use, the fry pan should be turned off so that the glue will harden. Once the glue has hardened, the pan may be stored. It only takes a few minutes to melt the glue again when needed.

Glue Gun

The glue gun is a popular tool used in the flower shop. It offers greater control than pan glue because it allows one to apply glue directly to the surface of an object. Using a trigger glue gun in designs that will be refrigerated is not recommended because the glue tends to separate at temperatures less than 40 degrees. Because the tip of the gun is very hot, care must be used when handling the gun. The gun is designed with a standard brace to hold it upright when not in use. When the gun is laid on its side, the glue may run into the mechanism causing it to malfunction.

Glue Sticks

Glue sticks are inserted into glue guns and melted in a chamber when the trigger is pulled. Glue sticks come in 4-inch and 10-inch lengths. Cool melt glue guns, which melt a special glue at a lower temperature, are also available.

Floral Adhesive

Floral adhesive is a rubber cement that contains no chemicals that are harmful to fresh flowers. Since floral adhesive is not affected by humidity or temperature, it may be used in fresh designs that will be stored in a cooler. Wedding and corsage work are types of designs in which floral adhesive is often used. Floral adhesive takes longer to dry than pan glue or glue gun sticks.

Florist Clay

Florist clay is a material used predominantly to secure styrofoam in containers. It is available in green or white and is

Notes

Supplies and Containers

Notes

packaged on a roll with a piece of waxed paper between each layer to prevent it from sticking to itself. Since oil from the hands will cut down on the adhesive quality of florist clay, it is best to cut pieces off the roll and leave the waxed paper on it during handling.

Aerosol Sprays

Floral spray color is an important florist tool. Considered a novelty when first developed, it has proven to be a florist staple today. It is important to remember that floral sprays are intended to enhance flowers, not to cover up inferior products. It should always be used in good taste. There are three key types of floral sprays:

1. Regular colors which are pigmented for opaque coverings.

2. Tints which are dyes for transparent coloring.

3. Accessory sprays, including those that increase the life of the flower or add luster to foliage.

Refrigerator Containers

Refrigerator containers, both storage and decorative, are used to store fresh flowers. Storage containers are used in the work cooler and are not normally seen by customers. They are typically plastic buckets of a variety of colors and sizes. Decorative containers are used to store fresh flowers in the display cooler. Clear or colored glass, ceramic or high-quality plastic vases, and decorative buckets are often used for this purpose.

Floral Preservatives

Floral preservatives are used to extend flower life in the flower shop and in the customer's home. They consist of three primary ingredients: bactericides, sugars, and acidity controllers. Bactericides keep the water clean and prevent bacteria from attacking flowers. Sugars provide the food for flowers. Acidity controllers keep the pH level in the water low to enhance water uptake. With proper use, preservatives help reduce shrinkage, increase flower life, enhance color, and improve fragrance.

Floral Foam

Notes

There are three general types of floral foam: wettable foam, dry foam, and styrofoam. Each foam is used for a different purpose in designing; thus, all three should be kept in stock in the flower shop workroom.

Fresh Floral Foam

Wettable floral foam is a cellular foam consisting of membranes designed to hold water. There are different grades available that vary in density. The type of foam needed is determined by the flowers to be used. Dense foams are used for heavy, thick-stemmed flowers, while light foams can be used for soft-stemmed flowers.

Specialty Sizes

Fresh flower foam is typically produced in individual bricks that are purchased in cases containing thirty-six to forty-eight bricks. However, it is also available in a variety of shapes and sizes. Fresh flower foam cylinders are available in two sizes and can be used in round containers, thus eliminating waste. Floral foam is also available with plastic cages around it, making it convenient for use in sympathy and party work. Caged foam with suction cups makes it possible to mount designs on doors, windows, etc. Holders which hold a small piece of floral foam for use in constructing wedding bouquets are also available. These specialty foams are available from most wholesalers.

Dry Floral Foam

Dry floral foam will not absorb water and is used only for dried silk arrangements. It is available in different densities and in a limited number of specialty sizes.

Styrofoam

Styrofoam is harder and more coarse than dry floral foam. It can be cut into different shapes and used as a base in novelty arrangements. Styrofoam is available in many pre-cut shapes, such as hearts and stars, which are often used in sympathy work. In some areas, the use of styrofoam is restricted due to environmental concerns.

Supplies and Containers

Notes

Shredded Styrofoam

Because it is inexpensive, shredded styrofoam is often used to fill large containers, especially for funeral work. It holds flowers in place firmly enough so that blocks of floral foam are not needed. Shredded styrofoam does not absorb water; thus, a container filled with shredded styrofoam for fresh designs must be adequately filled with water, as well.

Anchoring Mechanisms

Appropriate anchoring mechanisms must be utilized to insure the quality and durability of a design. Without these mechanisms, flowers and foliage will not remain positioned as the designer intended.

Pin Holders (Floral Frog)

Pin holders are used in an old style of design that originated from Japanese floral design. They have a heavy base made of steel and numerous pins sticking upright out of the base. The pin holder is placed into a container, and flowers are then pushed onto the pins to create the design. Pin holders are available in a variety of sizes and shapes, but are rather expensive and not suitable for use in everyday designs.

Anchor Pins

Anchor pins are made of green plastic and have four short prongs attached to a flat base. They are attached to the bottom of a container with the prongs pointing upward. Floral foam is then pressed onto the prongs to secure it in the container.

Candle Stakes

Candle stakes are made of green plastic and are available in several sizes to fit candles of different dimensions. They have pointed prongs which are inserted into the floral foam to provide a secure foundation for each candle in the arrangement.

Packaging Supplies

Flower packaging is often considered as important as the design inside, since it makes the first impression on a customer. A variety of packaging materials should be kept in stock at all times to insure that products are properly wrapped.

Tissue Paper

There are two types of tissue paper available: waxed and unwaxed. Waxed tissue paper is preferred when working with products that may be damp or in water. This tissue paper is used to wrap loose flowers or as a liner in rose boxes.

Unwaxed tissue paper is available in a rainbow of colors. It is used to package items that are not damp. Some florists choose to use one color of tissue paper as a trademark of their shop. Both types of tissue paper are available in rolls and reams of 480 sheets.

Outer Wrap

Outer wrap is a thick paper which comes on a roll. It often has a floral design printed on it and may be ordered with individual shop names on it. It is used to wrap bouquets and acts as a protective covering in cool climates. There are two kinds of outer wrap available: paper and cellophane. Although cellophane is more decorative, it is typically more expensive and, therefore, not always cost effective.

Foils

Decorative aluminum foils are available in two key types. Lightweight foil is colored on one side and silver on the other. It is typically used to cover plant pots. Polyfoil is a thicker foil with a thin sheet of plastic on the silver side. Polyfoil is also used to cover plant pots and is useful for lining baskets or other containers that need protection from moisture.

Plant Sleeves

Plant sleeves are designed for wrapping flowering and foliage plants and are available in several sizes. The sleeves are pulled down over a sleeving stand and a plant is placed on the stand. The sleeve is then pulled up around the plant and the top of the sleeve is folded over.

Clear Bags

Clear bags are excellent packaging materials because they allow customers to view the product while it is packaged. They

Notes

# Supplies and Containers

Notes

are available in cellophane, plastic, and polypropylene and in a variety of sizes. Small bags are used to package corsages and boutonnieres while larger bags are used for arrangements and wedding bouquets.

Boxes

Boxes, usually made from white cardboard, are available in a multitude of sizes and shapes. There are boxes for boutonnieres, corsages, orchids, nosegays, roses, bouquets, and wedding flowers. They may be ordered in a specific color or with a company logo printed on them.

Delivery boxes are less expensive and are used to hold arrangements during delivery. They are usually made of corrugated cardboard and are available in many different sizes.

Stationery and Tags

There are several types of stationery needed for the flower shop. The design of these items is important since they communicate the shop's image to every customer.

Company Stationery

Company stationery should have the name, address, and phone number of the flower shop printed on it. Specific items of stationery would include business-size envelopes, statement-size envelopes, paper for business letters, and business cards. White enclosure envelopes can be purchased with or without a company logo printed on them.

Enclosure Cards

Enclosure cards and envelopes may be printed with the flower shop name and logo on the back. Cardettes are used to hold cards upright in arrangements. They resemble plastic forks with long handles, and are available in clear, white, and green. Cardettes come in different stem lengths and can be purchased in packages of one hundred and cases of one thousand.

Care and Handling Tags

Pre-printed care and handling tags are available from wholesalers for most plants and flowers sold in flower shops. Delivery tags, for use when customers are not home, are also available.

Ribbon

Ribbon is available in various widths which are referred to by number, as shown in Table 1 below. The ribbon most commonly used in flower shops is satin acetate. Decorative laces and prints, used primarily for wedding work, are also available. Ribbons with wire edges for precise positioning of loops and streamers are also available. Paper ribbon comes in a variety of colors on 50-yard rolls and is available twisted, untwisted, or wired.

TABLE 2

RIBBON SPECIFICATIONS

Size Number	Width in Inches	Yards per Bolt
# 1 1/2	5/16	100
# 2	7/16	100
# 3	5/8	100
# 5	7/8	100
# 9	1 7/16	100
# 16	2	50
# 40	2 3/4	50
#100	4	50

Containers

Containers are available in many sizes, shapes, and price ranges. Containers that are used for everyday design work (sometimes referred to as utility containers) may be made of glass, pottery, wicker, plastic, or brass. Prices vary among the different types, depending on quality. When shopping for utility containers, price should not be the primary concern. Some containers are attractively priced but of poor quality. For example, glassware which often seems very reasonably priced may not withstand the pressure of water when filled. Also, there are many different types of plastic. Some less expensive plastics may look very cheap. When shopping for containers, it is important to keep in mind how functional, practical, and deliverable the container will be in relation to cost.

Notes

Supplies and Containers

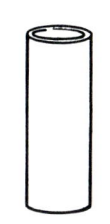

Figure 2.1a Cylinder Vase

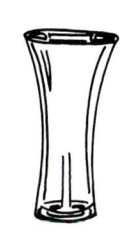

Figure 2.1b Tall Vase

Figure 2.2a Low Bowl

Figure 2.2b Oblong Suiban

Figure 2.3a Urn

Figure 2.3b Classic Low Urn

Container Styles

There are four basic container styles: cylinders, bowls and trays, urns, and novelty containers.

Cylinders *(Figures 2.1a and 2.1b)*

Tall cylinders are vases that are used to accommodate long-stemmed flowers, such as gladioli, roses, and garden flowers. These containers are also used to hold vertical stylized arrangements.

Bowls and Trays *(Figures 2.2a and 2.2b)*

Bowls are commonly used for basic, everyday arrangements, including round arrangements, centerpieces, and high style designs.

Urns *(Figures 2.3a and 2.3b)*

Urns are elegant-looking, footed containers. They may have handles and often reflect the Roman Period.

Novelty Containers

Many novelty containers are available for various occasions, such as a new baby and get well. Mugs with humorous sayings written on them are also popular. Containers designed for children, such as a teddy bear holding a bud vase, are also placed in this category.

Miscellaneous Containers *(Figures 2.4a and 2.4b on page 36)*

A variety of containers are spinoffs of other styles. Miscellaneous containers include bud vases, challis', and compotes.

Composition of Containers

Floral designers should always consider the composition of a container before choosing it for a design. Containers of a specific composition may lend themselves to some design styles and may be completely inappropriate for others. Factors to consider include the physical limitations of containers, as well as, the connotations associated with specific types.

Papier-maché

Papier-maché containers are temporary containers used primarily for sympathy work. They are sized to hold a full one half or one quarter block of floral foam. After a period of time, moisture may leak through papier-maché.

Plastic

Plastic containers are very popular and affordable. They are available in many colors and styles. When purchasing plastic containers, it is important to look for quality.

Glass

Several industry manufacturers offer inexpensive glass containers that can be used for everyday designs. These are normally available in clear, green, and frosted glass.

Inexpensive Pottery

Containers made of inexpensive glazed pottery can be used for utility designs. Pottery is manufactured in all of the container styles discussed above.

Wicker

Many types and grades of wicker can be used for design work. When selecting wicker containers, check the following:

1. Is a liner available?

2. Is the wicker heavy enough and constructed well enough to support the weight of a design?

3. If the wicker gets wet, will it withstand the moisture?

Liners

Some containers require a liner to hold saturated floral foam. Some wholesale florists carry generic liners that may be purchased for these containers. If generic liners are not available, polyfoil or heavy plastic is an alternative. Arrangements designed in a liner should be checked for leaks before delivery.

Figure 2.4a Shallow Compote

Figure 2.4b Weed Pot

Supplies and Containers

Supplies and containers are the basic ingredients of every arrangement. For this reason, it is imperative that florists have a thorough understanding of the products used in design, and the prices and quantities at which they are sold. A visit to a wholesaler can be an enlightening experience in product knowledge. If the buyer studies products and their packaging, efficient ordering is a likely result. Determining a shop's need for supplies and securing a knowledge of purchasing procedures may, in the end, save a considerable amount of money.

Basic Floral Design

Notes, Photographs, Sketches, etc.

Supplies and Containers

Notes, Photographs, Sketches, etc.

Design Mechanics

Chapter 3

The quality of a floral design is only as good as the design's mechanics. An arrangement or corsage must look fresh during and after delivery and while in the recipient's possession. A solid foundation is vitally important to the construction of any design, whether created with fresh flowers or silk and dried materials.

The proper use of items, such as ribbons, paints, and novelties, may add the finishing touch to a design. Attention given to detail is often considered an indication of a florist's professionalism. Secure placement of these items within a design will help insure their stability. Many mechanical techniques have been simplified as a result of availability of a wide variety of glues and adhesives.

This chapter will assist designers at all levels of skill in creating beautiful arrangements and corsages while implementing the appropriate mechanics into each design. The proper methods of color enhancing and gluing will also be covered. Sturdy mechanics are the foundation for every successful arrangement. The following mechanical techniques are the easiest and are best-suited for use by most florists.

Fresh Flower Arrangement Mechanics

There are many types of floral foam available. Each one has a specific purpose, but all of them are prepared in virtually the same way, following the guidelines listed here.

Soaking Floral Foam

Floral foam may be soaked before or after it has been secured in a container. However, total saturation is imperative, regardless of the manner in which a shop chooses to soak floral foam. The most efficient way to insure total saturation is to

Basic Floral Design

immerse the floral foam slowly into a sink or pail of preservative-treated water. The floral foam should remain in the water until it stops bubbling. Each manufacturer's foam has a different absorption rate, as do various densities of foam. Since air pockets may be trapped by water rushing into a block of foam, a knife may be inserted several times to check for air.

Sinks and pails used to soak foam should be free from any potentially hazardous residues, such as soap, tints, insecticides, or any other chemical residue that could harm fresh flowers. Any container used to soak floral foam should be cleaned thoroughly twice a week with the same soap and bleach solution used to clean flower buckets. The container should be rinsed thoroughly to wash away any soap residue.

Floral foam can be soaked after it has been secured into a plastic liner or container with pan melt glue. However, this method is not suggested for expensive containers or vases. When using this method, submerge the container at an angle. This allows the floral foam to absorb water from one side to the other. After it has been checked for trapped air, the soaked, foam-filled container is ready for use. The exterior of a plastic liner should be dried before being placed into a basket or decorative container.

Cutting Floral Foam

Floral foam must often be cut to an appropriate size for a specific container. When cutting foam, florists should be as economical as possible. Wet or dry floral foam can be cut with a floral knife, a long bread knife, a taut piece of wire, or a hacksaw blade with a small handle at one end. Many utility containers will accommodate various portions or an entire block of floral foam. Excess trimming is rarely required when using a container that has been designed for floral foam use. The trimming of excess foam is almost always necessary when using giftware or a container supplied by a customer.

When cutting floral foam, it is best to have no more than 1 inch of foam above the lip of the container. Most floral foams are unable to wick water at a level higher than 1 inch above the water line. One inch of foam should provide designers with plenty of room for any necessary horizontal insertions. To insert large stems, such as those of gladioli, as much as 1 1/2 inches of foam may need to be left above the lip of a container. Large arrangements that will utilize many large stemmed flowers should have the foam reinforced with chicken wire.

Space must be allowed between the floral foam block and the sides of the container in which it is placed. This space is referred

<u>Notes</u>

Design Mechanics

to as a water well. Floral foams require a constant source of water so that it can be transferred through the block to flowers and foliage. The water well makes it easy to replenish this water supply as needed.

Securing Floral Foam

It is important to properly secure floral foam in containers. The chances of damaging the flowers in a design are greatly increased when the foam can shift in the container. There are many methods used to secure floral foam in containers before designing begins. The following list includes techniques that are frequently used.

Waterproof Tape

One quarter inch waterproof tape (bowl tape) can be used to secure foam in most containers. The following steps demonstrate how waterproof tape is applied *(see Figure 3.1)*.

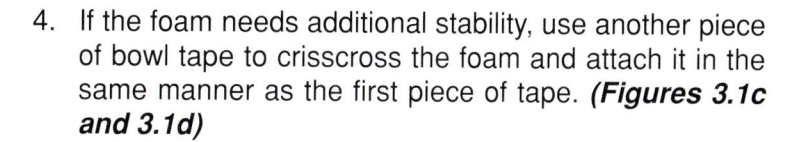

1. Press the end of the tape to the side of a clean, dry container.

2. Stretch it across the foam and attach it to the opposite side of the container. *(Figures 3.1a and 3.1b)*

3. Insure that the tape is properly secured by pressing it against the container firmly, so that it will not release.

4. If the foam needs additional stability, use another piece of bowl tape to crisscross the foam and attach it in the same manner as the first piece of tape. *(Figures 3.1c and 3.1d)*

Taping tips:

- It is suggested that the tape run only as far down the sides of the container as is absolutely necessary. It is difficult to disguise mechanics that are blatantly obvious.

- Wide bowl tape is designed for use on large containers and papier-maché. It is most effective to staple bowl tape to the lip of papier-maché containers. This prevents the tape from slipping or releasing.

Figure 3.1a Waterproof Tape Application - Side View Step 2

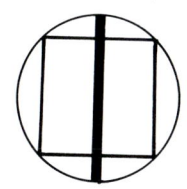

Figure 3.1b Waterproof Tape Application - Top View Step 2

Figure 3.1c Waterproof Tape Application - Side View Step 4

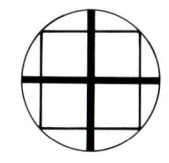

Figure 3.1d Waterproof Tape Application - Top View Step 4

Basic Floral Design

- If dirt or an oily residue prevents the tape from adhering to the container, clean the area with hand cleaner or nail polish remover. The tape will stick after the area dries.

- Chicken wire can be secured over floral foam when the foam needs to support large flower stems or a large number of stems. It should be molded over the top of the foam, then taped as before.

Pan Melt Glue

Pan melt glue can secure dry foam in many containers, thus providing designers with an unobstructed surface on which to work *(see Figure 3.2)*.

1. Dip a piece of floral foam into the glue. To guarantee proper adherence, a thin coating of glue should appear on the bottom and edge of the foam. Excess glue can be scraped off the bottom into a pan. *(Figure 3.2a)*

2. Press the glue-coated portion of the block down into the container. *(Figure 3.2b)*

3. Allow the glue to cool and set; then submerge the container and foam into a pail or sink of water.

   Tips:

   - Containers can be pre-filled with dry foam in preparation for large orders, holidays, or parties. The pre-filled containers can then be soaked as needed.

   - Always dip the four corners of the block in the glue to insure a secure bond in containers with rounded bottoms.

Figure 3.2a Pan Melt Gluing Step 1

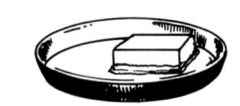

Figure 3.2b Pan Melt Gluing Step 2

Anchor Pins *(Figure 3.3)*

Some containers need to have the foam secured so that it and the flowers can be easily removed. Anchor pins can do just that. They are made of plastic and are reminiscent of a small, round, four-legged table.

Design Mechanics

Figure 3.3a Anchor Pin

Figure 3.3b Anchor Pin Step 1

Figure 3.3c Anchor Pin Step 2

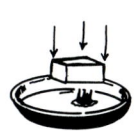

Figure 3.3d Anchor Pin Step 3

1. Position the anchor pin *(Figure 3.3a)* with the prong side up. Dip the round, flat part of it in the pan melt glue. *(Figure 3.3b)*

2. Place it in the container at the desired location. *(Figure 3.3c)*

3. When the glue has cooled, place the soaked piece of floral foam onto the anchor pin. *(Figure 3.3d)*

Tips:

- Anchor pins can also be attached by using floral clay instead of glue.

- Full blocks of foam may require two or three pins for a secure hold.

Special Container Tips

Some containers require additional preparation before being used for fresh flower arrangements. The proper preparation of containers may prevent water damage to a recipient's furniture. The following list of containers and techniques may assist designers in preparing containers quickly and efficiently.

Baskets

A heavy plastic liner that fits well is essential when arranging fresh flowers in any basket. Liners hold floral foam and water safely because stems cannot puncture them. If the liner does not fit well, however, the following is suggested.

1. Line a basket to the edge of the lip with a single or double layer of polyfoil before inserting the liner.

2. When a basket has flared sides, a length of crumpled foil wedged between the basket and the liner's sides will help prevent the liner from moving in the basket.

Securing a Foam Filled Liner in a Basket *(Figure 3.4 on page 46)*

1. Tape a length of #24 gauge wire, which measures longer than the width of the basket's opening. The color of floral tape used on the wire should match the basket whenever possible.

2. Insert the wire's first end through the weave at the basket's lip. *(Figure 3.4a)*

3. Loop the end of the wire around the weave at the basket's lip. *(Figure 3.4b)*

4. Pull the length of taped wire over the foam and secure the wire's other end to the opposite side of the basket's lip using the same method as before. The taped wire should cut into the foam slightly to prevent it from moving. *(Figure 3.4c)*

Raising a Liner in a Basket

Sometimes liners sit too low in baskets. At such times, the foam will not be at an appropriate level in the liner relative to the basket's lip. When this is the case, a piece of hard foam (styrofoam) can be attached to the liner's bottom with pan melt glue using the following steps *(see Figure 3.5)*.

1. Cut a piece of hard foam large enough to support the liner's bottom. Insure that the piece of hard foam is the proper height and size before gluing it into place.

2. Dip the fitted piece of hard foam into pan melt glue. Scrape off the excess glue into the pan.

3. Place the side of the hard foam with glue on it onto the bottom of the liner. Let it cool and then set. *(Figure 3.5a)*

4. Place the entire unit in the basket and secure it with the proper length of taped wire. *(Figure 3.5b)*

Non-glazed Pottery

Some pottery and ceramic containers will not hold water because they have not been glazed inside. They can either be sealed with a waterproof sealant or be fitted with a liner of some type. The liner will allow a fresh arrangement to be placed into one of these containers. Liners are usually necessary when the container belongs to a client. Plastic basket liners, plastic cups, and glass cylinders can make ideal liners for this type of pottery. The following steps may assist in the process of fitting the liner.

Figure 3.4a Securing a Foam Filled Liner in a Basket Step 2

Figure 3.4b Securing a Foam Filled Liner in a Basket Step 3

Figure 3.4c Securing a Foam Filled Liner in a Basket Step 4

Figure 3.5a Raising a Liner in a Basket Step 3

Figure 3.5b Raising a Liner in a Basket Step 4

Design Mechanics

1. Find the appropriate size and shape of liner for use in the container. Insure that the fit will allow for the addition of water within the liner.

2. Fill the liner with floral foam, and place it into the container.

3. Use hard foam to raise the liner up to meet the container's lip if the liner's lip is not even with the lip of the container.

Pottery that is not watertight can also be sealed with three to five coats of Thompson's® Water Seal. The entire interior of the container must be completely coated each time a layer of sealer is applied. This task is time-consuming and should not be done unless time and the container's price permit.

Clear Glass and Crystal

Some of the basic arrangement styles are easier to create in floral foam. This may be a problem when using clear glass or crystal vases. A piece of silver mylar sheeting, or the back of a broken mylar balloon, can make a perfect liner to hid the floral foam from view *(see Figure 3.6)*. The mylar allows the line and beauty of the container to be seen without distraction from the foam.

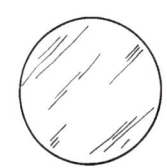

Figure 3.6a Mylar Lining Step 1

Figure 3.6b Mylar Lining Step 1

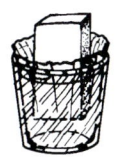

Figure 3.6c Mylar Lining Step 2

Figure 3.6d Mylar Lining Step 3

1. Cut and fit the mylar *(Figure 3.6a)* so that it is slightly larger than needed to line the container. If the mylar is large enough to cover the outside of the container, it should properly fit the inside. *(Figure 3.6b)*

2. Place a soaked piece of floral foam into the mylar-lined vase. *(Figure 3.6c)*

3. Fill the container with water. The weight of the water will cause the mylar to take the shape of the container, thus filling in all curves and corners. *(Figure 3.6d)*

4. Pull up gently on the excess mylar that is around the edge of the vase. This excess mylar may be left above the lip to act as a ruffle, or it can be trimmed even with the container's edge.

5. If needed, clear bowl tape can be used to hold floral foam in place. Be sure that the edge of the glass or crystal is clean and dry before applying waterproof tape.

Some designers prefer to use shredded hard foam or floral foam chips or sticks in containers such as rose vases. These types of foam provide more stability when fewer flowers and foliage pieces are used. The vase should be freely filled with either product by simply pouring it into the vase. Little room is left for water and stems if the foam bits are packed into the vase. When using these foam products, the mylar should be used as follows.

1. Place the mylar in the vase.

2. Freely fill the mylar-lined vase with the foam pieces.

3. Fill the container with preservative water.

4. Finish the mylar edge as before.

Milk glass and other opaque containers do not need to be lined with mylar. These containers can be freely filled with foam and used after the water is added.

Clear-water Design Mechanics

The goal of a clear-water design is to have the beauty of the stems visible through the sides of a clear glass or crystal container. There are several ways to create a design in clear water successfully. Tall or medium height, narrow-necked vases are best suited for this type of design. The use of a grid makes clear water designing easier. Many glass manufacturers have designed plastic grids that snap over the lip of vases and cylinders. These are convenient, but they do not fit every container that is available. Grids can be made by using the following methods.

Clear Tape Grids

Clear bowl tape can be used to grid containers of any type and size *(see Figure 3.7 on page 49)*.

1. Make sure that the outer edge of the container is clean and dry.

Notes

Design Mechanics

Figure 3.7a Tape Grid - Top View Step 2

Figure 3.7b Tape Grid - Side View Step 2

2. Create a crisscrossed grid with clear tape by placing a set of tape strips in a horizontal pattern. Then do the same in a vertical line pattern. *(Figures 3.7a and 3.7b)*

3. Arrange foliage to hide any tape that shows, so that all mechanics will be covered.

Chicken Wire Grids

Chicken wire can also be used to create a grid for glass containers. It is one of the oldest mechanical methods employed in the floral industry.

1. Cut a piece of chicken wire so that it fits the opening of the selected container. The piece should be slightly larger than the opening.

2. Bend the edges of the chicken wire over so that the formed piece fits just inside the lip of the vase. The formed piece of chicken wire should be large enough to prevent it from slipping down into the container.

3. Hold the wire in place with three to five beauty clips, depending on the size of the vase's opening.

4. The chicken wire can also be held in place with waterproof tape.

Lacing Greens for a Grid

Another successful grid for rose vases or other narrow-necked containers can be created by lacing greens *(see Figure 3.8)*. Fern, salal, huckleberry, and other foliage can be used to create a laced-foliage grid. Lacing is a technique that was brought to America by European designers. It is a very quick and easy technique. The following steps will assist designers in making a foliage grid.

1. Hold a piece of fern in one hand. Take a second piece and insert its stem in between the last and next-to-last frond at the bottom of the first piece. The tips of the two pieces of fern should be directly across from each other. *(Figure 3.8a)*

Figure 3.8a Lacing Greens for a Grid Step 1

2. The third fern stem is then inserted in between the last and next-to-last fronds on the second piece of fern. *(Figure 3.8b)*

3. The fourth piece is inserted in the same location on the third piece of fern. The tips of the third and fourth pieces of fern should be directly across from one another and perpendicular to the first and second ferns' tips. If a line were drawn from tip one to tip two, and a second line were drawn from tip three to tip four, a plus sign would result. *(Figure 3.8c)*

4. The next layer continues the pattern which has just been completed, but the next four pieces are placed so that their points are in between the first four. *(Figure 3.8d)*

5. Place the fifth piece of fern stem in the same position on the fourth piece of fern. *(Figure 3.8d)*

6. The sixth piece of fern is then positioned into the fifth piece in the same way. Its tip is directly across from that of the fifth. *(Figure 3.8d)*

7. The seventh piece of fern is positioned into the sixth piece and the eighth piece into the seventh. These two fern tips will also be directly across from each other and between those that were first placed. *(Figure 3.8d)*

8. If the tips for the last four pieces of fern were connected as explained in step 3, the result would be a diagram which looked like eight spokes on a wheel. When completed, the foliage should closely resemble a small fern plant. *(Figure 3.8e)*

9. Cut the fern stems to approximately 2 inches shorter than the vase's height; they need to be as long as possible while allowing the foliage to rest within the opening of the vase. The laced foliage should not move about on the lip of the container; it should sit securely inside the lip.

It is also possible to use only the first four pieces of leatherleaf or baker fern and then complete the grid with other foliage, such as oregonia, salal, or plumosa.

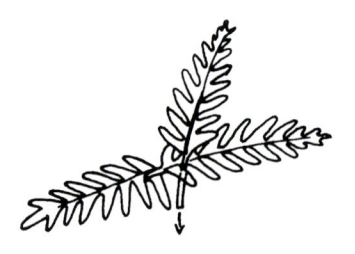

Figure 3.8b Lacing Greens for a Grid Step 2

Figure 3.8c Lacing Greens for a Grid Step 3

Figure 3.8d Lacing Greens for a Grid Steps 4 - 7

Figure 3.8e Lacing Greens for a Grid Step 8

Design Mechanics

Notes

Silk Flower Arrangement Mechanics

Many of the basic mechanics used for fresh designing are also applicable to designing with silk and dried materials. The properties of the foams used here are different; however, there is a need for additional materials and techniques when preparing a container for this type of work.

The two types of foam used for silk and dried work are hard foam (styrofoam) and dry foam. They can be used separately or together, depending on the designer's needs. Mechanical techniques are slightly different in silk and dried arrangements because of their permanent nature. The mechanics are also different because there is no need for a water well or water.

Cutting Foam

Both hard foam and dry foam can be cut with a quality florist knife. Hard foam can also be cut with a narrow hacksaw blade with a small handle at one end. There are also heated cutters made especially for use with hard foams. These simply melt through the foam.

Cutting dry foam is similar to cutting fresh floral foam. Dry foam is more dense, but its density does not make it difficult to cut. Pieces should be cut so that they fit the container similar to the fit of floral foam. It is suggested that the top of a piece of foam be approximately 3/4 inch above the lip of a container for proper control of horizontal insertions. Larger stems may require that the foam remain slightly higher: 1 to 1 1/2 inches at the most. If the foam is positioned too high in a container, the visual proportion and balance of the arrangement will not be correct.

Securing Foam for Silk Designs

It is important for dry foam to be attached securely in place for silk design work. It is best to secure the foam with pan melt glue. Both hard foam or dry foam can be secured in almost any type of container with pan melt glue. The same procedures as suggested for designing with fresh foam should be followed. The following is a list of gluing tips that can be used.

- Foam that is glued into a basket should have a thicker layer of glue on it than foam glued into pottery. Wide-weave baskets should have the foam glued into a liner. The wide-weave baskets may also have the foam secured with taped wires in the same manner as with fresh foam.

- Blocks of hard foam or any foam can be glued together to raise or widen them since they do not have to carry water to fresh flower stems.

- Glue a piece of hard foam under a piece of dry foam when working with a combination of heavy branches and fine-stemmed drieds. The heavy branches are then secured by inserting them through the softer foam and into the hard foam. The fine attached stems are inserted only into the soft foam.

- Anchor pins can be attached with floral clay or pan melt glue into opaque containers for more flexibility and easier cleaning.

Weighting Glass, Crystal, and Plastic Containers

Mechanics are often more complicated when working with clear or translucent containers made of glass, crystal, or plastic. Clear crystal and glass can be lined with mylar sheeting to hide the foam inside. Marbles, rocks, and/or silk foliage can also be used to hide the foam. Hard foam and dry foam are very lightweight. Therefore, plastic, glass, or crystal containers may need to have weight added to them for stability. The following techniques may be used to give weight to containers of this kind.

Bowls

Designers might add weight to the bottom of the foam to add stability to the design in a low bowl or dish. The weighted foam can simply be set in the base of the container. This enables the entire arrangement and mechanics to be removed as a complete unit so that the bowl may be cleaned.

Tall Vases and Cylinders

Foam and mylar can be secured into tall containers using an alternate technique.

1. Cut the foam to the proper size.

2. Dip it into the pan melt glue. Scrape most of the glue back into the pan.

3. Press the part of the foam that is covered with glue into the mylar sheet.

Notes

Design Mechanics

Notes

4. Place the whole unit into the vase. Center the unit, if needed.

5. Pour sand around the core of the foam. The sand will stabilize the container and add weight to it. The sand will also make the mylar conform to the shape of the container.

Marbles can also be used to secure the core of the foam. With this technique, the mylar is not necessary. Instead, the visible marbles add an elegant look to the container.

Plastic Containers

Plastic containers and hard or dry foam are too light to support silk designs. These containers need to be weighted when used for designing. Adhering to the following steps will make this possible.

1. Secure the foam into the plastic container with pan melt glue.

2. Pour sand, grave marbles, or pebbles into the container. Use only enough weighting material to create a steady base.

Disguising Mechanics and Foam

A professionally-finished design is symbolic of a good designer. Moss or a similar material should be used to cover the foam and any other part of a container that needs to be hidden. Moss is the least expensive and most natural material to use. A variety of mosses will hide mechanics and add depth to designs. Each type of moss can convey a mood, as well as, become an integral part of a design. When using moss, it is helpful to mist it so that it will be more pliable. The moss can then be shaped around the foam and container.

Corsage Mechanics

Corsages must be designed with the proper mechanics to insure that designs remain in tact while being worn. Following is a discussion of several wiring and taping methods that are frequently used by designers.

Basic Floral Design

Basics of Wiring

Flowers for corsages and bouquets are wired to eliminate bulky stems and to provide flexibility in flower positioning. The gauge of wire used is determined by the weight of the flower and the distance it will be from the binding point of the design. Heavy flowers close to the binding point require heavier wires than small flowers at the perimeter of the design.

The most common wire gauges used in corsage work are #24, #26, and #28. Number 24 gauge wire is typically used for wiring roses, carnations, and heavy-stemmed flowers. Number 25 gauge wire and #28 gauge wire are used for wiring delicate flowers and filler flowers. For efficiency and convenience, a chart listing flowers used to create corsages, the proper wire gauge, and the wiring technique for that flower is provided at the end of the book. This chart is perforated and may be removed from the book and placed in the flower shop as a reference to insure that flowers are wired correctly.

Chenille stems may also be used to wire some types of flowers. Moistened chenille stems may be inserted into flower stems, providing a wicking action which brings water to the flower. The chenille fibers along the chenille stem help grip the stem and prevent the flower from falling off. A simple rule to help decide when and how to wire flowers is to use wire in order to lengthen, strengthen, or control stems.

Extending Flower Life with Cotton

When working with special flowers, it is helpful to apply a piece of wet cotton to the end of the stem after wiring and just before taping. This provides the flower with needed moisture and helps extend flower life. Flowers that respond particularly well to this treatment are:

Roses
Orchids
Alstroemeria
Gardenias
Lilies

Wiring Techniques

Following are the seven basic techniques for wiring flowers and foliage. Some materials may be wired with more than one of

Notes

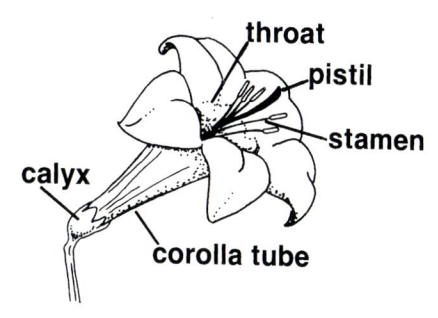

Design Mechanics

Figure 3.9 Basic Parts of the Flower

Figure 3.10a Pierce Wiring Method Step 2

Figure 3.10b Pierce Wiring Method Steps 3 & 4

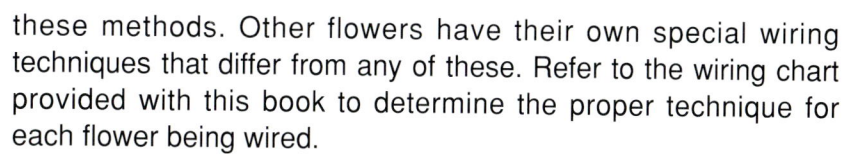

Figure 3.11 Insertion Wiring Method

these methods. Other flowers have their own special wiring techniques that differ from any of these. Refer to the wiring chart provided with this book to determine the proper technique for each flower being wired.

An understanding of basic flower morphology is helpful in following the steps in many of the wiring techniques described. The flower diagram in **Figure 3.9** shows the basic parts of the flower.

Pierce Method

Flowers with a thick calyx beneath the flower head, such as roses and carnations, are wired by piercing, as shown in **Figure 3.10**.

1. Trim the flower stem to a length of 1/2 to 1 inch.

2. Push one end of a wire horizontally through the calyx using half the length of the wire. **(Figure 3.10a)**

3. Bend both ends down parallel with the stem. **(Figure 3.10b)**

4. Tape, starting just above the pierce. **(Figure 3.10b)**

5. For heavy flowers in need of additional support, a second wire may be inserted through the flower so that the two wires are crisscrossed. This method is called cross-piercing.

Insertion Method

This method can be used for flowers with the heads firmly fastened to the stem, such as asters. Use wire 6 to 9 inches long and strong enough to hold the flower head erect **(see Figure 3.11)**.

1. Cut the flower stem to about 1 inch in length.

2. Push the wire inside the stem and up into the flower head until it is firm. The wire should not be visible from the top of the flower. **(Figure 3.11)**

3. Tape the stem and the wire tightly together.

Hook Method

This method can be used with any flower that has a hard disc-like center, such as daisies and mums. It may also be used with a light gauge wire on individual florets, such as those of delphinium or hyacinths **(see Figure 3.12)**.

1. Cut the flower stem to about 1 inch in length.

2. Push a wire along or through the stem until the wire has emerged through the center of the flower to a height of about 1 1/2 inches. **(Figure 3.12a)**

3. Form a hook 1/2 to 3/4 inch long and pull the wire gently back down into the flower, making sure that the hook is concealed in the blossom. The end of the hook should emerge back through the base of the flower. **(Figure 3.12a)**

4. Tape the stem, beginning at the base of the flower and making sure to catch the end of the hook within the tape. **(Figure 3.12b)**

Figure 3.12a Hook Wiring Method Steps 2 & 3

Figure 3.12b Hook Wiring Method Step 4

Wrap-around (Clutch) Method

Almost any flower can be wired with this method, but is especially effective for small flowers in clusters, such as baby's breath and statice **(see Figure 3.13)**.

1. Cut the flower stem or stems to 1 to 1 1/2 inches.

2. Wrap a light wire around the stem or cluster tightly to create a "bunchy" appearance. **(Figure 3.13)**

3. Bend the two wire ends parallel to the stem and tape.

Figure 3.13 Wrap-around (Clutch) Wiring Method

Stitch Method

This method is used almost entirely for broad-leaved foliage, such as camellia, ivy, or salal **(see Figure 3.14)**.

1. Cut the stem of the leaf to approximately 1/2 inch.

2. Pierce a wire through the back of the leaf near the center rib. Pierce the wire high enough on the leaf to

Figure 3.14a Stitch Wiring Method Step 2

Design Mechanics

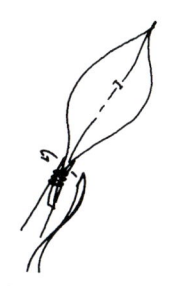

57

Figure 3.14b Stitch Wiring Method Step 4

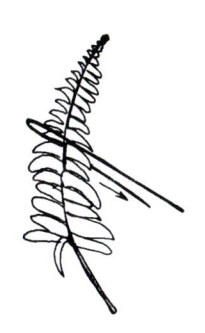

Figure 3.15a Hairpin Wiring Method Step 2

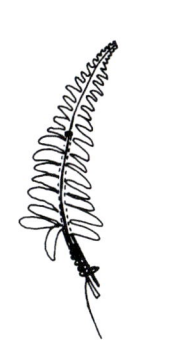

Figure 3.15b Hairpin Wiring Method Step 4

Figure 3.16 Splinting Wiring Method

gain complete control of the leaf, but not so high that the wire will show in the bouquet (about half the length of the leaf). *(Figure 3.14a)*

3. Push the wire halfway through the leaf and bend the wire ends down.

4. Wrap one wire around the leaf stem and around the second wire for extra security. *(Figure 3.14b)*

5. Tape the stem.

Hairpin Method

This method is used to wire multi-flowered stems or fern-like foliage when support is needed high on the stem *(see Figure 3.15)*.

1. Bend a wire in half to form a hairpin.

2. Straddle the hairpin over the stem near the center or top, depending on the amount of control desired *(Figure 3.15a)*

3. Pull the wire down until the bend of the hairpin rests on the stem.

4. Wrap one wire around the stem and the second wire. *(Figure 3.15b)*

5. Tape the stem.

Splinting Method

This method is used primarily when creating a design that features the flowers' natural stems, such as a hand-tied bouquet or a design in a foam bouquet holder. The splinting method adds strength to the stem and allows the stem to be slightly bent for design purposes *(see Figure 3.16)*.

1. Insert a full-length wire vertically into the base of the calyx.

2. Loosely wrap the wire around the full length of the stem in a gentle spiral. *(Figure 3.16)*

3. Trim any excess wire from the end of the stem.

4. If desired, tape the stem to cover the wire. (Do not tape over the end of the flower stem.)

Basics of Taping

Floral tape is a lightweight wax crepe paper. The adhesive is activated when the tape is stretched and wrapped tightly around wire or other design elements. A certain amount of adhesiveness remains after the tape is wrapped around an item. This adhesiveness causes individual, taped wires to stick together until the group can be bound by a separate piece of floral tape.

Floral tape is available in a wide variety of colors, including several shades of green, which is the most widely used color. Two widths of floral tape are also available: 1/2 inch and 1 inch. One-half inch tape is frequently used to bind wired stems together in bouquets. Floral tape is a staple item in wedding design, and it is imperative that designers learn to use it well.

Taping a Wired Stem (Figure 3.17)

1. With the wired flower in hand, start at the calyx of the flower and wrap a piece of tape around the top of the wire, pressing it securely into place. **(Figure 3.17a)**

2. Twirl the flower stem with one hand while stretching and pulling the tape on a downward angle with the other hand. The tape should be tightly wrapped around the wire with no buckles or gaps along the stem. **(Figure 3.17b)**

3. When the end of the wire is reached, tear the tape off the roll and wrap the remaining piece around the wire. **(Figure 3.17c)**

Figure 3.17a Taping a Wired Stem Step 1

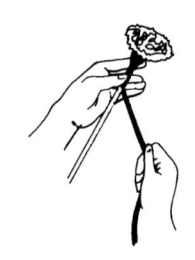

Figure 3.17b Taping a Wired Stem Step 2

Figure 3.17c Taping a Wired Stem Step 3

Wireless Taping

This method of taping is used primarily for small flowers or accessories. It is used to create free-flowing pieces from a corsage or hairpiece. Only lightweight materials should be used with this technique since there is no wire to support the item.

1. Cut the stem of the item to be taped to approximately 1 inch in length.

Design Mechanics

2. Wrap a piece of floral tape around the top of the stem the same as if the flower were wired.

3. Twirl the flower in one hand and twist the tape tightly around itself. The resulting "stem" will be soft and pliable.

4. Continue taping until the "stem" reaches the desired length.

5. For added support and control, the stem may be taped a second time.

Wiring Techniques for Special Flowers

Certain types of flowers are either too delicate or unusually shaped to be wired using any standard method. The following are techniques for wiring commonly used corsage flowers.

Cattleya, Cymbidium, and Japhet Orchids

Although these flowers are traditionally wired using the pierce method, the following method may be used when additional support is needed *(see Figure 3.18)*.

1. Cut the orchid stem to a length of 1 to 1 1/2 inches.

2. Insert a chenille stem up through the orchid stem as far as possible without entering the throat of the orchid. *(Figure 3.18a)*

3. Pierce-wire the orchid stem at the base of the flower with a #24 gauge wire. *(Figure 3.18b)*

4. Begin taping at the base of the flower and tape all the way down, binding the stem, wire, and chenille into one unit.

Dendrobium and Cypripedium (Lady Slipper) Orchids

These flowers may be wired in more than one way depending on how they will be used in design. The following steps are for wiring individual blossoms for bouquets or body flowers *(see Figure 3.19 on page 60)*.

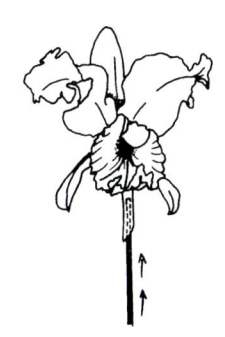

Figure 3.18a Wiring Cattleya, Cymbidium, and Japhet Orchids Step 2

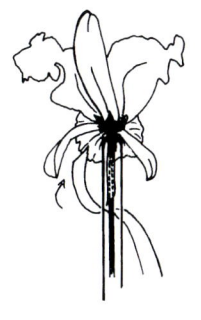

Figure 3.18b Wiring Cattleya, Cymbidium, and Japhet Orchids Step 3

1. Pierce a #24 to #26 gauge wire vertically into the orchid where the stem and the flower meet. **(Figure 3.19a)**

2. Push the wire out through the throat of the flower and bend the end into a small hook. **(Figure 3.19a)**

3. Pull the wire hook back into the orchid until it reaches the flower base. The end of the hook should protrude through the back of the flower. **(Figure 3.19b)**

4. Tape the end of the hook to the flower stem, and continue taping to the end of the wire.

NOTE: The pierce method may also be used to wire individual dendrobium blossoms by inserting a wire through the thick chin at the base of the flower. Full-length dendrobium orchid sprays with multiple flowers on a stem may be wired using the wrap-around method with a #22 gauge wire.

Figure 3.19a Wiring Dendrobium and Cypripedium (Lady Slipper) Orchids Step 1

Figure 3.19b Wiring Dendrobium and Cypripedium (Lady Slipper) Orchids Step 2

Phalaenopsis Orchids

Phalaenopsis orchids are extremely delicate and must be handled carefully when designing. The following wiring technique is used to provide support without damaging the flowers **(see Figure 3.20)**.

1. Tape the center 1 inch of a #26 or #28 gauge wire with white tape.

2. Bend the wire in half to form a "U" in the middle of the white-taped section.

3. The lip of the orchid is connected to the rest of the flower by a delicate narrow membrane. Place one end of the bent wire on each side of the narrow membrane. **(Figure 3.20a)**

4. Gently pull the wire down until the taped center rests against the membrane. The wire should not be inserted through any part of the flower.

5. Align the wires with the stem on the underside of the orchid. It may be necessary to bend the wire slightly where it meets the narrow membrane.

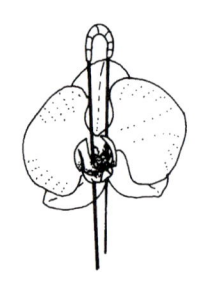

Figure 3.20a Wiring Phalaenopsis Orchids Step 3

Figure 3.20b Wiring Phalaenopsis Orchids Step 6

Design Mechanics

6. Wrap one wire around the flower stem and the second wire a few times to secure the wire in place. **(Figure 3.20b)**

7. Tape the wire from top to bottom.

Gardenias

Gardenias may be wired using the cross-pierce method described previously or with a chenille stem as described below **(see Figure 3.21)**. Gardenias are fairly easy to wire, but are very fragile and easily bruised. Bruising can be reduced by keeping the hands wet while working with the flowers. Avoid touching the petals of a gardenia if at all possible.

1. Turn the flower upside down and cut the stem about 1 inch below the collar and remove the calyx.

2. Place a chenille stem up into the stem until secure. **(Figure 3.21a)**

3. Use a #24 gauge wire to pierce wire the stem directly under the collar. **(Figure 3.21b)**

4. Bend the wire parallel to the stem and tape. **(Figure 3.21c)**

5. After the gardenia has been prepared, a wet tissue may be placed over the flower to help maintain freshness and reduce bruising.

NOTE: If the gardenia is not already tailored, wire as directed and edge the gardenia blossom with wired camellia leaves or create a self-made collar as outlined below. If the gardenia is collared with plastic leaves, clip them off and staple fresh galax or other broad-leaved foliage into place. Be sure the ends of the staples face the flower to prevent scratching.

Gardenia Collar *(Figure 3.22)*

1. Cut a circle about 1 1/2 inches in diameter out of thin green or white cardboard.

2. Bend the cardboard slightly and clip crisscrossed slits through the center to provide an opening for the flower stem. **(Figure 3.22a)**

Figure 3.21a Wiring Gardenias Step 2

Figure 3.21b Wiring Gardenias Step 3

Figure 3.21c Wiring Gardenias Step 4

Figure 3.22a Creating a Gardenia Collar Step 2

3. Staple flat, broad-leaved foliage, such as camellia or salal, around the edge of the cardboard circle with the backside of the leaf against the cardboard. The base of each leaf should overlap the cardboard about 1/3 inch. **(Figures 3.22b and 3.22c)**

4. Slide the flower stem through the center opening of the cardboard. Gently position the collar underneath the gardenia so that it will support the petals.

5. Wire and tape as directed.

Camellia

Traditionally, camellia flowers are cross-pierced through the flower petals about 1/4 inch above the calyx. The following method is also effective for these delicate blossoms **(see Figure 3.23)**.

1. Bend the top 1/2 inch of four #24 gauge wires down toward the wire at a 45-degree angle to create a hook. **(Figure 3.23a)**

2. Gently insert the hooks of the wires, one at a time, into the base of the flower petals on four sides of the flower. **(Figure 3.23b)**

3. Pull the wires together under the flower and tape.

Delicate Blossoms

Small, delicate flowers, such as pansies, violets, and begonias, are often requested for wedding bouquets. Many of these blossoms are quite fragile and difficult to work with. The following techniques may be used to simplify designing with these flowers.

Gluing Delicate Blossoms

Floral adhesive glue (not hot glue) may be used to add delicate flowers directly into a bouquet. For more precise placement of these flowers, the following technique may be used **(see Figure 3.24 on page 63)**.

1. Select a fresh broad-leaved foliage (such as salal). The leaf should be approximately the same size as the

Figure 3.22b Creating a Gardenia Collar Step 3

Figure 3.22c Creating a Gardenia Collar Step 3

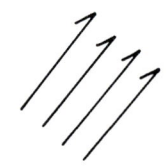

Figure 3.23a Wiring Camellias Step 1

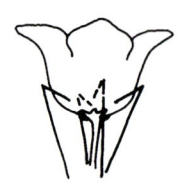

Figure 3.23b Wiring Camellias Step 2

Design Mechanics

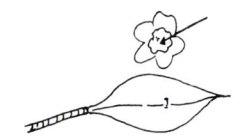

63

Figure 3.24a Gluing Delicate Blossoms Step 2

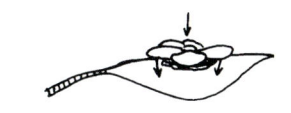

Figure 3.24b Gluing Delicate Blossoms Step 3

flower. Wire the leaf using the stitch method and tape. Make sure the wire is heavy enough to support the weight of the leaf and flower.

2. Apply a generous amount of floral adhesive glue to the back of the flower. *(Figure 3.24a)*

3. Lay the flower on the leaf and set it aside for about 30 minutes to allow the glue to dry. *(Figure 3.24b)*

4. Use the wired leaf to incorporate the flower into the design.

Using Gelatin with Delicate Blossoms

A diluted gelatin mixture may be used to coat delicate blossoms and make them more firm. The flowers may be wired and taped before or after the coating is applied. The gluing method described above may be used to secure them into a design.

1. Mix one envelope of clear gelatin with 1 cup of boiling water until dissolved.

2. Allow the mixture to cool to room temperature.

3. Paint the gelatin mixture onto the flowers and place them in the cooler to stiffen.

4. Wire the blossoms individually or secure them to a leaf as described in the gluing technique above.

Feathering Carnations

Feathering is the term used to describe the process of making a series of smaller carnation florets out of a standard carnation. A carnation can be broken down into a few petals or can be used in halves, thirds, or quarters, depending on florists' needs. Insuring that tape is wrapped tightly is important to the success of this technique. The following steps should be followed to create feathered carnations *(see Figure 3.25)*.

Figure 3.25a Feathering Carnations Step 1

Figure 3.25b Feathering Carnations Step 1

1. Cut the stem off at the base of the calyx. A rich green dot will be visible at the location where the stem was attached. *(Figures 3.25a and 3.25b)*

Basic Floral Design

2. Hold the blossom upside down. Slice through the base of the calyx from the bottom to where it visually ends and the petals begin *(Figure 3.25c)*. The blossom may be cut in half, in thirds, or in quarters, depending on the desired size of the finished floret. *(Figures 3.25d and 3.25e)*

3. Pull the pieces apart carefully, so that the petals stay connected to the calyx. Remove the piece of calyx with its attached petals. *(Figure 3.25f)*

4. Tape the piece of calyx tightly around its attached petals. This will create a flower similar to a miniature carnation. Tape from the top of the calyx to its base. *(Figure 3.25g)*

5. Pierce-wire the created flower and tape it. *(Figure 3.25h on page 65)*

6. The feathered carnation is now ready to be used as an individual blossom in a corsage. *(Figure 3.25i on page 65)*

<u>Wiring Silks for Corsage Work</u> *(Figure 3.26 on page 65)*

The stems of most silk flowers are too heavy to use as the stem for a corsage flower. There are many ways to wire silk flowers, but few allow the stem to look slim and sleek. The simplest method, which allows the most control, is a four-step process *(see Figure 3.26a on page 65)*.

1. Cut the stems of the flowers to approximately 3/4 inch in length.

2. Dip the end of a #26 or #28 gauge wire into pan melt glue. Use only a fine bead of glue. Large amounts of glue will detract from the appearance.

3. Lay the glued wire along the stem of the flower.

4. After the glue has dried, tape tightly from the base of the flower down the wire.

Silk foliage is prepared in a similar manner. *(Figure 3.26b on page 65)*

1. Cut the stems of the foliage or leaf to approximately 3/4 inch below the base of the leaf.

Figure 3.25c Feathering Carnations Step 2

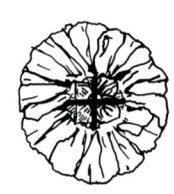

Figure 3.25d Feathering Carnations Step 2

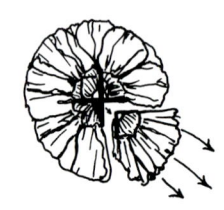

Figure 3.25e Feathering Carnations Step 2

Figure 3.25f Feathering Carnations Step 3

Figure 3.25g Feathering Carnations Step 4

Design Mechanics

Figure 3.25h Feathering Carnations Step 5

Figure 3.25i Feathering Carnations Step 6

Figure 3.26a Wiring Silk Flowers

Figure 3.26b Wiring Silk Foliage

2. Dip a #26 or #28 gauge wire into pan melt glue. Use only a fine bead of glue. Large amounts of glue will detract from the appearance.

3. Lay the glued wire along the back of the leaf, 3/4 inch above the base of the leaf, along the vein of the leaf.

4. After the glue has dried, tightly tape from the base of the leaf and down the wire.

How to Make a Bow

Many designs are far more effective without a bow, while other designs need bows or ribbon treatments to have a finished look. The majority of the floral-buying public prefers ribbon in most designs. In the eyes of the average consumer, ribbon adds a perceived value to an arrangement or corsage. Therefore, the floral industry has created ribbon treatments for almost every occasion. A variety of bow styles is used in floral design. Each style can be created with any available width of ribbon. This allows florists to incorporate each style into corsages, arrangements, and other designs.

Bow Making Tips

Following are tips for making various types of bows that can be used in all types of floral designs.

- Bows should be held in one hand while feeding the ribbon into it with the other.

- During construction, hold the bow with the thumb, index finger, and middle finger. The thumb stays on the top center, while the other two fingers act like a shuttle, as the ribbon is worked back and forth from underneath.

- Practice is necessary to become proficient at making bows. To improve this skill, designers should be encouraged to make bows often.

- A bow without a center loop is best in situations where it will be tucked under a flower or placed deep inside an arrangement.

Basic Floral Design

- It is best not to make bows with large, loose loops. They crush easily and do not hold their shape well.

- Bows can be tied off or finished with chenille stems, bare wire, taped wire, or narrow matching ribbon.

- It is better to use ribbon directly from a bolt instead of cutting the ribbon prior to beginning the bow. A series of bows will appear more uniform.

- Any bow with or without a center loop may have as many or as few loops as desired.

- A bow's tail length is usually measured in proportion to the width of the ribbon. Long tails may be used in bud vases, rose vases, or on football mum corsages.

Making a Bow with a Center Loop *(Figure 3.27)*

1. Pull a few yards of ribbon from a bolt. Measure the length of one streamer and twist the ribbon at this point while holding it between the thumb and index finger. When the ribbon is twisted, it will change from the shiny side to the dull side. **(Figures 3.27a and 3.27b)**

2. Pull the ribbon from the bolt over the thumb and tuck it between the thumb and index finger. A small loop, which is shiny and covers the thumb, will be made. **(Figure 3.27c)**

3. Twist the end of the ribbon half way so that the shiny side is visible. Make a loop to the side of the center loop. Tuck the end of the ribbon loop between the index finger and thumb. Twist the ribbon again so that the shiny side is visible. **(Figure 3.27d)**

4. Make another loop of the same size on the other side of the center loop. Tuck the ribbon between the thumb and index finger. Twist the ribbon. **(Figure 3.27e)**

5. Continue to make loops on each side of the center loop until a total of eight to ten loops have been formed. **(Figures 3.27f and 3.28g on page 67)**

6. Slide a wire along the side of the thumb through the center loop. Pull the wire down between the index and

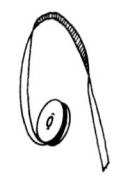

Figure 3.27a Making a Bow with a Center Loop Step 1

Figure 3.27b Making a Bow with a Center Loop Step 1

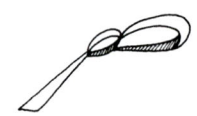

Figure 3.27c Making a Bow with a Center Loop Step 2

Figure 3.27d Making a Bow with a Center Loop Step 3

Figure 3.27e Making a Bow with a Center Loop Step 4

Figure 3.27f Making a Bow with a Center Loop Step 5

Design Mechanics

Figure 3.27g Making a Bow with a Center Loop Step 5

Figure 3.27h Making a Bow with a Center Loop Step 6

Figure 3.28a Making a Bow without a Center Loop Step 1

Figure 3.28b Making a Bow without a Center Loop Step 2

Figure 3.28c Making a Bow without a Center Loop Step 3

middle fingers, and make sure that all of the loops are caught by the wire. **(Figure 3.27h)** Twist the wire tightly around the ribbon. Cut the ribbon from the bolt so that the second tail is approximately the same length as the first.

7. Pull the loops and arrange them so that the bow looks balanced, full, and lush.

Making a Bow without a Center Loop *(Figure 3.28)*

1. Pull ribbon from a bolt. Measure off the appropriate tail length, and pinch it at that point between the thumb and index finger. *(Figure 3.28a)*

2. While the ribbon is still on the bolt, shiny side up, make a loop at one side of the thumb. Pinch the ribbon between the thumb and index finger. *(Figure 3.28b)*

3. Twist the ribbon so that the shiny side is up; then, make a loop on the opposite side of the thumb. Tuck the ribbon between the thumb and middle finger. ***(Figure 3.28c on page 68)***

4. Twist the ribbon so that the shiny side is up; then, continue to make loops, first on the index finger side and then on the middle finger side. Make four or five loops on each side of the thumb. ***(Figure 3.28d on page 68)***

5. Place the wire next to the thumb and insert it between the index and middle fingers. Pull the wire around the ribbon and twist it tightly to secure the bow. Cut the ribbon from the bolt so that the second tail matches the first. Then shape the bow as before. ***(Figure 3.28e on page 68)***

Making a Three Loop Tuck-in Bow

When this bow is completed, it will have two loops on one side of the wire and two tails and one loop on the other.

1. Pull the ribbon from a bolt. Measure the desired tail length and twist the ribbon at that point.

2. Make a loop to the opposite side of the thumb. Tuck the ribbon between the thumb and index finger.

3. Twist the ribbon so that the shiny side is up. Make another loop on the same side of the thumb as the tail. Tuck the ribbon between the thumb and middle finger.

4. Twist the ribbon so that the shiny side shows. Make the last loop on the same side as the first one. Tuck the ribbon between the index finger and thumb. Twist the shiny side up.

5. Put the wire next to the thumb. Pull it down between the index and middle fingers. Pull the wire around the ribbon and twist it to secure the bow. Cut the ribbon from the bolt so that the second tail matches the first.

6. Place the bow in a design so that the three loops lie on top of each other with the tails below them.

Figure 3.28d Making a Bow without a Center Loop Step 4

Figure 3.28e Making a Bow without a Center Loop Step 5

Making a Double Loop Tuck-in Bow

This bow is similar to a shoestring bow, but has no center loop.

1. Pull some ribbon from the bolt and measure the desired tail length from the end; twist at the point.

2. Make a loop on the side of the thumb opposite the tail. Tuck the ribbon between the thumb and index finger. Twist the ribbon so that the shiny side shows.

3. Make a loop on the same side as the tail.

4. Twist so that the shiny side of the ribbon is showing, except on the last tail.

5. Place the wire next to the thumb; pull it down between the index and middle finger and twist it tightly to secure it. Cut the second tail so that it is the same length or shorter than the first.

When the bow is inserted into a design, the two loops will be positioned between the two tails.

Making a Single Loop Tuck-in Bow

1. Pull some ribbon from the bolt. From the end, measure off a tail of the desired length and twist.

Design Mechanics

2. Make a loop on the opposite side of the thumb. Tuck it between the index finger and thumb.

3. Twist so that both tails and the loop are shiny side up.

4. Place the wire next to the thumb, and pull it between the index finger and middle finger. Twist it tightly, and cut the ribbon from the bolt so that the second tail matches the first.

5. Place it in the design so that the loop rests on top of the tails.

<u>Making Tail Tuck-ins</u> *(Figure 3.29)*

1. Cut the desired length of ribbon from the bolt.

2. Attach a pick to the tail with a wired wood pick or a pick machine. Double tails can have a wire twisted around the center so that the two tails are divided.

3. Tails can be cut at an angle, as shown in **Figure 3.29a**, or with two points. A two-pointed tail is made by cutting a *V* out of the ribbon's end. *(Figure 3.29b)* The finished tail will look like a *W*.

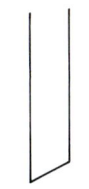

Figure 3.29a Making Tail Tuck-ins - Angle Cut

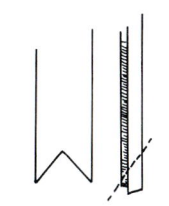

Figure 3.29b Making Tail Tuck-ins - W Cut

Paint and Dye Techniques

Paints and dyes are of an immense value to floral designers. They may be used to enhance or alter the color and or textural appearance of flowers and containers. Several types of floral sprays are available. Spray paints are most often opaque-based colors that will completely cover any color underneath. Spray tints are translucent colors that allow the base color to show through to a limited degree. Glitter sprays and similar products add a dust coating or texture to the sprayed surface. It is important to read labels and familiarize oneself with each product and its use before utilizing them in daily design work.

Using Spray Paints

The methods used to apply spray paints, tints, and glitters are similar. The following steps will assist florists in using these products successfully.

1. Shake the can to mix the paint completely. Shake new cans or cans that are not frequently used for an extended period of time.

   2. To check the flow of paint, test the can by spraying it into a trash can or box.

   3. Hold the can so that its spray nozzle is about 12 inches away from the item being painted.

   4. Press the nozzle down in quick bursts, while moving the can from side to side to insure even coverage.

   5. A single light coat of paint or tint is usually preferred on fresh or silk flowers, while several light coats are recommended for containers, foliage, and dried materials. Applying one or two light coatings of glitter spray is more effective than one heavy application.

   6. Allow all sprayed items to dry thoroughly before using them.

   7. After finishing with a can of paint, turn it upside down and press the nozzle until only air is discharged. This clears the nozzle of paint that might dry and block the nozzle.

Stem Dyes

Stem dying relies on the flower's transport system to carry dye to the petals. The flower's need for nutrition causes the dye to travel up the stem and throughout the bloom. Wholesalers use this method of coloring flowers more frequently than retailers. Stem dying is more successful if done with white or light-colored flowers. It is suggested that only fresh flowers be dyed. Old flowers do not dye evenly. The procedures for dying are as follows.

   1. Flowers to be colored should be removed from water and cold storage approximately 3 hours before processing. They need to come to room temperature and be thirsty to properly take up the dye. Flowers that have been in dry storage or that are shipped dry absorb dye quickly and may over-stain; therefore, it is important to check flowers frequently while in the solution.

Design Mechanics

Notes

2. Instructions for mixing stem dye may vary, so labels should be read before beginning. Most often the solution is a mixture of 2 teaspoons of dye to 1 quart of 90 to 100 degree water. If the water is too hot, it may scald the stems.

3. Remove all of the lower foliage from the stems. Cut the stems at an angle with a sharp knife or blade cutter.

4. Place the stems into the solution immediately. The flowers should absorb a sufficient amount of dye in 15 to 30 minutes. Long-stemmed flowers should be removed from the dye as soon as color appears above the calyx. At this point, there will be enough dye in the stem to color the bloom completely. Short-stemmed flowers may require more color to insure total and even coloration.

5. Rinse the stems. Re-cut them, and place them in warm, preservative-treated water. At room temperature, the blooms will be colored in about 2 hours.

It is best not to refrigerate stem-dyed flowers for several hours. They can remain out of the cooler overnight if processed late in the day. Refrigeration can stop or slow the completion of coloring, as well as, the development of the flower.

Dip Dyes

Dip dyes tint flowers through the direct dipping of flower heads into the color solution. Dip dyes are semitransparent and should be used on white or light-colored flowers. Fresh flowers accept the dye best. The following steps explain how to dip dye flowers.

1. Dip the flower heads into the dye solution for a few seconds.

2. Shake off any excess dye.

3. Rinse the bloom in clear water.

4. Shake the bloom again to remove excess water and promote faster drying. As with sprays, it is best to

Basic Floral Design

allow the flower to dry thoroughly to prevent staining other flowers and clothing.

If a lighter color of dip dye is desired, dilute it with the appropriate thinner, not water. To darken the shade of color, dip the bloom again and repeat the entire process after it has dried from the first treatment.

Special Decoration Mechanics

Florists might wish to add balloons, plush animals, candles, or other gift-related items to an arrangement. It is important to place such items securely in a design to prevent flower breakage. Secure placement will help insure that designs reach recipients undamaged. The following are tips and steps that can assist florists in designing with gift items.

Balloons

Shops can save valuable time by properly anchoring balloons into an arrangement. The following steps will help prevent losing balloons in the wind **(see Figure 3.30)**.

1. For best results, use a 4-inch, wired wood pick. Take three balloons and lay their ribbons on one side of the pick. (Ribbon ends should fall past the pick's point. It is best to put no more than three balloons on a single pick.)

2. Wrap the pick's wire around the pick and ribbon one or two times.

3. Pull the ends of the balloon ribbons up to create a small loop just below the wire's anchoring point. **(Figure 3.30a)**

4. Finish wrapping the wire around the second layer of ribbons and the pick. The balloons will be held securely in the wet foam because the pick will expand slightly after insertion. **(Figure 3.30b)**

Figure 3.30a Anchoring Balloons Step 3

Figure 3.30b Anchoring Balloons Step 3

Plastic Novelties

Hard plastic novelties, such as animals, birds, and ornaments, are often only available without a wire stem. Without this stem it is

Design Mechanics

very difficult to keep them in place within a design. A wire stem can be easily attached to these items using the following method.

1. Light a candle and hold the point of a #18 gauge or #20 gauge wire in the flame. To hold short pieces of wire, use a pair of needle-nose pliers to avoid burns.

2. When the wire's end is red hot, quickly insert the hot wire point into the bottom or base of the plastic novelty. If needed, add a bead of glue from a glue gun to the point of insertion for added security.

3. Cut the wire to the desired length and insert the novelty item into the design.

4. A wire wood pick may need to be added to the wire stem to insure that it is straight in the foam.

Plush Animals

Plush animals are popular with both young and old. It is important to keep them clean and dry when placing them in an arrangement. To protect a plush gift, a piece of clear cellophane can be used by following the techniques below *(see Figure 3.31)*.

1. Pull a piece of cellophane up around the animal's waist.

2. Place a matching length of ribbon around its waist and tie it to hold the cellophane in place. *(Figure 3.31a)*

Figure 3.31a Protecting Plush Animals with Cellophane

Plush animals can also be secured in a design with a hyacinth stick by utilizing the following technique.

1. Cut a hyacinth stick 1 inch shorter than the height of the animal.

2. Tape the stick with floral tape which matches the color of the plush animal.

3. Insert a few pieces of foliage to cover the area of foam that the animal will rest on.

4. Place the plush animal on the bed of foliage. Insert the hyacinth stake through the ribbon at the animal's waist and into the foam.

Figure 3.31b Anchoring Plush Animals with Hyacinth Sticks

5. A second length of ribbon should be tied around a large animal's neck, as well as, to the stake to keep it from falling over. **(Figure 3.31b)**

The same principles apply when florists wish to attach an animal to the handle of a basket. Protect the animal with the before-mentioned cellophane wrap if the animal will sit on any part of the floral foam.

1. Secure the animal's neck, and possibly waist, to the handle with ribbon.

2. If the animal swings around the handle, use a hyacinth stake to correct the movement.

3. Follow the instructions above to use a hyacinth stake in the basket.

Candles

Candles should be secure in any type of foam that is being used. There are several plastic devices that will hold candles of various sizes in place. These should be used in silk designs so that the candles can be replaced or changed as desired. It is advisable to place candles in some type of chimney when using them with silk and dried materials. Florists should check with local authorities to determine local fire codes which might apply to these circumstances. The following tips will assist a designer when using candles in silk, dried, and fresh arrangements.

Silk and Dried Arrangements

- Large pillar candles can be secured with pan melt glue applied directly to hard foam for silk work.

- Dry foam should have plastic candleholders for the proper support of the candles.

- It is best to insert candleholders before covering the foam with moss to insure a secure hold.

Fresh Arrangements

Plastic candleholders may be utilized in fresh flower arrangements. In addition, the following methods, which are less costly but just as efficient, may also be used.

Notes

Design Mechanics

Figure 3.32a Taper Candles

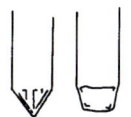

Figure 3.32b Cutting Tapered Candles

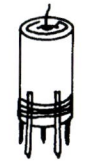

Figure 3.33 Securing Pillar Candles

Taper Candles

At room temperature, taper candles can be cut at the base with two angled cuts. The finished candle bottom will resemble a three dimensional "V" or the end of an axe blade. Never use candles pointed like a pencil; they may rotate and loosen too easily. After the candle is trimmed, insert it into at least half the depth of the foam block. Push the candle straight down as it is inserted. Do not turn or twist the candle while inserting it into the foam.

Large Pillar Candles

Large pillar candles may have 4-inch or 6-inch wood picks attached around their base to insure a secure hold in foam. Four-inch picks are recommended for 3-inch pillars. Six-inch picks are best for pillars that are 9 inches or taller.

1. Attach the 4-inch picks with waterproof tape about 1 inch from the bottom of the candle. This leaves 3 inches of pick to insert into the foam. Six-inch picks should be placed approximately 1 1/2 inches from the base of the candle, leaving 4 to 4 1/2 inches of pick to insert into the foam. The longer pick gives the candle a more stable hold in the foam. Cut a small piece off the bottom if the picks are too long.

2. Use five or six picks for each pillar candle. The tape should be wrapped around the pillar and the picks about three times so that the picks cannot move.

3. When florists are inserting pillar candles into arrangements, the base of the candles should rest on the foam, with at least 3 inches of pick in the foam. It is important to have a large enough base to hold these candles, which may be top heavy.

Florists will lose many customers if their arrangements are not well constructed. To assure a client's happiness, all floral products must be properly secured within a design. The proper wiring and taping techniques, coupled with properly-soaked floral foam, will extend a flower's longevity in any arrangement. Once mastered, the techniques in this chapter will assist florists with the basics of design, and as a result, will enhance the customer's satisfaction.

Basic Floral Design

Notes, Photographs, Sketches, etc.

Design Mechanics

Notes, Photographs, Sketches, etc.

Fresh Flower Care and Handling

Chapter 4

*H*ealthy, long-lasting flowers are a necessity in any successful floral business. Studies show that consumers want long-lasting products. Price is not their only concern. Since there is an increasing number of floral outlets for consumers to choose from, providing long-lasting product gives the florist an edge over the competition. It also proves to the consumer that the florist is a floral professional who has mastered the business, the art, and the science of flowers.

To create beautiful and long-lasting designs, the floral artist must thoroughly understand the products he or she is working with. Flowers are perishable, living, and ever-changing, and they require special care to insure a healthy and long life. There are thousands of species and varieties of flowers in every shape, form, and color. Floral knowledge can be overwhelming, but it helps to begin with a solid foundation, including basic flower structures and life-prolonging techniques (often referred to as care and handling or Chain of Life procedures). This chapter provides a series of charts and checklists to assist in categorizing flowers that have similar needs and in organizing the entire care and handling process.

Flower Structures, Classifications, and Names

Despite the overwhelming variety of flowers, they all have much in common despite differences in appearance. The primary similarity is structural, particularly of the essential reproductive organs: pistils, or female organs, and stamens, or male organs. The stamen is a collective term for the anther and filament. The pistil is a collective term for the stigma, style, and ovary. Basically, the stamen produces pollen grains which, through fertilization, enable the ovules in the pistil to develop into seeds. Around these basic fertile parts, flowers usually have a ring of conspicuously colored petals. Sometimes the petals are fused into a tube. The sepals are a ring of small, normally green, bracts below, or outside, the petals. They enclose the other flower parts in the bud. All of the sepals combined form the calyx. Often the petals and sepals look the same or are fused together and are referred to as the perianth. *Figure 4.1* illustrates the basic anatomy of a complete flower, which is a flower that has both male and female reproductive parts, plus petals and sepals. *Figure 4.2* illustrates the location of structural parts on a hybrid lily.

Some flowers, such as orchids, are referred to as irregular flowers because some parts, such as petals, are fused, or because other variations occur. The large showy part of some flowers is actually another structure (frequently a modified leaf) and the true flowers are smaller and less obvious. Examples include the anthurium, calla (the showy, colorful part is called a spathe) and poinsettia (the showy colorful parts are called bracts). *Figure 4.3* diagrams the arrangement of structural parts on an anthurium.

These variations in the number and arrangement of pistils and stamens, plus the color and shape of petals and sepals, not only make flowers unique and distinctively beautiful, but are important parts of flower identification and design. This terminology is frequently used in educational materials, reference books, and even conversations between growers, flower suppliers, designers, and others. Indeed this flower morphology forms the basis of the true classification of flowers.

Ordering flowers would be truly bewildering without classification and nomenclature (naming) to organize and simplify flower names. Basically, classification is the placing of similar things together. The earliest classifications simply distinguished plants harmful or useful. Today, there are a number of practical systems of classification, including those based on growth habit, such as bulbs or woody shrubs, life span of the actual plant (annual, biennial, perennial), and arbitrary classifications, such as tropical flowers, garden flowers, and European or Dutch flowers. These classifications are useful because they categorize flowers into groups that may assist florists in planning production, utilization, and marketing. However, regional differences may lead to confusion when using practical classifications. To avoid this, a standard worldwide scientific plant classification has been established.

The foundation for modern scientific classification was developed by the Swedish botanist Linnaeus, who divided all flowering plants into classes based on the number and arrangement of their reproductive organs. As knowledge improved and ideas changed, more categories were added to this

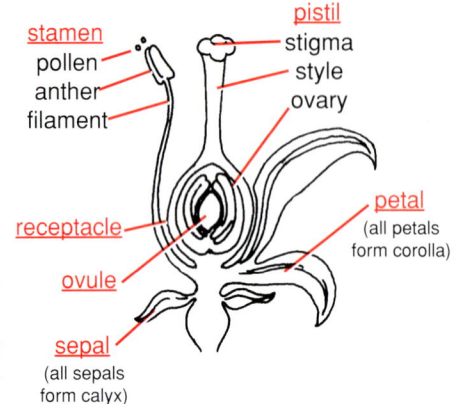

Figure 4.1 Basic Anatomy of a Complete Flower

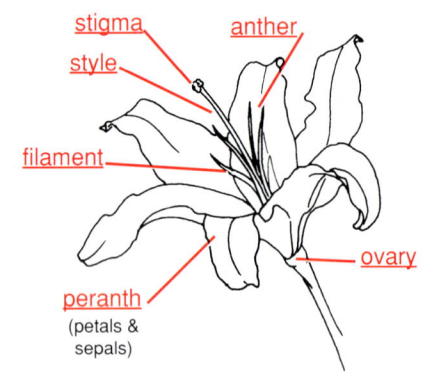

Figure 4.2 Arrangement of Structural Parts of a Hybrid Lily

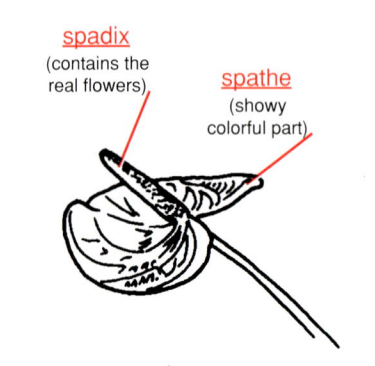

Figure 4.3 Arrangement of Structural Parts of an Anthurium

Fresh Flower Care and Handling

Notes

framework, incorporating the concept that plants are placed in categories because they have a close genetic relationship. Key categories and their corresponding relationships are listed below.

- Families - Broad groups of genera with similar traits.

- Genus - A group of similar, genetically-related species that have many major characteristics in common.

- Specific epithet (otherwise known as the species) - A group of plants that have definite and constant characteristics in common; this actually distinguishes specific qualities of a genus.

There are common terms that are often confused: variety and cultivar. A variety is a botanical collection, referring to a group of plants within a species that shows marked differences in nature. A cultivar is a variety which exists because it is cultivated or grown for horticultural purposes.

In other words, a cultivar is a group of flowers within a species that shows marked differences when grown under the supervision of man. Without man's influence, these plants or flowers may not continue to exist. For example, plant "sports" or throw backs must be propagated by cuttings or asexual reproduction methods (cultivation practices); otherwise, the plant is likely to return to its original state. The terms variety and cultivar are often used interchangeably when discussing ornamental crops. However, in actuality, many plants used in commercial floriculture are simply cultivars.

The binomial nomenclature is based on a two-part classification. Essentially, it means that plants acquire two Latin names. The first represents the genus and the second represents the specific epithet. Remember, the specific epithet is also known as the species. The scientific names genus and specific epithet each describe the species. If the flower is a variety or cultivar, the name has three parts. In communication, scientific names are most commonly written as follows.

Genus species 'cultivar' (only genus and species underlined or italicized; cultivar name in single quotes)

Example:

Dianthus caryophyllus cv. White Sim (a common white carnation cultivar)

or

Dianthus caryophyllus 'White Sim'

Basic Floral Design

Knowing or being familiar with Latin names is a great advantage and asset to flower ordering and care. Scientific names are used internationally, a practice which is vitally important with the increasing worldwide production of flowers. Packing lists, especially for direct orders of imported items, may be written with Latin names, and design magazines and books are more frequently using this nomenclature. Also, flowers within a certain genus have similar needs; therefore, knowing the genus of a certain flower and its needs will provide a fairly good idea of how to take care of the flower. This can be especially helpful with all the "new" flowers that are coming on the market. Examples are the carnation (<u>Dianthus caryophyllus</u>) and the Sweet William (<u>Dianthus barbatus</u>), which are both sensitive to ethylene and benefit from ethylene reduction treatments.

Several additional points should be kept in mind regarding use of variety and cultivar names and common names. Knowledge and use of variety and cultivar names can be very helpful, especially since there can be tremendous differences in appearance, as well as, performance. The florist should not simply request red roses, for example, but should specify 'Samantha,' 'Royalty,' 'Cara Mia,' 'Visa,' 'Gabriella,' or another. Keep in mind, however, that these names can vary among regions and countries. This goes for common names too. Common names, such as carnation and baby's breath, are those most frequently used because that is what most people know. This can sometimes lead to confusion, however. For example, the term protea is often used to order members of the Proteaceae family, when not all of them are true protea. The commonly called King Protea is <u>Protea cynaroides</u>, but the Pincushion is not truly a protea, but a <u>Leucospermum nutans</u>. It helps to know and use scientific names, especially when ordering an unusual flower or a specific flower for specific use, such as a wedding.

Basic Flower Needs

Designers must always remember that they are working with living products. Just like human beings, animals, and other living things, flowers have basic needs for a healthy, long life. Cut flowers require special care because they have been removed from the mother plant and the ideal conditions of the growing environment. Therefore, for the flower to live in bouquets, arrangements, and other designs, the needs must be fulfilled in other ways. An understanding of providing special care is an important foundation for proper floral care. Table 3 on page 83 reviews basic flower needs.

Notes

Fresh Flower Care and Handling

Notes

TABLE 3

BASIC FLOWER NEEDS

What Are Flower Needs	Why Are They Necessary
Water	Flowers are composed of more than 90 percent water! Water is needed to carry dissolved nutrients through the network of tiny vessels, up the stem and leaves, to the flower. Water keeps the flower firm, fresh, and alive after it has been separated from its mother plant.
Food	Flowers need an energy source (food) to carry on life-giving processes. When cut from the mother plant, a flower loses its source of nourishment; therefore, food must be provided by the florist.
Healthy Environment	Flowers need air to support life-giving processes. Air must be clean and fresh because pollutants, including gases such as ethylene, can inhibit life and cause damage. Temperatures also affect life-giving processes. Warm temperatures, like those during the growth process, encourage growth and development. Cool temperatures, like those in a cooler, slow down development and help flowers live longer. Excessively hot or cold temperatures will cause damage.
Hygiene (Sanitation)	Clean water, environment, and tools help prevent the growth of stem-clogging, disease-causing organisms that inhibit flower life.

Not Meeting Flower Needs

Designers and customers are greatly frustrated when maximum flower life is not realized. It is particularly frustrating when a typically long-lasting flower, such as a standard carnation (<u>Dianthus</u> <u>caryophyllus</u>) lasts only a few days. The most common cause for early deterioration and short life is a failure to meet flower needs. Sometimes this failure occurs at several points along the distribution chain, and sometimes it happens at only one point, such as the retail flower shop. Floral designers must learn to recognize and prevent these problems. The causes of early flower deterioration are reviewed in Table 4 on page 84.

Basic Floral Design

TABLE 4

CAUSES OF EARLY FLOWER DETERIORATION

Why There Is Early Deterioration and Short Life	How This Happens
Inability of Stems to Absorb Water	Stems are dirty and clogged with debris, soil particles, or bacteria; flower stems probably were not cut during processing; dirty or improper solutions may have been used.
Excessive Water Loss	Flowers were not unpacked quickly enough, were stored dry too long, and/or were exposed to drafts, high temperatures, or low humidity.
Not Enough Food	The improper type or amount of flower food (preservative) is used, or it is not used at all.
Disease and Microorganism Development	Rigid pest and disease control is not used during the growing process and/or flowers are kept in unsanitary or improper conditions (wet and warm) during shipping or holding.
Ethylene Gas	Sensitive flowers are not treated properly or are not treated at all with an ethylene-reduction treatment, and/or they are exposed to high temperatures, poor ventilation, poor sanitation, or ethylene-producing machinery or crops.
Improper Environmental Conditions	Flowers are poorly packaged and/or are shipped, held, or displayed in improper conditions, such as warm temperatures, low humidity, and poor ventilation (which can be found in trucks and coolers not made for floral use and in many home situations).

Meeting Flower Needs

The key to delaying deterioration and prolonging flower life is meeting flower needs. This involves a series of life-prolonging procedures which incorporate specific tools and techniques. A tools, equipment, and chemicals checklist is provided in Appendix A to assist the designer in preparing for these procedures. Sometimes these life-prolonging procedures are called the Chain of Life, because each person in the flower distribution chain (grower-wholesaler-retailer-consumer) must follow these steps before maximum flower life can be realized. Retail florists are a

Fresh Flower Care and Handling

Notes

very important link in this chain because they help the flowers recover from shipping and prepare them for the enjoyment of the consumer. Floral designers should maintain a positive attitude and never assume that cut flowers will last only a few days, regardless of the care given them. The life-prolonging techniques described here are absolutely essential for all cut flowers, even those that are in the shop for a short period of time (1 to 2 days). Working to insure maximum flower life can result in success that is twofold: minimal shrinkage and waste, and maximum customer enjoyment of floral purchases. Flowers that are long lasting may provide valuable advertising.

To insure maximum flower life, florists must be aware of the potential longevity of flowers (often called vase life or decorative life). Some flowers are naturally short-lived (3 to 4 days) and others may last 2 weeks or more. A longevity chart in Appendix A lists the expected vase life for several varieties of flowers and provides instructions for insuring that potential vase life is realized.

Prelude to Care and Handling

Designers cannot create beautiful, long-lasting designs with inferior flowers. The initial step in insuring the proper care and handling of fresh flowers is purchasing quality flowers. This involves two elements:

1. Select a reputable supplier who follows reliable purchasing, handling, and shipping practices.

2. Purchase quality flowers. Following is a list of characteristics to look for.

    a. Flowers should be firm, not limp.

    b. They should be free of disease, insects, and breakage.

    c. Stems should be clean, not dark and slimy on the ends.

    d. Good coloring should be visible in flower and foliage (no excessive yellowing, browning, blackening, bluing, or other severe mottling or discoloration).

    e. The flower's stage of development will permit long life. The following general rules of thumb apply to various flower types.

Basic Floral Design

- Cluster or spike flowers - Purchase with one or two buds open.

- Filler flowers (baby's breath, for example) - Purchase with one third to one half of the flowers open.

- Single-stemmed flowers (roses, for example) - Purchase with buds showing color and just ready to open.

- Flowers similar to daisies - Purchase with flowers open, but with green centers or with only one or two rows of pollen showing.

Additional purchasing considerations include the following:

- Storage potential - Flowers with minimal storage potential should be purchased 24 to 48 hours before the floral event. Those with good or excellent potential can be purchased earlier in the week.

- Source of flowers - Find out country of origin and grower, if possible. This can affect harvest stage, packaging, special treatments given, and overall quality. Certain growers tend to harvest flowers at a tighter stage than others. Extra time is needed to allow tight buds to open.

- How flowers are packed - Flowers that are sensitive to bruising and shattering (such as orchids, gardenias, anthuriums, gerbera, daisies, roses, fuji chrysanthemums, delphinium, and snapdragons) must have protective packaging to minimize flaws and mechanical damage.

- Previous treatment - It is common for flowers to move through the distribution system dry (out of water). This is especially true for whole or half boxes of one type of flower. Extra time must be allowed to condition these flowers

Notes

Fresh Flower Care and Handling

Notes

before designing. Flowers that have been in water, on the other hand, are sometimes more developed and may be opened too much to be useful. It is also beneficial to find out if flowers have received special treatments to prevent problems such as wilting, leaf yellowing, or ethylene damage.

Care and Handling Steps

An overview or flow chart of the entire care and handling process, from arrival in the shop to purchase by the customer, is provided here. The tools, equipment, and chemicals checklist in Appendix A will also help in acquiring good care and handling habits. The overview here shows how proper care and handling include a series of important steps that work together to promote long flower life. The overview is ideal for placing in flower shop workrooms for use by everyone involved in processing, handling, or designing flowers.

Care and Handling: Sequence of Events Overview

A. Prepare for arrival of flower shipment:

1. Make room in coolers by discarding old flowers and combining buckets of remaining flowers.

2. Sanitize buckets and fill them with a clean, warm, preservative solution that has been properly mixed.

B. Unpack and inspect flowers immediately upon their arrival:

1. Remove wilt-sensitive flowers first.

2. Place other flowers in a cooler if processing can not be completed for 1 to 2 hours.

C. Prepare and process:

1. Prepare flowers that will be dry-stored.

    a. Keep them in wrappers or other special boxes.

    b. Place boxes in cool storage until needed.

2. Process flowers that will be stored in solution or used for display or design.

Basic Floral Design

Notes

    a. Remove lower leaves.

    b. Insure that stem ends are even.

    c. Cut the stems again.

D. Pre-treat and condition:

  1. Pre-treat flowers that require special treatment for leaf-yellowing, stem clogging, wilt sensitivity, ethylene sensitivity, or other special problems.

  2. Condition flowers in floral preservative solution.

    a. Keep flowers moist in solution for at least 2 hours.

    b. Exceptions: Flowers that open quickly, such as tulips, or those that are open or are going to be stored in solution for a few days can be put directly in the cooler.

E. Place flowers in a floral cooler:

  1. Flowers that are stored dry should be placed in a cooler immediately after preparation.

  2. Observe other flowers and place them in coolers based on their stage of development and the manner in which they will be used.

  3. Label all buckets with a code that specifies arrival date.

F. Use flowers properly in design, display, and sales:

  1. When designing, remove only those flowers from the cooler that will be needed within a short period of time. Do not remove entire buckets or boxes of flowers.

    a. Soak floral foam bricks and bouquet holders in floral preservative solution, and add pre-mixed solution to vases and other containers.

    b. Use special dips and sealers for shatter-sensitive flowers.

Fresh Flower Care and Handling

Notes

      c. Apply finishing spray to designs, if desired.

      d. Place finished designs back in a cooler.

  2. For display, label all buckets with proper names.

      a. Do not place too many flowers in a bucket.

      b. All buckets can be kept in the cooler, or selected ones may be placed prominently to attract impulse shoppers, then rotated into the cooler for 6 to 12 hours.

  3. At the time of a sale, package flowers to protect them from weather and damage. Include care information and floral preservative packet(s), and use water tubes, especially for wilt-sensitive flowers if they will be out of water for 2 hours or more (1 hour or more in hot weather).

G. Follow a strict sanitation schedule:

  1. Sanitize buckets, tools, and coolers according to the hygiene checklist, Table 5, page 99.

  2. Keep fruits, vegetables, and other food out of the cooler.

  3. Remove dying, diseased, and broken flowers, leaves, and other debris from the cooler on a daily basis.

H. Maintain flower storage and display regularly:

  1. Check store and cooler displays daily.

      a. Add preservative solution to arrangements.

      b. Make sure all flowers are placed in buckets so that all stems are in the solution.

  2. Re-cut stems every 2 to 3 days.

  3. Reorganize cooler stock weekly to prepare for upcoming flower shipments.

Basic Floral Design

Detailed Care and Handling Steps

It is imperative that florists follow proper care and handling procedures when working with fresh cut flowers. If applied, the following procedures and techniques will enable florists to insure that only quality fresh flowers leave their shops.

Re-cutting Stems

Re-cutting stems maximizes water uptake by removing blockage caused by air, bacteria, and debris.

For regular re-cutting, make sure stem ends are even so they will all be cut. Next, hold the bunch securely with one hand and cut 1/2 to 1 inch off the stems with a sharp floral tool. Using hand-held floral cutters or bench-mounted cutters is suggested. Avoid using dull knives, wire cutters, or ribbon-cutting scissors that are dull. (Hint: It may prove beneficial to have specific tools for each job in a floral shop, such as a tool for cutting stems only, a tool for cutting ribbon only, and a tool for cutting wire only, etc.)

Re-cutting stems underwater insures that they will initially take up water rather than air. This helps prevent air bubbles and greatly facilitates water uptake. Underwater cutting is especially beneficial for flowers with tight buds, flowers that have been dry for a long time, and flowers that are wilt-sensitive. A chart of wilt-sensitive flowers appears in Appendix A. Some florists actually re-cut all flower stems underwater.

To re-cut flowers underwater, fill a sink, tub, bucket, or similar container with warm water. Make sure that the stem ends are even; then, hold the bunch so that the lower several inches are underwater, and cut 1/2 to 1 inch off the stems. A water droplet will form on the cut ends and prevent air from entering the stems when they are transferred from one bucket to another. Use a hand-held floral cutter or a commercial cutter designed specifically for underwater cutting. Avoid holding flowers under running water during this procedure.

Warm Water Storage

Water ranging from 100 to 110 degrees Fahrenheit facilitates uptake into stems better than cold water. Warm water also contains less air, which can contribute to blockage in flower stems.

Place water in buckets just before flowers are added. The temperature of the water should be 100 to110 degrees Fahrenheit

Notes

Fresh Flower Care and Handling

Notes

only when the stems are first placed in it; then it will naturally cool to room temperature or cooler temperature without harming the flowers.

Avoid using water that is excessively hot. Water that is too hot may actually cook flower stems. Use a thermometer to insure that the water is 100 to 110 degrees Fahrenheit.

If warm water is not available, fill buckets with water 2 hours or more before they are needed and keep them out of the cooler.

Clean Stems

Stems clogged with bacteria and debris, either visible or invisible, will not work efficiently. Clean stems have open, water-carrying vessels and better uptake, which insures healthier flowers and longer life.

Clean water and buckets are necessary to insure clean stems. Some florists use chlorine bleach or cleanser in water to insure cleanliness. Commercial stem-sanitizing dips and solutions are recommended. They are especially effective with flowers that are likely to have dirty or clogged stems, such as gerbera and baby's breath. Treatment may range from an instant dip to a 1-hour treatment, depending on the brand used. After treatment, place flowers in a floral preservative solution.

Floral Preservatives

Commercial floral preservatives are special mixtures that have been developed and perfected to prolong flower life. They are not gimmicks or flukes. They are special chemical mixtures that are proven to be effective. The fact that some brands have been in existence for more than 50 years is proof of this.

Preservatives offer multiple benefits. They contain a sugar base which provides food to keep the flower's energy level high, as well as, ingredients to inhibit bacteria (which keeps water and stems clean). They also contain ingredients which lower pH and enhance water uptake. Plain sugar, chlorine bleach, or other mixtures do not contain the ideal combination of ingredients needed to serve all of the functions. When used correctly, floral preservatives help prolong the lives of most flowers and foliage. There are numerous brands of floral preservatives available in a variety of forms, including dry powder and liquid concentrate. Each form has unique characteristics; therefore, one brand may be more effective in a particular shop than another brand. Since the effectiveness of floral preservatives is influenced by water quality, some companies test water and recommend a preservative that will provide the best results when used with that water. Most importantly, remember to use floral preservatives consistently and correctly.

The proper use of floral preservatives is vital. Using improper amounts, especially lesser amounts, does not help and can actually harm the flowers. Using less than the recommended rate can mean that a sugar base is added without enough ingredients to inhibit bacteria growth, leading to dirty water. On the other hand, "the more the better" is not always true and can be expensive. To eliminate problems and insure best results, follow the tips below when using floral preservatives.

1. Read label directions carefully. Post the mixing instructions near the flower-processing area.

2. Sanitize buckets.

3. Place the proper amount of preservative and water into buckets according to package directions. Amounts may vary, but 1 tablespoon of dry powder per quart of water (or 4 tablespoons per gallon) is common.

4. Utilize measuring devices to insure that proper amounts are used. Measuring scoops are usually included with preservatives. Never measure preservatives by adding a pinch or a handful.

5. Preservative solutions can be used for several days. Mixing fresh solution for new flower shipments is recommended. For long-lasting flowers, it is beneficial to place fresh solution in storage buckets once a week.

Mixing Preservative for Bud Opening

To promote bud opening, twice the recommended amount of preservative (generally twice the amount is equivalent to 2 tablespoons per quart) can be used for 24 to 48 hours, then flowers are placed in a warm location. To speed up the process, some florists cover the flowers with a sheet of plastic, then remove it for ventilation once or twice a day. Flowers that are shipped as tight buds and need this treatment include carnations, miniature carnations, gladioli, and gypsophila (baby's breath).

Notes

Fresh Flower Care and Handling

<u>Notes</u>

Some florists only use floral preservatives in specific instances. In actuality, floral preservatives should always be used when handling, storing, and designing with fresh flowers. Use floral preservatives in the following items.

- Storage buckets
- Bud vases
- Vases of arranged flowers
- Water tubes
- Arrangements with wet foam bases
- Bouquet holder designs which include wet foam

To make the use of floral preservatives easier and more effective, keep the following tips in mind.

- Mix solution in a large watering can or pitcher for adding to bud vases and replenishing the water supply in pre-made arrangements that are on display.
- Post mixing directions near the sinks.
- Have a large container handy with cup, quart, and gallon markings to measure water into buckets.
- For buckets of the same size, mark a ruler at the 1/2 gallon and 1 gallon marks so the ruler can be placed in buckets and water filled to the correct point.
- Do not use metal containers. A chemical reaction between metal and certain preservatives may reduce the effectiveness of the preservative.

Supplements or Pre-treatments

Supplements or pre-treatments are special treatments that assist in preventing special flower problems and greatly extend vase life. They are used prior to floral preservatives in the care and handling process and are, therefore, referred to as pre-treatments. Sometimes called supplements, they are used in addition to regular floral preservatives.

Basic Floral Design

Ethylene Reduction Treatments

Ethylene reduction treatments help reduce ethylene gas action and minimize damage to sensitive flowers. A popular treatment is STS or silver thiosulfate. It is best used by the growers and wholesalers, but should be used by retail florists if flowers arrive untreated. If uncertain whether a flower has been treated or not, a second treatment is advised and should not be harmful. Various types of commercial solutions are available.

During ethylene reduction treatments, flowers are processed, placed in a supplement (treatment time is normally 1 hour), then placed in a floral preservative solution. Supplemental solutions should be used with environmental awareness in mind. Manufacturers' directions for their safe mixture, use, and disposal must be carefully followed. Special disposal kits are available from some manufacturers. For quick reference, ethylene-sensitive flowers are listed in a chart in Appendix A. More information regarding ethylene is provided on pages 95 and 96.

Growth Regulator Treatments

Growth regulator treatments are special solutions used by growers to prevent problems such as leaf-yellowing on alstroemeria, lilies, and chrysanthemums. Growers who use these treatments are often known for producing excellent product. Their flowers not only last longer, the foliage stays firm and green much longer than products purchased from other growers. It is important to determine who these growers are so that their product can be specifically requested.

Hydrating Solutions

Hydrating solutions can be used by growers, wholesalers, and retail florists and are used to encourage hydration, or water uptake, and help prevent water stress problems, such as bent neck in roses. They are pH-lowering solutions that work by reducing pH to the optimum range of 3.5 to 4.5 for water uptake. Citric acid is a common hydrating solution. Florists should consider using citric acid solution if large quantities of roses are shipped dry from long distances or if wilting and bent neck are recurring problems. Commercial powders and pre-mixed solutions are also available. To use, process flowers and place them in the solution (treatment only takes 30 minutes to 1 hour); then, place in floral preservative solution.

Notes

Fresh Flower Care and Handling

Notes

Conditioning Techniques

This step maximizes solution uptake and enhances firmer, longer-lasting flowers. The uptake is often referred to as "giving the flowers a drink," but is more accurately called hydration. Flowers need to hydrate with preservative solution to replace moisture lost during shipping and handling and in preparation for design or display.

Generally, flowers should be kept out of the cooler for at least 2 hours to maximize uptake of solution. They should then be placed in the cooler for another few hours to finish hardening off.

Conditioning times vary for specific types of flowers:

- Allow flowers to condition from 6 hours to overnight before designing with them.

- Flowers that have been shipped dry in boxes, especially those from other countries, or flowers that feel soft and limp, should be conditioned for 24 to 48 hours before use.

- Tulips may be placed in cool preservative water and placed directly into the cooler so they will not blow open.

- Roses that are beginning to open should be kept out of the cooler for no more than 1 hour.

Avoid taking flowers, especially wilt-sensitive flowers, such as roses, directly from shipping boxes to the design bench. Overall, conditioning times in and out of the cooler are dependent upon the period of time flowers have been dry, how well they are developed, and how quickly they will be used. Proper conditioning requires careful observation and practice.

Environmental Conditions for Storage and Display

Proper refrigeration and storage procedures are an integral part of keeping flowers and designs at their peak by delaying further development (opening), minimizing water loss, minimizing bacteria and other microorganism development, and minimizing ethylene production.

The first key to creating proper environmental conditions is a combination of low temperature and high humidity. The second key is utilizing a cooler that was specifically designed for use with flowers. Experts suggest having at least one floral cooler that maintains a temperature of 34 to 36 degrees Fahrenheit and relative humidity of 85 percent or more. The cooler should be equipped with low velocity fans that circulate air, but keep water loss low. If florists have minimal or improper refrigeration, such as a household refrigerator or a beverage cooler, it will be difficult to keep flowers fresh. Tips for storing flowers in the proper environmental conditions are given below. Charts listing the storage potential of specific flowers and signifying flowers that are sensitive to chilling are provided in Appendix A.

- Certain flowers are sensitive to chilling and may be damaged at temperatures above freezing, even between 40 and 60 degrees. These flowers should never be placed in a regular floral cooler. Some florists have a special cooler for such flowers, or they keep them in a separate area of the shop, preferably an area with high humidity.

- For short-term holding, flowers are usually placed in buckets containing preservative solution. After an initial 1 to 2 hours of conditioning in the shop, flowers are placed in the cooler to harden off and hold until used for design or sale.

- Flowers that blow open quickly, such as tulips, or that are already open, can be placed in the cooler immediately after processing and administering the preservative treatment.

- Flowers that have good storage potential may be purchased in advance and stored. If storage is planned for an extended period of time, they can be kept dry. It is best to keep flowers in plastic sleeves and shipping boxes when placed in the cooler. Do not place unprotected flowers and foliage directly on the floor or cooler shelf without protection. Check for molding and limpness periodically. After storage, process and condition flowers for at least 24 hours before using.

- Some flowers respond to gravity by bending upwards if they are kept in a horizontal position. These flowers, which include snapdragons, gladioli, and Star of Bethlehem, should be stored upright.

Notes

Fresh Flower Care and Handling

Notes

- Wilt-sensitive flowers and those with poor or minimal storage potential should never be stored dry or held for more than 24 to 48 hours.

- The storage potential of floral designs is always a question. Many florists design flowers for weddings and special occasions 2 or 3 days in advance. If flowers are properly conditioned and packaged, this will not create a problem. However, pre-made designs must be stored in a floral cooler until the event.

- Some florists use an extra room or some other area for holding and storing during peak periods, such as holidays. If this is necessary, ideal temperature and humidity must be maintained, if possible. A humidifier can be used to add humidity. Flowers that are wilt-sensitive, short-lived, or already open should be kept in the cooler. Other flowers may be kept in an extra room.

Sanitation (Cleanliness) and Ethylene Prevention Program

Cleanliness helps prevent dirt, bacteria, and debris from clogging stems and inhibiting uptake. It also helps prevent ethylene damage. Ethylene is a major problem when dealing with cut flowers. It is an odorless, colorless gas that is called the "aging hormone" because it stimulates the aging process in flowers and plants, causing petals to drop, leaves to fall, and fruits to ripen. It can drastically shorten vase life and cause premature death when present in extremely low levels. Carnations exhibit "sleepiness," or a wilted, soft, browning appearance, when exposed to ethylene.

Ethylene is produced by all plants, flowers, and fruits, although some produce higher amounts than others. Damaged and dying flowers produce more ethylene than healthy flowers. The gas is also a by-product of the burning of fuels, such as kerosene, diesel oil, propane, and gasoline. Therefore, it is often found near loading docks and in shops where kerosene space heaters are used. Ethylene can also be produced by microorganisms, similar to bacteria, that breed in dirty buckets.

Not all flowers are equally sensitive and show symptoms of injury. A chart of flowers that are ethylene-sensitive appears in Appendix A. If measures are not taken to prevent ethylene damage, these flowers are likely to be short-lived in designs.

They may start browning or dropping petals and leaves in the shop or shortly after delivery to the customer.

Strict sanitation is a multi-step program that involves a combination of procedures. One step alone does not prevent all problems. The following steps outline the recommended procedures for insuring proper sanitation.

Notes

1. Properly sanitize buckets, benches, and tools. Sanitation involves more than rinsing out buckets; it involves strict procedures for cleaning and sanitizing. Sanitizing procedures and products are listed below.

    a. Three primary elements are needed: hot water, a scrub brush, and a cleaning agent. A scrub brush gets into scratches and creases better than a sponge cloth or hands. Cleaning agents designed specifically for floral use are ideal. Some florists use chlorine bleach, but specially-mixed agents are more effective. Avoid using cleanser, dishwashing liquid, or plain water.

    b. Mix the cleaning agent with hot water and scrub the bucket thoroughly, including the inside bottom, bottom edge, inner walls, upper edge, outer walls, and outer bottom. Rinse the bucket with clear water and place it upside down. (This mixture and method of sanitization may also be used to clean floors.) Place tools in a bucket of cleaning solution, then scrub and rinse. The cleaning agent can also be placed in a spray bottle and used to spray design benches and cooler walls, prior to scrubbing and rinsing them with a clean sponge.

2. It is important to sanitize frequently. Table 5 on page 99 suggests cleaning frequency for key tools and floral areas.

3. Follow these steps to avoid ethylene problems:

    a. Remove dead and dying flowers and other debris from design and display areas and coolers.

    b. Do not store fruit or any other food in the cooler.

Fresh Flower Care and Handling

Notes

    c. Remove flowers from sleeves and boxes upon arrival to prevent ethylene build-up.

    d. Do not store flowers near loading areas where they are exposed to engine exhaust.

    e. Some florists use scrubbers, or filters, in the cooler which scrub ethylene from the air by absorbing it and changing it into a form that is not detrimental to flowers. If scrubbers are used, they should be active units, as opposed to passive units, such as packets and blankets that hang in the cooler or are placed in a box. Scrubbers are not meant to be used as an independent means of controlling ethylene. They should be used in combination with other control measures.

TABLE 5

HYGIENE CHECKLIST

Tools and Areas	Cleaning Frequency
Display and storage buckets	At least once a week (every time the bucket is emptied).
Flower displays	Daily (remove broken stems and leaves, dying flowers, debris).
Counter tops	Daily.
Floor	Sweep clean daily; disinfect at least once a week.
Processing Tools (floral knife, stem cutters, etc.)	Daily.
Counter-mounted cutters	Wipe clean daily; disinfect once a week.
Portable underwater cutters	Each time they are used.
Sinks	Wipe clean daily; disinfect at least once a week.
Foam soaking bins	Wipe clean daily; disinfect at least once a week.
Flower fixtures and coolers	Clean and disinfect once a week.

Packaging Stems and Finished Designs

Proper packaging assists in retaining humidity and minimizing water loss, particularly during storage. Packaging floral purchases can also prevent breakage and temperature damage. Listed below are tips for proper packaging.

- Wilt-sensitive flowers that are stored, including baby's breath, gardenias, and camellias, which are frequently used for weddings, should be wrapped. Baby's breath can be placed in a bucket of preservative solution and then wrapped in a plastic bag. Gardenias and camellias should be kept on moistened cotton in shipping boxes until needed. Some special flowers, like gloriosa lilies and anthuriums, are shipped in special packages that prevent water loss and damage during storage.

- It is common to place bouquets and body flowers in a plastic or cellophane bag, mist them with water, blow into the bag, seal it, and place it in the cooler. This is essential if the design is made a few days in advance. It helps prolong life by minimizing water loss, and the breath of air provides extra carbon dioxide (CO_2). Designs may be placed in boxes for added protection. Bags in the cooler should be opened daily to allow for ventilation and to be sprayed with additional water. This practice should be followed until the day of the special event, at which time excessive misting should cease so the flowers will not wet clothing, etc.

- Every floral purchase and delivery should be wrapped in floral wrapping material before leaving the store. When outdoor temperatures fall below 55 degrees Fahrenheit, extra wrapping should be used for flowers that are chill-sensitive. When temperatures are below 32 degrees Fahrenheit, extra wrapping should be used for all flowers. This includes heavy floral paper or plastic bags instead of tissue paper. Openings in the paper should be folded or stapled shut. Add extra layers of wrapping according to greater drops in temperature. If temperatures fall below 20 degrees Fahrenheit, even flowers in boxes should be wrapped in layers of paper or plastic.

Notes

Fresh Flower Care and Handling

Notes

Care and Handling During Design

Florists must follow proper care and handling procedures to insure that flowers last as long as possible. Below are tips on proper care and handling to be used during design work.

1. Use finishing sprays and dips to seal flowers and minimize water loss so flowers will stay firm and bright for longer periods of time. These sprays and dips are especially useful for designs created in advance and designs created with wilt-sensitive flowers. They should only be applied to fresh, firm flowers. Do not apply to those that are already wilted. Allow sprays and dips to dry before packaging flowers or placing them in the cooler. Following is a discussion of finishing sprays and dips.

    a. Aerosols, such as Design Master Clear Life and Floral Life Clear Set, are sprayed on to seal pores and minimize water loss.

    b. Light glues are used to prevent petals from shattering, including Floral Life Mum Tite and Oasis® Mum Mist. Note: If the special sprays listed above are not available, a light mist of glitter glue can be used. Spray glues made for other purposes, such as photo mounting, should never be used. They will damage flowers.

    c. Liquid anti-transpirants, such as Crowning Glory®, may be used as sprays or dips that coat flowers or foliage and minimize water loss. These sprays can help prolong life if used properly by covering all surfaces rather than simply misting the flower. Read label directions on anti-transpirants before using.

    d. Self-made glue dip is made by mixing one part white glue, such as Elmer's Glue-All™, to three parts water. Flowers are dipped into this mixture to seal and prevent shattering of flowers, such as chrysanthemums, and prevent browning on other flowers, such as gardenias.

e. Self-made gelatin sealer is made by dissolving one envelope of flavorless gelatin in 1 cup of boiling water. Allow the mixture to cool to room temperature, then paint it onto the backs of delicate flowers and set them in the cooler to stiffen.

There are several tips for using special finishing sprays and dips other than water.

- Do not apply to flowers that are already wilted.

- Remove items from the cooler and allow to dry completely before application.

- Items with moisture-free surfaces can be dipped once or misted with several light coatings.

- Items should be allowed to dry completely after application before they are packaged and returned to the cooler or prepared for delivery.

- Treated items should not be oversprayed with water.

2. Soak floral foam in preservative. Floral foam bricks and bouquet holders should be soaked before designing. A floral preservative solution can be mixed in the proper proportions in a tub, bin, sink, or bucket. Drop foam in and allow it to soak on its own. Do not force it down. A fresh solution should be mixed every 1 to 2 days.

3. When creating designs, leave a water well in the arrangements. Leaving a small amount of space at the side or back of a design makes it easier to add additional preservative solution in the shop and in the customer's home.

4. Remove only the flowers needed for one design from the cooler, rather than removing a full bucket.

5. Keep flowers in a bucket of solution at the design bench so flower stems will not become dry and limp.

Notes

Fresh Flower Care and Handling

Notes

Organizational Tips

Following are tips that will help assure that flower care and handling is more efficient and effective.

- Assigning specific duties, such as unpacking, processing, preservative and pre-treatment mixing, sanitizing, and display maintenance, helps insure that each job is completed in a timely and efficient manner.

- Labelling or date-coding flower shipments with arrival dates assists in organizing the cooler and encourages better turnover of flowers. Some florists even label with discard dates so the flowers will be thrown out at the proper time. There are numerous labelling methods, including colored stakes and dots and plastic markers labelled with grease pencils. Actual dates may be used or a special code may be developed using letters of the alphabet to designate days of the week. Using a special code that customers do not understand and posting a reference chart for employees is recommended.

- Although labelling is beneficial, flowers must still be rotated in the cooler so older flowers are in front and will be used first. New shipments should always be placed in the back to eliminate confusion.

- Some florists have a designated area where all care and handling materials are kept and all procedures are performed. This results in less confusion and greater efficiency.

Proper care of flowers at the retail level is absolutely essential if florists want to supply the long-lasting products that customers demand. Care actually begins with the purchase of superior quality products that have received the proper care. This care should continue from the moment a flower enters the shop until the moment it leaves. To be effective at floral purchasing and handling, florists must first have an understanding of flower structure, classification, and naming; then build on this foundation with the knowledge of how to meet the needs of flowers with water, food, healthy environment, and hygiene. This information

Basic Floral Design

should be incorporated as an integral part of the training of every shop employee. The designer, in particular, should master this information, along with basic design techniques, proceeding to higher levels of creativity.

Flower knowledge and care does not have to be overwhelming. To make the challenge easier and more effective, the material in this chapter can be incorporated into a manual for training and review and kept handy for frequent reference. If care is incorporated into an organized daily schedule, so that all flowers used in designs are properly treated, florists will enjoy an outstanding reputation and repeat sales, and the customer will benefit from the maximum enjoyment of long-lasting flowers.

Notes

Fresh Flower Care and Handling

Notes, Photographs, Sketches, etc.

Basic Floral Design

Notes, Photographs, Sketches, etc.

Fresh Flower Care and Handling

Notes, Photographs, Sketches, etc.

Flowers to Wear

Chapter 5

Ladies and gentlemen often complement their outfits with floral accents. A woman might choose to wear a corsage, to place a flower in her hair, or to carry a single blossom. A gentleman usually selects a boutonniere for his lapel.

Flowers are worn for weddings, proms, holidays, and many other social events. Proms provide florists with wonderful opportunities to acquire loyal customers. Most teenagers appreciate the florist's interest and professional guidance in selecting flowers for this very important occasion and are likely to return to the same florist in the future. Holidays, such as Easter and Mother's Day, along with other special days, are excellent times to market flowers to wear.

Florists should be able to professionally design flowers to wear for any event. Florists must possess a thorough understanding of conditioning and handling flowers and foliage before using them to create designs to wear. Providing the customer with a product that is exceptionally fresh and long lasting is one of the keys to success. Florists can gain the confidence of their customers by providing well-designed, quality products, which will usually result in future orders. Flowers to wear, such as corsages, hairpieces, and boutonnieres, should be designed to be light and comfortable so that they are a pleasure to wear rather than a burden.

Conditioning

Conditioning is essential for insuring beautiful, long-lasting flowers. It is especially critical for flowers that will be wired and taped. The goal of flower conditioning is to encourage and maximize the uptake of food and water which have been lost in transit and which are needed to prolong the flower's life. Specific information that is important for maintaining the quality of flowers can be found in the conditioning segment of Chapter 4.

Boutonnieres

Wedding, formals, proms, and other functions, such as civic organization banquets, are occasions when many men wear boutonnieres. The boutonniere may be a single flower, a cluster of blooms, or a sophisticated foliage grouping. Regardless of the occasion, florists should provide gentlemen with masculine boutonnieres. Typically, boutonnieres are small, usually no larger than a standard carnation.

Florists should coordinate flowers that are being worn with the other flowers used for specific events. When a young man is planning to attend a formal or prom, florists might suggest a boutonniere made of flowers that will match or blend with those chosen for his date.

Proper design mechanics and conditioning of flowers are essential in providing professional designs. No matter how small or insignificant lapel flowers may seem, they deserve a florist's expertise. Boutonnieres should be quality, professional designs created with fresh flowers.

Flowers and Foliage for Boutonnieres

The size of the flowers and foliage used in a boutonniere is important. Large flowers or leaves should not be used excessively. It is best to use one large flower or a few small ones to create a boutonniere that is proportionate to the size of the person wearing it. Table 6 lists some of the most popular types of flowers and foliage used to create boutonnieres.

TABLE 6

POPULAR BOUTONNIERE FLOWERS AND FOLIAGE

Flowers	Foliage
Roses (Standard and Sweetheart)	Ivy
Carnations (Standard and Mini)	Camellia
Freesia	Lemon Leaf
Stephanotis	Ming Fern
Alstroemeria	Pittosporum
Dendrobium Orchids	Plumosa
Cornflowers	Cedar

Notes

Flowers to Wear

It is important to use proper mechanics and construction techniques when designing boutonnieres. Following are the steps for constructing popular types of boutonnieres. The same steps apply regardless of the type of flower used.

Single Flower Boutonniere *(Figure 5.1)*

Roses and carnations are two of the most commonly requested flowers for the single flower boutonniere. Medium-sized flowers are most desirable for this type of design. Smaller flowers are better used in clusters. Large flowers are usually avoided to prevent a corsage-like appearance.

1. Wire and tape a single flower, such as a rose, and a single leaf of a broad-leaved foliage, such as camellia.

2. Place the leaf behind the flower so that the tip of the leaf extends about 1/2 inch above the flower.

3. Tape the stems of the flower and leaf together.

4. Trim the stem to a length to 1 1/2 to 2 inches.

Three Flower Boutonniere *(Figure 5.2)*

Generally, all of the flowers used in a three flower boutonniere are small, so that the finished design is not too large.

1. Wire and tape three small flowers, such as stephanotis, and three small leaves, such as ivy.

2. Begin with the smallest flower in a vertical position. Place the second flower about halfway below the first and angle it slightly to the left. Tape the two stems together. *(Figure 5.2a)*

3. Position the third flower about halfway below the second flower and angle it slightly to the right. Tape the flower to the boutonniere stem. *(Figure 5.2b)*

4. Position a leaf behind the first flower so that the tip extends about 1/2 inch beyond the flower. Tape the leaf to the stem. *(Figure 5.2c)*

Figure 5.1 Single Flower Boutonniere

Figure 5.2a Constructing a Three Flower Boutonniere Step 2

Figure 5.2b Constructing a Three Flower Boutonniere Step 3

Figure 5.2c Constructing a Three Flower Boutonniere Step 4

5. Arch the two remaining leaves slightly by bonding the wire stitched through the leaf.

6. Position one leaf behind each of the remaining flowers and allow the leaves to arch to the left and right, following the angle of the flowers. Tape the leaves to the stem. **(Figure 5.2d)**

7. Add wire pieces of filler, such as baby's breath, between the flower placements, as desired.

8. Trim the boutonniere stem to a length of 1 1/2 to 2 inches.

Figure 5.2d Constructing a Three Flower Boutonniere Step 6

Garden Style Boutonniere *(Figure 5.3)*

A variety of small blossoms should be used when creating a garden style boutonniere. A mixture of small blossoms, florets, and pieces of filler and foliage create interesting garden style boutonnieres. Flower selection is the only limitation when creating boutonnieres of this style.

1. Wire and tape 3 to 5 blossoms or florets, 3 to 5 pieces of filler, and 3 to 5 pieces of foliage. Be sure to tape each wire to the end.

2. Arrange the florets and blossoms into a loose, miniature nosegay-type cluster between the thumb and index finger. **(Figure 5.3a)**

3. Add filler, as desired, between the flower placements. **(Figure 5.3a)**

Figure 5.3a Constructing a Garden Style Boutonniere Steps 2 & 3

4. Arrange pieces of foliage behind the flowers to provide a green background for the flowers and to hide the mechanics. **(Figure 5.3b)**

5. Tape all of the stems together at the point where they are held by the thumb and index finger. Do not tape the wires together all the way down the stems.

6. Trim each individual stem to a length of approximately 1 1/2 inches.

Figure 5.3b Constructing a Garden Style Boutonniere Step 4

Flowers to Wear

Notes

Corsages

Ladies attending social events, weddings, or proms may choose to wear a corsage to compliment their outfits. Corsages can be very traditional, involving flowers, fillers, foliage, and ribbons. They can also be contemporary, featuring the sleek look of one flower accented with a touch of foliage or dry material.

Flowers should offer the proper contrast by blending colors and textures to enhance a lady's outfit. Selecting flowers that provide the appropriate color and texture is characteristic of a quality designer. Florists should keep a vast number of flowers, fillers, and foliage in stock so that every customer's needs can be met.

Flowers and Foliage for Corsages

A corsage should be proportionate to the size of the person wearing it. Therefore, flowers for corsages must be chosen carefully. Flowers and foliage that are frequently used to create corsages are listed in Table 7.

TABLE 7

POPULAR CORSAGE FLOWERS AND FOLIAGE

Flowers	Foliage
Roses (Standard and Sweetheart)	Ivy
Carnations (Standard and Mini)	Camellia Leaves
Freesia	Lemon Leaf
Stephanotis	Ming Fern
Alstroemeria	Pittosporum
Chrysanthemums	Plumosa
Gardenias	Cedar
Gladioli Blossoms	Leatherleaf
Cattleya Orchids	
Cymbidium Orchids	
Phalaenopsis Orchids	
Dendrobium Orchids	

To construct corsages properly, florists should follow the appropriate steps, regardless of the type of flower being used. Following are the steps for constructing ten types of corsages.

Single Flower Corsage *(Figure 5.4)*

The single flower corsage may be designed simply by constructing a single flower boutonniere and adding a bow. Construction steps for a slightly more decorative single flower corsage follow.

1. Wire and tape a single flower and three pieces of foliage. Carnations, camellias, gardenias, and orchids are the flowers most often selected to create a single flower corsage.

2. Place one leaf behind the flower so that the tip of the leaf extends about 1/2 inch above the flower. Tape the two stems together.

3. Arch the two remaining leaves slightly by bending the wires stitched through the leaves.

4. Position one leaf to the left and one leaf to the right of the flower. Tape the leaves to the stem.

5. Add wired pieces of filler around the flower, as desired.

6. Add a bow at the base of the flower.

7. Trim the corsage stem to a length of about 2 inches.

Figure 5.4 Single Flower Corsage

Double Flower Corsage *(Figure 5.5)*

Carnations, cymbidium orchids, and phalaenopsis orchids are often selected for use in a double flower corsage. Following are construction steps for a double flower corsage.

1. Wire and tape two flowers and five pieces of foliage. Wire and tape filler flowers, if desired.

2. Hold a single flower in a vertical position and place the second flower just below it. Tape the two stems together. *(Figure 5.5a)*

Figure 5.5a Constructing a Double Flower Corsage Step 2

Flowers to Wear

Figure 5.5b Constructing a Double Flower Corsage Step 3

Figure 5.5c Constructing a Double Flower Corsage Step 5

3. Place the leaves behind the flowers so that about 1/2 inch of each leaf can be seen beyond the edges of the flowers. Tape the leaves into place. **(Figure 5.5b)**

4. Add the wired pieces of filler where desired. Tape them securely into place.

5. Add a bow at the base of the second flower. Tape it into place. **(Figure 5.5c)**

6. Trim the corsage stem to a length of about 2 inches.

Triple Flower Corsage

Carnations, roses, and chrysanthemums are frequently selected when designing a triple flower corsage. Following are instructional steps for designing this type of corsage.

1. Wire and tape three flowers and five to seven pieces of foliage. Wire and tape filler flowers, as desired.

2. Hold a single flower in a vertical position and place the second flower just below it. Tape the two stems together.

3. Place a leaf behind each flower so that about 1/2 inch of each leaf can be seen beyond the flowers. Tape the leaves into place.

4. Add the wired pieces of filler where desired. Tape them securely into place.

5. Place the third flower just below the second flower so that the second and third flowers overlap slightly. Tape the flower into place.

6. Repeat Steps 3 and 4 around the third flower.

7. Add a bow between the second and third flowers. Tape it into place.

8. Trim the corsage stem to a length of about 2 inches.

Triangular Corsage *(Figure 5.6)*

The triangular corsage typically incorporates a variety of small flowers. Foliage and filler material are used to soften the lines and provide relief from a strict geometric appearance.

1. Wire and tape seven to nine small flowers and six or seven pieces of foliage.

2. Hold a single small flower in a vertical position and place a second flower just below it so the two overlap slightly. Tape the two stems together. *(Figure 5.6a)*

3. Design two more units of two flowers each as instructed in step 2. *(Figure 5.6b)*

4. Create a triangular shape by positioning one of the three units vertically. Place a second one sideways to the left and the third unit downward and to the right (bent over the thumb). Tape the three stems together.

5. Add one to three flowers in the center of the corsage as needed to fill out the shape of the triangle. *(Figure 5.6c)*

6. Add foliage around the back of the corsage in the manner described for creating a single flower corsage. Additional foliage may be inserted through the center of the corsage so that only the tips show. *(Figure 5.6d)*

7. Add filler flowers, if desired.

8. Attach a bow at the base of the triangle. *(Figure 5.6e)*

9. Trim the corsage stem to a length of about 2 inches.

Crescent Corsage *(Figure 5.7 on page 117)*

The crescent corsage has a soft, curved line which lends a gentle feminine quality to the design. The curve of the corsage may be styled in either direction, but is particularly flattering when curved inward toward the face.

1. Wire and tape six to eight small flowers and six or seven pieces of foliage.

Figure 5.6a Constructing a Triangular Corsage Step 2

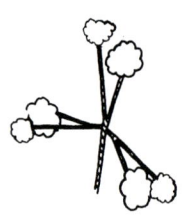

Figure 5.6b Constructing a Triangular Corsage Step 3

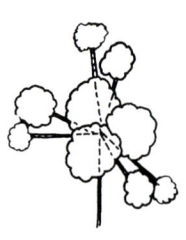

Figure 5.6c Constructing a Triangular Corsage Step 5

Figure 5.6d Constructing a Triangular Corsage Step 6

Figure 5.6e Constructing a Triangular Corsage Step 8

Flowers to Wear

Figure 5.7a Constructing a Crescent Corsage Step 3

Figure 5.7b Constructing a Crescent Corsage Step 4

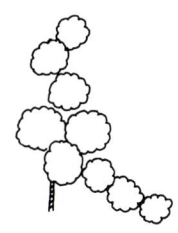

Figure 5.7c Constructing a Crescent Corsage Step 5

Figure 5.7d Constructing a Crescent Corsage Step 6

2. Create 2 two-flower units as described in step 2 of the triangular corsage instructions.

3. Position one unit vertically and the second one downward and to the right (bent over the thumb). Tape the two units together. *(Figure 5.7a)*

4. Add two to three focal flowers in the center between the two units. *(Figure 5.7b)*

5. Use additional flowers to connect the center flowers to the end points in a crescent shape. *(Figure 5.7c)*

6. Add foliage around the back of the corsage so the tips show approximately 1/4 inch beyond the flowers. Use the foliage to disguise the mechanics on the underside of the corsage. *(Figure 5.7d)*

7. Add filler flowers, as desired.

8. If a bow is needed, it should be positioned on the lower outside curve of the crescent.

9. Trim the corsage stem to a length of approximately 2 inches.

Double Spray Corsage

Double spray corsages are very popular. Originally designed as a hair decoration, the double spray corsage became a popular style because of its structure and flexibility. This style of corsage is referred to as the double spray corsage because of its structure.

1. Wire and tape approximately ten small flowers and six or seven pieces of foliage.

2. Begin with the smallest flower in a vertical position and tape a second flower about two-thirds of the way below and to the right of the first flower.

3. Position the next flower about two-thirds of the way below and to the left of the second flower. Tape the flower to the stem.

Notes

4. Continue staggering flower placements left and right until five flowers are in position. Each flower should be slightly larger than the one above it.

5. Add the sixth flower in the same staggered manner, but at a slightly downward angle. The sixth flower should be the largest in the design.

6. Add the remaining four flowers, one at a time, below the sixth flower. Bend each one over the thumb and position it to the left or right of the previous flower. The size of these flowers should taper in the reverse of the rest so that the bottom flower is about the same size as the top flower in the corsage.

7. Add foliage to the back of the corsage to cover mechanics and provide a strong background.

8. If a bow is desired, it should be tucked under the sixth flower.

9. Trim the corsage stem to a length of approximately 2 inches.

Over-the-shoulder Corsage

Over-the-shoulder corsages are designed to rest on the top of the shoulder and cascade slightly down the front and back of the body. The over-the-shoulder corsage is constructed in the same way as the double spray style with the following exceptions.

- The smallest flowers at the points of the design should be wired with a very light gauge wire so they will cascade freely over the shoulder and provide motion.

- The last two or three flowers are positioned farther apart than usual, approximately 2 inches apart, to make the tips of the corsage more graceful. The design will look sparse and elongated at both ends as it is constructed, but, once curved over the shoulder, it will look more appropriate.

- Once the corsage is designed, it should be place on the shoulder of an average size person and curved to follow the lines of the body.

Flowers to Wear

Nosegay Corsage

The nosegay corsage is a Victorian-style design in a circular form. It is usually created with a variety of petite flowers and/or buds and may be designed in a pattern of concentric rings or in a mixed manner.

1. Begin with a single flower, such as a sweetheart rose, as the center flower.

2. Add a ring of flowers around the center placement and tape them at a single joining point, leaving the ends of the wires free.

3. Continue adding rings of flowers to the design in the same manner until it reaches the desired size (usually about 3 inches in diameter).

4. Add a row of foliage under the last row of flowers to disguise the mechanics and provide a background for the flowers.

Glamellia Corsage

A glamellia corsage is a composite flower made with gladiolus florets. It is designed to resemble a cammellia blossom. The blossoms are wired or glued together, starting with a bud in the center and then gradually increasing in size using open florets, until a flower resembling an open camellia has been created.

Creating a Glamellia *(Figure 5.8)*

1. Select gladiolus florets in each of the following sizes.

    - A tight bud displaying color. *(Figure 5.8a)*

    - A partially open bud displaying color. *(Figure 5.8b)*

    - A floret that is partially open. *(Figure 5.8c)*

    - A floret that is halfway open. *(Figure 5.8d)*

    - One to three florets that are fully open. *(Figure 5.8e)*

Figure 5.8a Creating a Glamellia Step 1

Figure 5.8b Creating a Glamellia Step 1

Figure 5.8c Creating a Glamellia Step 1

Figure 5.8d Creating a Glamellia Step 1

Figure 5.8e Creating a Glamellia Step 1

2. Allow the florets to warm to room temperature.

3. Strip the green spathes off all of the florets.

4. Do not remove the stem portion of the tightest bud. Wire the bud, using the cross-pierce method, and pull the wires down to resemble a stem. Tape the stem down with floral tape.

5. Prepare the remaining florets for assembly by holding each floret with the thumb inside the floret while the index and middle fingers support the outside. Using a sharp knife, cut the stem and lower 1/8 to 1/4 inch of the floret off so that the stamens fall out. If the stamens do not fall out on their own, carefully pull them out through the center.

6. Insert the wired bud into the center of the partially open bud until the bases of the two flowers meet. Pierce-wire, using #26 gauge wire, through the two buds to secure them in place. Pull the wire down and tape. **(Figure 5.8f)**

7. Insert the two-bud unit into the partially open floret. Pierce-wire through the three florets and pull the wires down against the others and tape. **(Figure 5.8f)**

8. Insert the three-floret unit into the half open floret. Pierce-wire through the four florets and pull the wires down against the others and tape. **(Figure 5.8f)**

9. Insert the four-floret unit into the fully open floret. **(Figure 5.8f)**

10. Pierce wire through the five florets with three pieces of fine wire. Pull the wires down against the others. **(Figure 5.8g)**

11. Tape the base of the flowers down to the end of the wires to finish the glamellia.

12. Wired broad-leaved foliage, such as camellia leaves, should be added to provide a supportive background

Figure 5.8f Creating a Glamellia Steps 6 - 9

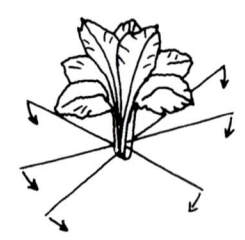

Figure 5.8g Creating a Glamellia Step 10

Figure 5.8h Creating a Glamellia Step 12

Flowers to Wear

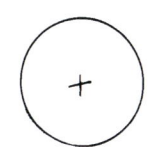

Figure 5.9a Creating a Larger Glamellia Step 2

Figure 5.9b Creating a Larger Glamellia Step 4

Figure 5.9c Creating a Larger Glamellia Step 4

Figure 5.9d Creating a Larger Glamellia Step 5

Figure 5.9e Creating a Larger Glamellia Step 7

to the corsage. A bow may be added, if desired. **(Figure 5.8h)**

13. Cut the stem to a length of approximately 2 inches.

Creating a Larger Glamellia *(Figure 5.9)*

1. Make a glamellia, following Steps 1 through 11 above. Refrigerate the corsage in a sealed bag until needed.

2. Cut a circle out of lightweight cardboard 1 inch smaller than the desired size of the finished glamellia. The cardboard circle from an empty bolt of ribbon may also be used. Cut a small X in the center of the circle of cardboard with a florist knife. **(Figure 5.9a)**

3. Prepare five to seven additional open florets for use, following step 5 above. Cut each floret into three individual petals.

4. Spread a layer of floral adhesive glue around the outer edge of the cardboard circle to a width of 1 inch. **(Figures 5.9b and 5.9c)**

5. Lay the individual gladiolus petals on the cardboard with the tips extending approximately 1/2 inch beyond the cardboard. The base of each petal should point toward the X in the center. Work around the cardboard, overlapping the petals slightly, until a complete ring of petals is in place. **(Figure 5.9d)**

6. Spread another layer of floral adhesive glue over the base of the petals that have been placed on the cardboard circle. Place another row of petals onto the cardboard overlapping the first set of petals about halfway.

7. Add more rows of petals in the same way to cover the cardboard completely. Note: The X in the center should not be covered up. **(Figure 5.9e)**

8. Put a layer of glue around the center X. Insert the stem of the pre-made glamellia through the X and pull it down until the glamellia rests on the cardboard. The flower petals should create a smooth transition from the edges to the center bud.

9. Wire and tape several large camellia or salal leaves. Position the leaves under the cardboard for support and tape the leaves to the stem. Individual camellia or salal leaves can also be glued to the cardboard to hide the mechanics.

10. Cut the stem to a manageable length. If desired, wrap the stem with ribbon to finish.

Poinsettia Corsage

Corsages featuring poinsettias are often requested during the Christmas season. The poinsettia is a member of the Euphorbia family. Its flower has a stem that is similar to a straw. When a flower is cut from the poinsettia plant, white sap may drain out of the stem. This occurs more often with old varieties of poinsettias. When using poinsettia flowers in corsages, a special conditioning process is necessary to seal the cut stems before they are used in designs. Once the stems have been cut and sealed, it is best not to re-cut them or the sap will begin to flow again. Poinsettias have often been sealed by burning the ends of the stems in an open flame. However, research has shown that alternate techniques yield better results. The following conditioning methods are recommended.

Conditioning New Varieties with Little or No Sap Flow

Cut the poinsettia flower from the plant, and place it in a solution of 2 teaspoons of 10 percent liquid chlorine bleach per gallon of water. (A 10 percent chlorine solution is made by mixing one part bleach to nine parts water.)

Conditioning Old Varieties with Heavy Sap Flow

Cut the poinsettia flower from the plant, then place it in plain water for 1 hour. After removing the poinsettia from the water, place it in 90 percent isopropyl alcohol for 10 minutes. Remove it from the alcohol, and place it in a floral preservative solution.

Creating a Poinsettia Corsage

1. Poinsettias are delicate. The bracts can break off easily. Use extreme care when working with them.

2. Wire a poinsettia with a #24 gauge, taped wire, using the wrap-around wiring method. Tape the wired stem.

Notes

Flowers to Wear

3. Wire and tape three to five pieces of holiday foliage, such as holly or pine tips.

4. Arrange the foliage around the flower in the same manner used to create a single flower corsage.

5. Add a bow underneath the flower. Velvet ribbon is a popular choice for this type of corsage.

6. Cut the stem of the corsage to a length of approximately 2 inches. Be sure not to cut the stem of the corsage above the point where the poinsettia stem was originally cut for conditioning.

Prom and Party Flowers to Wear and Carry

Corsages and boutonnieres of any type may be worn to proms, parties, football games, and other festive events. However, the following types of corsages, boutonnieres, and hair and hand-held flowers are most frequently requested for these special occasions.

Nestled Boutonniere *(Figure 5.10)*

A novelty boutonniere frequently designed for proms is a rose nestled in the center of a carnation. To design a boutonniere of this style effectively, it is recommended that the carnation be a different color than the rose. For example, a white carnation with a red sweetheart rose in the center is very effective.

1. Wire a sweetheart rose with a #22 gauge wire using the pierce method. Do not tape the wired stem.

2. Remove the pistil from the center of the carnation. This provides room to insert the wired rose down through the center of the carnation and through the calyx. Once inserted, position the rose so that it is nestled into the center of the carnation. *(Figure 5.10)*

3. Pierce-wire the carnation and tape the stem.

4. Finish the boutonniere as described in the instructions for creating a single flower boutonniere on page 111.

Figure 5.10 Creating a Nestled Boutonniere

Wrist Corsages

A wrist corsage is constructed by designing a lightweight corsage and attaching it to some type of wristband with a holder. There are a number of wristlet holders available. Some have elasticized wristbands; others have a plastic latch similar to that found on a watchband. The corsage is usually attached to these bands with a metal clamp or ribbon. Another type of wristband, often considered more secure and comfortable to wear, can be created with ordinary florist products.

Attaching a Commercial Wristlet

A commercial wristlet is attached after the corsage has been completely constructed. There are two popular types: the ribbon tie wristlet and the elastic band wristlet. The ribbon tie wristlet usually has a lace backing attached to plastic or cardboard. It is attached to a corsage by placing it behind the corsage with the ribbon ties facing the corsage. The ribbons are then tied around the shank of the corsage in two places using a double knot. A shoestring bow can be used to finish the ribbon ends.

The elastic band wristlet is also frequently used. It is attached to the finished corsage by bending the four wire prongs on the wristlet up so that they are U-shaped, or resemble the legs of a table. The prongs are then placed against the center portion of the back of the corsage and pinched around the shank of the corsage with a pair of needle-nosed pliers. Once attached, the band should be pulled on slightly to insure that the prongs will remain securely in place.

Constructing a Wristlet *(Figure 5.11)*

Another type of wristband often considered more secure and comfortable to wear can be created with ordinary florist products using the following steps.

1. Cut a 16-inch length of satin or velvet covered wire tubing.

2. Bend both ends in toward the center of the wire and use a taped #24 gauge wire to bind the ends of the tubing to the center. This should create a figure 8. *(Figure 5.11a)*

Figure 5.11a Constructing a Wristlet Step 2

Flowers to Wear

Figure 5.11b Constructing a Wristlet Step 3

3. Tape the ends of the binding wire to the corsage stem at the midway point. *(Figure 5.11b)*

4. To secure the band around the wrist, slip one loop of the figure *8* through the other, and bend the loop backward to tighten the design on the arm.

NOTE: Two chenille stems may be taped together and used to form the same type of figure *8* band.

Hand-held Flowers

Young ladies may choose to carry a single long-stemmed rose with a touch of baby's breath and ribbon, or a scepter of nerine lilies bound with braided ribbon. Whatever the size or style, hand-held designs are usually most effective when designed with a few interesting botanical specimens rather than a mass of everyday flowers.

Miniature nosegays are also popular for high school formals in some geographical areas. These hand-held flowers should be lightweight and easy to carry. Flower combinations for these bouquets may range from a few sweetheart roses with a touch of baby's breath and fern to a collection of tiny florets. Regardless of the flowers that are chosen, the bouquet should be small so it will not appear to be a bridal bouquet.

Creating a Single Rose to Carry

1. Remove all thorns from a long-stemmed rose. If the neck is weak, wire it using the splinting method. Leave the foliage on the top half of the stem. One may also wish to re-cut the rose and place a water tube on the stem to provide a water source. This tube should be taped to the stem to insure security and to hide the mechanics.

2. Select a filler, such as baby's breath, to use as an accent. Position the filler so that it surrounds the stem just below the flower head. Tape the stem of the filler to the flower about halfway down the stem.

3. Position one to three pieces of foliage, such as leatherleaf, around the stem so that the tips are just below the filler. Tape the foliage to the flower stem at the same point that the filler was taped.

4. Prepare a bow with streamers. Tape it to the flower stem at the same point as the filler and foliage stems.

5. Trim the filler and foliage stems to a length equal to the flowers.

Creating a Miniature Nosegay

1. Wire and tape six to twelve small flowers or florets. The number and type of flowers used will determine the size of the finished bouquet.

2. Wire and tape eight to ten pieces of filler and eight to ten pieces of foliage.

3. Arrange three or four flowers into a cluster. Hold the cluster in one hand and tape the stems together, starting 3 to 4 inches down the wires.

4. Position a ring of flowers around the cluster. Tape these stems into place. Finish the back of the bouquet with additional foliage placements, as needed.

5. Insert foliage and filler materials between and behind the flowers, while maintaining a round shape.

6. Ribbon, tulle, or lace backing may be added to complete the bouquet.

7. Create a handle for the bouquet by cutting the stem to a comfortable length, usually about 5 inches. Wrap the stem in ribbon, following the steps on pages 132 through 133.

Football Mum Corsage

In some geographical regions, football mum corsages are considered a must for college and high school football games. They are especially popular for homecoming games and dances. The typical football mum corsage is designed simply with a single standard mum, foliage backing, and a bow. It may also be decorated with school letters and football accents for a more spirited look. In a few areas, more elaborate corsages are popular. They sometimes include two or three mums with an abundance of streamers, lettering, and accessories. The following methods for creating football mums may be adapted to create corsages from simple to extravagant.

Notes

Flowers to Wear

Figure 5.12 Football Mum Corsage

Making a Football Mum Corsage *(Figure 5.12)*

1. Cut the stem of a standard chrysanthemum to a length of 1 1/2 inches, and wire with a #20 gauge wire using the insertion method. Use a #22 gauge wire to pierce-wire the stem. Tape all of the wires to the stem.

2. Insert the wired mum through the *X* in the pre-made collar. (Instructions for creating a mum collar are given on page 128.) Spread floral adhesive glue around the top of the mum stem. Pull the collar up the stem until it sticks to the glue. (The glue will assist in keeping the collar securely in place.) Tape the back of the collar to the stem.

3. Make a long, looped ribbon bow and streamers with #5 ribbon. Tape the wire into place so that the bow is under the base of the collar and mum.

4. Finish the stem, as desired. The stem can be left long and carried, or cut short and worn on the shoulder.

Accessories for Football Mum Corsages

- Footballs - Small plastic footballs can be attached to the mum by inserting a wire through the center of the flower and attaching the football to the end of the wire before hooking it back through the flower.

- Chenille Letters - School letters can be made out of colored chenille stems. Letters should be made with a small loop of chenille, so that the hook can be passed through them. This attaches letters to the mum in the same way as the football is attached. When forming a letter, a small loop should be shaped near the center. This loop is used to attach the letter to the mum, using the technique described for attaching the footballs.

- Ribbon Accents - Ribbon of different widths and various colors may be combined to make bows and/or streamers as elaborate as desired. Miniature footballs, bells, and other accessories may be tied to the ends of the streamers. Braided ribbons may also be used to create a unique look.

Football Mum Collars

The large size and fragile nature of standard mums makes it difficult to design and wear without damage. For this reason, mum collars are often used to provide a decorative and supportive backing for the flowers. These backings may be constructed of either foliage or ribbon in the following ways.

Making a Collar with Foliage *(Figure 5.13)*

1. Cut out a circle of lightweight cardboard approximately 1 inch smaller than the mum. Cut an *X* in the center of the circle with a florist knife. The cardboard from an empty bolt of ribbon can also be used. *(Figure 5.13a)*

2. Select approximately seven uniformly sized salal leaves. Staple them onto the cardboard, one at a time, around the circle with the tips extending about 1 inch over the edge of the cardboard. Allow each leaf to overlap slightly. Trim a bit of the leaf base if it hides the *X* in the center of the cardboard.

3. The finished collar can be made in advance and stored in the cooler in a plastic bag. Water should not be sprayed into the bag unless waxed cardboard is used to make the circle. *(Figure 5.13b)*

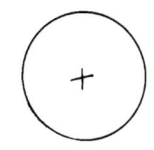

Figure 5.13a Making a Football Mum Collar with Foliage Step 1

Figure 5.13b Making a Football Mum Collar with Foliage Step 3

Making a Collar with Ribbon or Lace

1. Cut out a circle of lightweight cardboard about 1 inch smaller than the mum. Cut an *X* in the center of it with a florist knife. The cardboard from an empty bolt of ribbon can also be used.

2. Pleat the end of a piece of #40 ribbon or lace, and staple it to the edge of the cardboard so that the ribbon extends approximately 1 inch beyond the cardboard. Staple approximately 1/2 inch from the edge.

3. Continue pleating and stapling the ribbon until the entire circle of cardboard is covered. Cut the ribbon off the bolt.

Flowers to Wear

Notes

Hair Flowers

Flowers for the hair are especially popular for proms, weddings, and other formal occasions. A simple floral hair decoration might be a sprig of baby's breath tucked behind the ear. A more elaborate headdress might be a floral wreath or profile spray. There are a variety of ways to create floral hair decorations. The various methods are dependent upon the desired size and placement on the head. Regardless of what style is designed, it is important that the appropriate mechanics are used to provide a lightweight and secure floral piece that is comfortable to wear.

Single Flower Headpiece

1. Select a flower, such as an open rose or lily. Wire and tape the flower using the appropriate wiring method.

2. Wire and tape three or four small pieces of foliage and/or filler with a #26 or #28 gauge wire.

3. Position the foliage and filler around the flower and tape them into place.

4. Add accessories, such as ribbons or pearl sprays, as desired.

5. Trim excess wires from the stem so that only a thin stem remains. Tape the stem, and trim it to a length of 2 inches. Use the stem to secure the piece in place with hairpins.

Cluster Hairpiece

1. Wire and tape three to five small flowers or florets and a few pieces of filler and foliage. Tape each wire all the way to the end.

2. Arrange the flowers and filler into a cluster, and tape them into place at a single point.

3. Position the foliage behind the cluster to form a backing. Tape the foliage into place.

4. Trim the stems so that the cluster has a few thin wires left, each about 2 inches long. The cluster will be pinned into the hair at two points with hairpins.

Barrette Hairpiece *(Figure 5.14)*

1. Open the barrette and hot glue a piece of ribbon to the back side of the decorative bar. *(Figure 5.14a)*

2. Glue a second piece of ribbon across the top of the barrette. The two pieces of ribbon should overlap and create a completely sealed surface around the barrette. *(Figure 5.14b)*

3. Glue a light bed of greens onto the ribbon with floral adhesive glue. Elevate some of the greens, and position them at angles to give the design depth.

4. Add a bow or streamers to the barrette, if desired.

5. Begin gluing flower placements onto the center of the barrette, and work out toward the ends with smaller flowers, buds, and other fillers. *(Figure 5.14c)*

Hair Comb Hairpiece *(Figure 5.15)*

1. Use hot glue to secure a piece of ribbon on the upper front and back portions of a hair comb (opposite the teeth). The two pieces of ribbon should overlap and create a sealed surface along the edge of the comb.

2. Follow Steps 3 through 5 for designing a barrette.

Hair Clip Hairpiece

1. Place a piece of waxed paper between the teeth of a hair clip. This prevents the clip from being glued together during the design of the piece.

2. Hot glue a piece of ribbon over the metal forks on each side of the clip.

3. Follow Steps 3 through 5 for designing a barrette. Be sure to add flowers around the clamp to help disguise it.

4. When all of the glue has dried, remove the waxed paper from between the teeth of the clip.

Figure 5.14a Constructing a Barrette Hairpiece Step 1

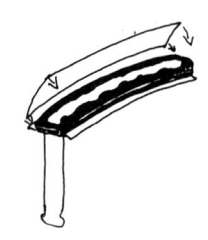

Figure 5.14b Constructing a Barrette Hairpiece Step 2

Figure 5.14c Constructing a Barrette Hairpiece Step 5

Figure 5.15 Hair Comb

Flowers to Wear

Figure 5.16 Floral Wreath

Figure 5.17 Floral Headband

Figure 5.18 Profile Hairpiece

Floral Wreaths and Headbands

Floral wreaths and headbands are designed in exactly the same manner. The difference between them is the position in which they are worn on the head. The floral wreath should be worn around the crown of the head, while the headband is wrapped straight across the forehead. These headpieces must be custom designed to fit the head of the individual. To insure a proper fit, measure the head with a tape measure or a piece of ribbon. Place the measure gently around the top of the head, approximately 2 inches above the ear for a wreath and 1 inch above the ear for a headband. Design headpieces of the appropriate length in the following manner.

Making Wreaths and Headbands *(Figures 5.16 and 5.17)*

1. Tape two #24 gauge wires together end to end.

2. Bend one end of the wire into a 1-inch hook.

3. Tape the end of the hook to the wire to create a small loop.

4. Beginning at the looped end of the wire, create a garland of foliage by binding 2- to 3-inch long clusters to the wrapped wire with a #28 gauge wire. The stems of the foliage should face the straight end of the wire.

5. When the greens reach the end of the wire, bind one more cluster to the wire in the direction opposite the rest.

6. Add flowers to the garland in a random pattern with floral adhesive glue.

7. Bend the garland into a ring and insert the straight end of the wire through the looped end. Bend 1 inch of the straight wire back over the loop to secure the ring.

8. Attach ribbons and streamers to the back of the ring to disguise the connecting point.

Profile Hairpieces *(Figure 5.18)*

A profile hairpiece is usually worn so that it creates a dramatic sweep of flower to one side of the face. This type of hairpiece is constructed in exactly the same manner as the double spray corsage described on pages 117 through 118. Because this hairpiece is usually large, it is important to keep the design as light as possible. This can be accomplished by using wire of the lightest weight possible and trimming excess wire from the design as it is constructed. The profile hairpiece is usually secured with hairpins attached at each end, as well as, at the center of the design.

Stem Finishes

There are a variety of ways to finish the stem ends of a boutonniere or corsage. The simplest method is to cut the stem and leave it straight. While this method is the easiest, it sometimes does little to enhance the design. The following three stem finishes lend themselves to creating more sophisticated corsages and boutonnieres.

Curled Finish *(Figure 5.19)*

A more interesting, less blunt finish can be achieved by curling the stem of a corsage or boutonniere. This can be done very simply by bending the stem end up to form a small loop. A fancier curl can be created by twisting the end around a hyacinth stake or pencil for a corkscrew effect. In either case, the stem should be cut 1/2 to 1 inch longer than usual to allow for the curl.

Figure 5.19 Curled Stem Finish

Garden Finish *(Figure 5.20)*

The garden stem finish is designed to look as if the natural stems of the floral materials are still attached. This effect is achieved by taping all of the wired stems at a single point during construction and leaving the ends of the individual wires free. The wires are then cut to the appropriate length and spread apart slightly. When creating the garden finish, it is important to tape each flower all the way to the end so that the wire will be covered, regardless of the length it is cut.

Ribbon-wrapped Finish *(Figure 5.21)*

Ribbon wrapping is a technique commonly used to finish the stems of bridal bouquets. This same technique can be used with narrow ribbon to create an interesting effect on corsages and boutonnieres. The ribbon color may be selected to match the

Figure 5.20 Garden Stem Finish

Flowers to Wear

Figure 5.21a Creating a Ribbon-wrapped Stem Finish Step 1

Figure 5.21b Creating a Ribbon-wrapped Stem Finish Step 2

Figure 5.21c Creating a Ribbon-wrapped Stem Finish Step 3

garment it will be worn with. The stem will then blend with the fabric, making it less noticeable. The following steps are used to create a ribbon-wrapped stem finish.

1. Using #3 ribbon, place the end of the ribbon 1/4 inch from the bottom of the stem. Work with the dull side of the ribbon showing. A drop of hot glue may be used to secure the end of the ribbon to the stem. **(Figure 5.21a)**

2. Pull the ribbon down over the stem end and up around the back side of the stem. Wrap the ribbon around the stem, working up toward the flower. Be sure that the ribbon is overlapped far enough so that none of the stem shows. **(Figure 5.21b)**

3. Secure the ribbon by pulling the end through the last wrapped-around section. This will create a knot just below the flower. Secure the knot with a drop of hot glue to prevent it from sliding. **(Figure 5.21c)**

4. Trim the end of the ribbon to approximately 1/4 inch in length.

General Tips for Constructing Flowers to Wear

- Trim excess wires from a corsage as it is constructed. This will keep it from becoming too bulky and heavy.

- Some foliage and fillers, such as plumosa or baby's breath, can be taped directly to individual flowers instead of being wired and taped.

- Lightweight foliage and fillers can be added to corsages by dipping the ends into floral adhesive glue and then positioning them in the corsage.

- Tape should always be stretched and pulled tightly to prevent pieces from shifting or falling out of the design.

- Pollen should be removed from the centers of lilies and alstroemeria to avoid stains on clothing.

- Flower life can be extended by placing a small piece of wet cotton on the end of each stem before taping.

Accessories and Accents for Flowers to Wear

Corsages and boutonnieres sometimes require special accessories to make them more appropriate for specific occasions or types of dress. Dried materials, for example, can be used to add an earthy or autumn look to a boutonniere. Lace ribbons and pearl sprays can be used to add a romantic look to a corsage. Touches of silk flowers or velvet leaves are ideal for use when a difficult color, such as blue, must be incorporated into a design. The following accents and accessories can be used to make flowers to wear more special.

Rhinestones and Pearls

Rhinestone and pearl sprays are appropriate for formal occasions of all types. Corsages for young girls might be accented with bees or butterflies made of iridescent materials studded with pearls or rhinestones. Adults might prefer elegant touches of pearl sprays woven between or within the flowers. Most of these accessories have wired stems which can be taped directly to the corsage during construction.

Glitter and Diamond Dust

Diamond dust and glitter sprays can also be used to accent a corsage. A light dusting of one of these sprays or glitters can be applied to the entire design or to parts of the design. Baby's breath that has been diamond dusted will add a bit of sparkle to corsages or boutonnieres.

Ribbon, Tulle, and Lace

Ribbon, tulle, and lace can be used to add a romantic look to corsages and hairpieces. These materials are relatively inexpensive, but they can provide a sophisticated look. Following are several effective uses for these common accessories.

Ribbon

- Streamers add movement and color. Knotting at different lengths adds interest.

- Bows create focal points and add color.

Flowers to Wear

Notes

- Braiding adds an interesting touch to stem ends and bouquets.

- Loops and tails provide accents to corsages and boutonnieres.

Tulle

- Streamers add softness and color.

- Bows add a cloud-like focal point.

- Puffs add support, softness, and color.

Lace

- Streamers add color and movement.

- Bows create a soft focal point.

- Loops and tails provide accents to corsages, boutonnieres, and bouquets.

Finishing Dips and Sprays

Finishing dips and sprays are used to assist in minimizing water loss in flowers used to create boutonnieres, corsages, and hairpieces. These dips and sprays help seal the flowers so that less water is lost through the pores, thus providing a longer-lasting product. Flowers, fillers, and foliage used for flowers to wear can be treated with a finishing spray or dye prior to design construction.

To prevent spotting, the dip or spray should be allowed to dry thoroughly before packaging and refrigerating. For more information on using finishing dips and sprays, refer to Chapter 4 in this book.

Packaging

Proper packaging of flowers to wear helps prevent moisture loss and may be just as important as the design it holds. Flowers that are sealed in cellophane or plastic bags can be placed in cardboard boutonniere and corsage boxes for presentation. Flowers can also be sealed in cellophane corsage boxes. The type of packaging used should be consistent with the shop's image. A pre-printed label placed on each box will assist in identifying the shop the flowers came from. A ribbon might also be tied around the box as a finishing touch.

Wearing Flowers Appropriately

Corsages and boutonnieres are traditionally worn on the left shoulder. This originated with the Victorian custom of wearing flowers over the heart.

Corsages are generally worn somewhat higher on the shoulder than boutonnieres. A corsage may be worn up and over the top of the shoulder so that it is slightly to the front of the body with the tip at about collarbone level. Corsages should be positioned to follow the natural curve of the shoulder and secured with two pins. **(Figure 5.22)** One pin should be placed through the corsage stem. The other pin should be used higher in the corsage, among the flowers, to help prevent the corsage from rocking side to side. For garments made of delicate fabrics, a piece of cotton, folded tissue, or matching felt may be placed on the underside of the fabric to provide more bulk for the pins to grip. The pins may be stitched through the bra strap for added security. White or pearl-headed pins are typically used for corsages, but should be matched to the garment appropriately.

Boutonnieres are usually smaller and worn lower on the shoulder, near the buttonhole of the jacket lapel about 6 inches below the shoulder. **(Figure 5.23)** Shorter, black-headed pins are usually used to secure boutonnieres, but again, the pins should be appropriately matched to the garment. For example, a man wearing a white tuxedo should wear a white-headed corsage pin instead of a black-headed boutonniere pin. Boutonniere pins may also be inserted from the back side of the lapel so the pinhead does not show.

Wristlets are generally worn on the left wrist; however, left-handed individuals may prefer to wear them on their right. A wristlet corsage should be worn comfortably near the wristbone rather than higher on the forearm. The corsage should not be so large that it interferes with the use of the hand.

Profile sprays of flowers for the hair are usually worn on the right. Bobby pins are effective for pinning wired floral sprays, wreaths, or headbands into most types of hair. One or two bobby pins secured through narrow stems at each end of the spray should hold it firmly in place. This is generally more effective than pinning through the bulky center of the spray. For fine hair, twist a

Figure 5.22 Corsage Placement

Figure 5.23 Boutonniere Placement

Flowers to Wear

Notes

small section of hair around itself a few times before pinning into it. Hair combs can be secured in any type of hair by teasing a section of the hair, misting it with hairspray, and inserting the comb after the spray has dried.

Flowers to wear can be designed in a wide variety of shapes and styles. It is the florist's role to share the many options with each customer to insure that the most appropriate design is created. When constructing flowers to wear, florists must follow proper wiring and assembly techniques. Accessories should be added only to enhance the design, not to dominate it. The final steps of sealing and packaging designs are vital to insuring long-lasting products. Attention to detail throughout all of these stages of production will result in a quality product and a satisfied customer.

Basic Floral Design

Notes, Photographs, Sketches, etc.

Flowers to Wear

Notes, Photographs, Sketches, etc.

Designing Basic Arrangements

Chapter 6

The objective of every florist should be to create designs that are well organized, well constructed, and harmonious. Such designs require a combination of the appropriate colors, textures, forms, and patterns. When selecting these components, the size and shape of the arrangement and the color and type of plant materials to be used must be considered. Knowledge of the principles and elements of design is essential for this creative process. When the principles of floral design have been applied to materials that were carefully chosen, a beautiful and pleasing flower arrangement will be the result.

To achieve success in any artistic endeavor, an artist must possess discipline and patience. The artist must practice continually and must attempt various styles of floral design. The style of design most frequently practiced in the United States is referred to as western style or line-mass style.

Line-mass design is often referred to as geometric design. These designs are constructed with line flowers and foliage, which complete a structure or framework similar to that created by 2- by 4-inch boards in a house. All other plant materials go inside the framework of the design to form the mass. The geometric designs in western design are:

- Symmetrical Triangle (three point formal)
- Asymmetrical Triangle (three point informal)
- Crescent
- Oval
- Horizontal
- Vertical
- Hogarth Curve

Basic Floral Design

Familiarity with the following list, often considered the "Rules of Arranging," will be of great assistance to floral designers.

- A floral design should be at least one and one-half times the height or width, whichever is greater, of the container.

- Small flowers and those of light colors should be placed at the outer edges of a design, while large flowers and those of dark colors should be placed inside the design near the focal area or lip of the container.

- The following rule of spacing should be followed. The closer flowers are to the focal point or area, the closer they should be placed to each other. Conversely, the farther flowers extend from the focal area, the farther they should be placed from each other.

- No two flowers should be positioned on the same level, unless they are developing or completing a pattern. This helps prevent flowers from appearing as if they are in a line.

- Flowers that are compatible, those with approximately the same vase life, should be used together in a design.

- Unity is achieved when a design and its container become one.

- A western style design usually has a focal area near the lip of the container. The design is three-dimensional; it has height, width, and depth.

Pre-design Considerations

A flower arrangement must be compatible with its surroundings, and it must be appropriate for the occasion at which it will be displayed. The selection of containers and flowers is very important, and in each case, careful consideration should be given to form, color, structure, size, and suitability. An

Notes

Designing Basic Arrangements

Notes

arrangement created for a formal dinner, for instance, would not satisfy these requirements if it were so tall that guests could not see each other across the table. A general rule of thumb is that a container and arrangement should not be more than 14 inches tall when used as a centerpiece. When selecting a container, consider the following factors.

- Does the color of the container harmonize with the flowers and the setting?

- Is the texture of the vase or container compatible with the flowers? There should be a complete contrast or a complete blend.

- Is the container proportionally sized in regard to its surroundings?

- Would a container with a flat base or a pedestal work better?

After a container has been selected, devices must be added to help secure plant materials that will be inserted into the design. In floral design, such articles are referred to as holders, stationing devices, or frogs.

The oldest known device for securing materials in floral designs dates back thousands of years to oriental floral design. This device has resulted in what is called a pin frog, or needlepoint holder. Needlepoint holders are frequently used by garden clubs and to a lesser degree by retail florists. Chicken wire, shredded styrofoam, floral clay, and waterproof and clear tapes are examples of other types of common holding devices. Floral foam is the most popular and most frequently used. Water-absorbent foam, often call wet foam, and water-repellent foam, often called dry foam, are manufactured by several companies. Innovative, quality methods of securing and stabilizing with foam materials are continually being developed.

The stability of an arrangement depends on how firmly the frog is secured to the container. Methods of securing designs are commonly referred to as mechanics. Regardless of how beautiful and appealing a floral arrangement may be, it is not a quality design if its mechanics are improperly executed. A floral arrangement without proper stabilization invites disaster. Chapter 3 provides additional information about the use of mechanics in floral design.

Basic Floral Design

Plant Materials

When choosing flowers for a floral design, careful consideration must be given to the four growth patterns of plant material: line, mass, filler, and form.

Line Flowers

Line flowers extend along a single line with florets growing on one side or surrounding the line or backbone of the flower. Line flowers are used to establish the structure of a floral design. They outline it by adding the height and width. Line flowers also provide direction, strength, and a design pattern. They are showy and give "looks value" to a design. Using line flowers is often considered profitable, because it may take as many as three carnations to create the line of a single gladiolus. Gladioli, snapdragons, delphinium, and stock are examples of line flowers.

Mass Flowers

Mass flowers add weight and volume to a design. They are almost always round flowers that are placed within the framework of a design. Carnations, roses, and asters are examples of mass flowers.

Filler Flowers

Filler flowers have clusters of blossoms on a single stem. These flowers add fullness to an arrangement. They are transitional flowers, which fill spaces between the line and mass flowers. Statice, pompons, waxflower, and gypsophila are examples of filler flowers.

Form Flowers

Form flowers are distinctive, uniquely shaped, and often quite expensive. They require strong spatial definition. When selecting these flowers for a design, it is important to select line, mass, and filler greenery to accompany them as a background. Anthuriums, irises, birds of paradise, and orchids are examples of form flowers.

When selecting and composing an arrangement, the designer should consider the placement, proportion, and form of a design. For instance, if an arrangement for a church is ordered, the most

Notes

Designing Basic Arrangements

appropriate form would be a symmetrical triangle. This three-point, formal type arrangement would blend well in such a symmetrical surrounding. So that proper proportion to the surroundings can be achieved, this type of design should be as large and showy as the price will allow.

Constructing Line-mass Designs

Floral designing can be very exciting. Each arrangement should be seen as a challenge to determine the ideal combination of form, color, and texture that will result in the desired appearance. Mastering the basics of floral design provides designers with a solid foundation. Additional study and continued practice will assist in developing the skills needed to become a competent and creative floral designer. Following are instructions for creating the designs which are most often requested in floral shops.

Placement, Proportion, and Scoring *(Figure 6.1)*

To assist beginning designers in insuring the proper positioning of initial flower placements in a design, foam can be lightly scored into four quadrants. This provides a visual pattern that may prove to be helpful. The scoring guidelines discussed below are recommended for the design styles listed.

Free-standing Arrangement *(Figure 6.1a)*

Foam for use in a free standing arrangement that is to be viewed from all sides should be scored with a knife vertically down the center of the foam. A second line should be scored horizontally in the center of the foam. When completed, the foam should be divided into four equal sections.

Asymmetrical Triangle *(Figure 6.1b)*

Since most asymmetrical triangles are read visually from left to right, scoring should also read from left to right. (To make an asymmetrical design that reads right to left, reverse the scoring.) Draw a vertical line two-thirds from the right and one-third from the left. Draw a horizontal line two-thirds from the front and one-third from the back. This division of plant material will provide visual balance.

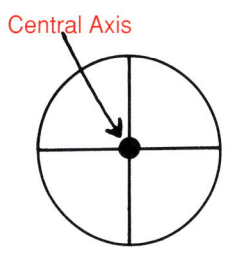

Figure 6.1a Placement, Proportion, and Scoring for a Free-standing Arrangement

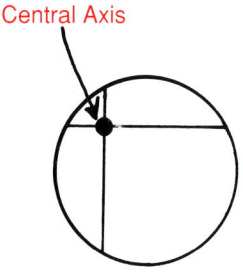

Figure 6.1b Placement, Proportion, and Scoring for an Asymmetrical Triangle

Symmetrical Triangle *(Figure 6.1c)*

Since the triangle is symmetrical (with equal amounts of material on each side of the central vertical axis), the first line is drawn vertically down the center of the foam; the second line is drawn horizontally two-thirds from the front and one-third from the back. This style of design is often requested for hospitals, churches, special occasions, and holidays. Many designs promoted by wire services are variations of this style of design. It is pleasing to most people and is easily designed. The two basic triangles most frequently used are the equilateral triangle and the isosceles triangle. Equilateral designs have three sides of equal length, and isosceles designs have two sides of equal length. A central vertical axis divides each of these triangles into equal halves, and flowers are placed equally on each side. In other words, one half is virtually a mirror image of the other.

To become familiar with this type of arrangement, two different approaches are recommended for study and practice. First, complete a small (15- by 15-inch) arrangement and a medium (18- by 18-inch) arrangement. Outline them with flowers first and complete them by adding a background of greenery. Secondly, complete a large (30- by 30-inch) arrangement that would be appropriate for use in a church or wedding service. Outline the design with large-line foliage first and complete it with flowers. In each of the two cases, the basic triangle will be equilateral. Be sure to respect the guiding principles of design, such as balance, placement, proportion, radiation, and unity, when practicing each approach.

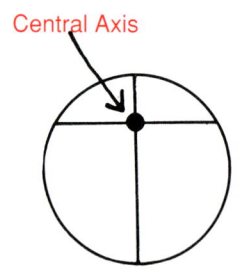

Figure 6.1c Placement, Proportion, and Scoring for a Symmetrical Triangle

Materials Needed for a Small Symmetrical Triangle

- Nine mass flowers (carnations, asters)
- Filler Flowers (statice, gypsophila)
- Foliage (leatherleaf, oregonia, ruscus)
- Four-inch pedestal container
- Floral foam

Constructing a Small Symmetrical Triangle *(Figure 6.2)*

1. Secure pre-soaked floral foam in a 9-inch container. Place the foam 1 inch above the lip of the container so that stem insertions can be made from the sides.

Designing Basic Arrangements

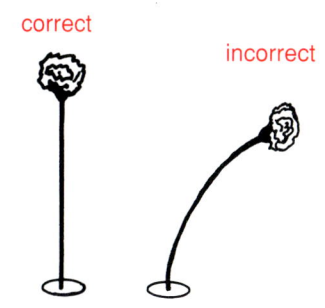

Figure 6.2a Constructing a Small Symmetrical Triangle Steps 3 & 4

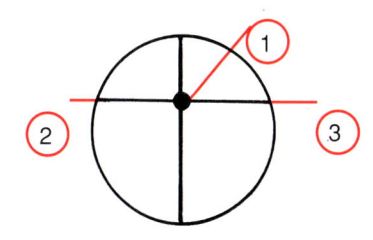

Figure 6.2b Constructing a Small Symmetrical Triangle Steps 3 & 5

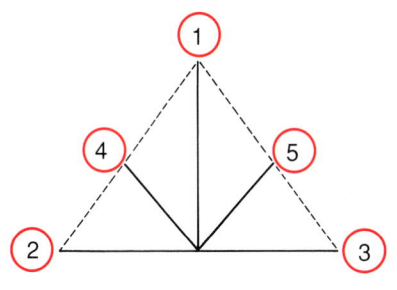

Figure 6.2c Constructing a Small Symmetrical Triangle Steps 6 & 7

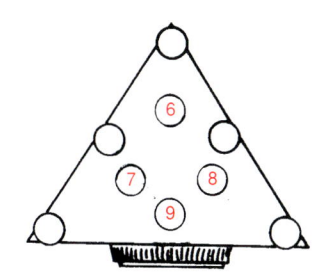

Figure 6.2d Constructing a Small Symmetrical Triangle Step 8

2. Score the foam to insure proper placement and proportion.

3. Cut a straight-stemmed flower to a length of 17 inches. (If necessary, wire may be used to keep the stem straight.) Cut the stem on a slant, and insert it at a point two-thirds back and on the center line of the container. The stem should be inserted into the foam 2 inches, making the height of the arrangement 15 inches. **(Figures 6.2a and 6.2b)**

4. The top of the first flower should be over its bottom. This establishes the central vertical axis of the design. If a plumb line were dropped from the top mass of the flower, it should fall to the base of the stem. **(Figure 6.2a)**

5. Cut two flowers to lengths of 7 inches and insert each stem 2 inches into the foam horizontally, one on each side of the container. These are placed on the lip of the container, two-thirds back and parallel to the table surface. These three flowers have established the structure of the design, giving it height and width. All other flowers are placed inside this framework. **(Figure 6.2b)**

6. Divide the space between the first and second flowers equally. Place the next flower with its blossom on the imaginary line that runs from the first to the second flower. Repeat this step on the opposite side. **(Figure 6.2c)**

7. Form a diamond shape in the center of the design with the four remaining flowers. **(Figure 6.2c)**

8. After completing the design with nine flowers, add greenery behind each. The greenery should follow the same lines as the flowers. **(Figure 6.2d)**

9. Insert filler flowers in empty spaces to add fullness, color, and transition.

NOTE: All flowers and greenery should be placed in an arrangement one type at a time. Also, each side of the central vertical axis should hold approximately the same amount of plant material.

10. If a bow is desired, remove the flower in the center (on the lip of the container), and insert the bow in its place.

Materials Needed for a Medium Symmetrical Triangle

- Thirteen mass flowers
- Filler Flowers (statice, gypsophila)
- Greenery
- Six-inch pedestal container
- Floral foam

Constructing a Medium Symmetrical Triangle *(Figure 6.3)*

1. Secure pre-soaked foam in a container. Make sure it is 1 inch above the lip.

2. Score the foam for a symmetrical triangle.

3. Cut the first flower to a length of 18 inches, and insert it two-thirds back and on the center line as in the previous design. *(Figure 6.3a)*

4. Cut the second and third flowers each to a length of 9 inches, and insert them 2 inches into the foam, two-thirds back to establish the width of the design. *(Figure 6.3a)*

5. The structure of the design has now been established, and all other flowers should be placed inside the framework.

6. Divide the space between the first and second flowers. Place two more flowers of equal distances from the first and second flowers in this space. The left side of the triangle will be divided into three equal angles. Repeat on the right side of the triangle. Make sure the blossoms are on the imaginary lines of the triangle. *(Figure 6.3b)*

7. Form a triangle inside the large triangle with five mass flowers. *(Figure 6.3c)*

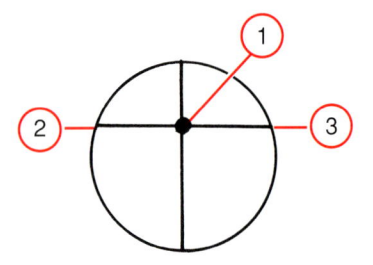

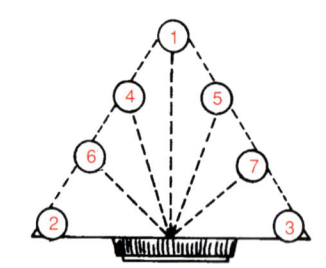

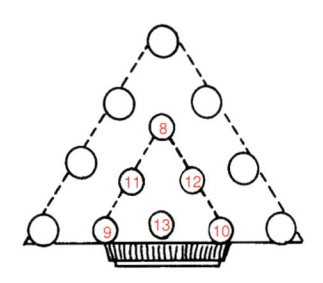

Figure 6.3a Constructing a Medium Symmetrical Triangle Steps 3 & 4

Figure 6.3b Constructing a Medium Symmetrical Triangle Step 6

Figure 6.3c Constructing a Medium Symmetrical Triangle Step 7

Designing Basic Arrangements

Notes

8. Add the remaining mass flowers to the center of this triangle. Place them near the lip of the container, and make sure that they are in line with the first flower. *(Figure 6.3c on page 148)*

9. Add greenery inside the design in the shape of a triangle.

10. Filler flowers can now be added to the arrangement, as desired.

11. If desired, substitute a bow for the last mass flower that was placed in the center of the triangle.

12. Inspect the arrangement, and make sure that all mechanics are covered and that there is visual balance on each side of the central vertical axis.

Materials Needed for a Large Symmetrical Triangle

Large symmetrical triangle arrangements are often used for church altars, weddings, or large parties. They should be large and showy. The construction of these designs usually starts with the introduction of greenery, followed by the addition of flowers. Selecting the proper line greenery and line flowers will contribute greatly to the success of a large symmetrical triangle arrangement. Following is a list of necessary materials.

- Ten line flowers (gladioli, delphinium, snapdragons)
- Line greenery (long myrtle, eucalyptus, etc.)
- Eight- or 10-inch high container
- Floral foam
- Chicken wire

Constructing a Large Symmetrical Triangle *(Figure 6.4)*

1. Place pre-soaked foam in a container. For large containers, it is wise to use old foam or scraps on the bottom and new, unused foam on top. Leave about 2 inches of foam above the lip of the container.

Basic Floral Design

2. Since the flower stems and foliage, along with the wet foam, become quite heavy in this type of design, extra precautions should be taken to insure that the container mechanics are properly constructed. Make sure that the foam is fully packed to the bottom. Cut a piece of chicken wire 1 inch larger than the circumference of the container. Cover the foam with the wire, and use floral shears to turn the jagged ends back into the foam. Secure the chicken wire with waterproof tape. *(Figure 6.4a)*

Figure 6.4a Constructing a Large Symmetrical Triangle Step 2

3. Estimate the one-third to two-thirds scoring as previously described for a symmetrical triangle arrangement.

4. To begin the arrangement, select the first piece of greenery and cut it to a length of 30 inches.

5. Insert it vertically with the top over the bottom and slightly behind the two-thirds back line. The first flower will be placed directly on the two-thirds line. *(Figure 6.4b)*

6. Cut the second and third pieces of greenery to lengths of 15 inches, and place them horizontally into each side of the arrangement, parallel to the surface of the table. They should stick straight out and rest on the lip of the container. *(Figure 6.4b)*

7. Divide the space between the first and second pieces of greenery, and fill this division with individual green spikes. Make sure that the top mass of material on each green spike is placed on the imaginary line of the design. *(Figure 6.4b)*

8. Repeat step 7 on the opposite side. *(Figure 6.4b)*

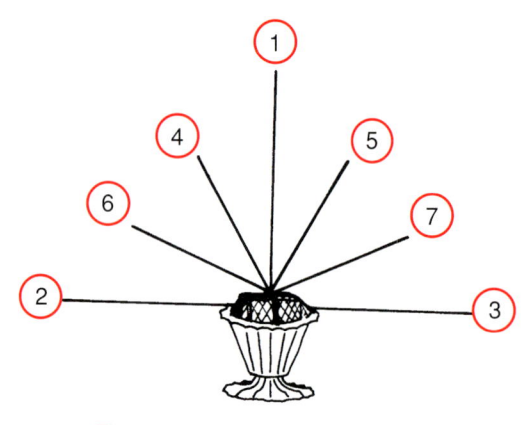

Figure 6.4b Constructing a Large Symmetrical Triangle Steps 5 - 8

9. Continue adding greenery until the triangle is complete. Place the greenery at angles so that it projects forward to form a rounded look. Make sure that the greenery virtually rests on the lip of the container.

10. Add filler greenery, such as leatherleaf. If gladioli are used, place their foliage in the back of the arrangement to add movement and weight.

Designing Basic Arrangements

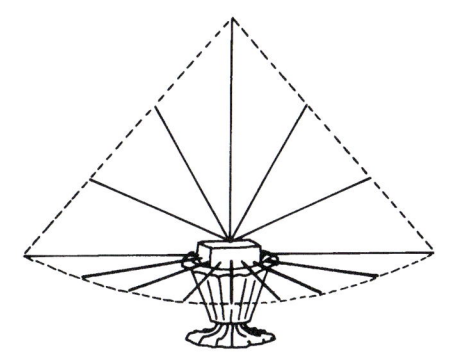

Figure 6.4c Constructing a Large Symmetrical Triangle Step 17

Figure 6.4d Constructing a Large Symmetrical Triangle Step 18

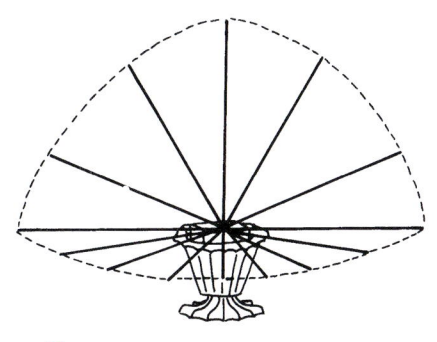

Figure 6.4e Constructing a Large Symmetrical Triangle with a Fan Shape

11. Use ten fully-opened gladioli to create this basic design. They are inexpensive, and they provide maximum show.

12. Cut the first gladiolus to a length of 33 inches, and place it two-thirds of the way back in the center of the container. Make sure its top mass is over its base. Gladioli should be inserted approximately 3 inches into the foam.

13. Cut the second and third gladioli to lengths of 15 inches. Insert these flowers in the foam on each side of the design, approximately two-thirds of the way back. Make sure that they are parallel to the table surface and that they rest on the lip of the container.

14. Place two gladioli between the first and second flowers. Make sure that they divide the space equally. Place the top bud on the imaginary line of the design.

15. Repeat step 14 on the opposite side.

16. Place the remaining gladioli equally on each side of the central vertical axis. Make sure that all flowers radiate from the focal point to the imaginary line of the design.

17. Complete the design by placing greenery throughout. Make sure that some greenery cascades gracefully over the lip of the container. This type of arrangement is usually displayed at a level higher than the audience; therefore, the greenery cascading over the lip of the container is especially important. ***(Figure 6.4c)***

18. Chrysanthemums, lilies, filler flowers, and other materials may be added to increase the value of the arrangement. ***(Figure 6.4d)***

19. If a bow is desired, place it in the focal area just above the lip of the container.

If a fan shape is desired instead of a triangle, use the same instructions, but alter the imaginary lines between the first three line flowers. The fan design often provides more show for the amount of plant material used. ***(Figure 6.4e)***

Asymmetrical Triangle *(Figure 6.5)*

In symmetrical triangle designs, true physical balance is achieved by placing identical materials in relative positions on each side of a central vertical axis. Asymmetrical compositions, however, achieve balance although plant materials are placed unequally on each side of its vertical axis. The axis is not central; rather, it is to the left of the center and two-thirds of the way back in the arrangement. This placement compensates for the unequal distribution of the material. **Figures 6.5 and 6.6** illustrate symmetrical balance and imbalance.

Additionally, these arrangements may appear to be balanced due to the proper placement of color or the appropriate use of size and texture. For example, a red flower is visually heavier than a white flower. Likewise, the coarse texture of yucca foliage appears heavier than the smooth leaves of the camellia. Two children of different weights balanced on a seesaw provide an example of asymmetrical balance. *(Figure 6.7)*

In these arrangements, the vertical line placed left of the center is joined by a horizontal line extending to the right, either straight out or diagonally forward. If the line is straight, the design is referred to as an *L*-form design. The diagonal line is more popular and is considered more artistic than the straight line. Asymmetrical triangle designs usually read from left to right.

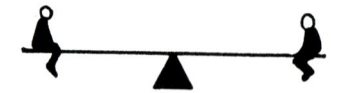

Figure 6.5 Symmetrical Balance

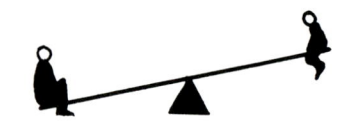

Figure 6.6 Symmetrical Imbalance

Figure 6.7 Asymmetrical Balance

Materials Needed for an Asymmetrical Triangle

- Three linear plant materials or three small branches

- Five specialty flowers (small lilies, pixie gladioli, miniature carnations)

- Filler foliage

- A pedestal, cylinder, or low bowl container

- Floral foam

Constructing an Asymmetrical Triangle *(Figure 6.8)*

1. Secure pre-soaked foam in a container. Make sure that the foam is 1 inch above the lip.

2. Score the foam for proper placement and proportion. Draw two intersecting lines, one two-thirds from the

Designing Basic Arrangements

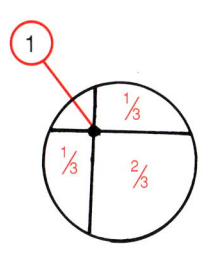

153

Figure 6.8a Constructing an Asymmetrical Triangle Steps 2 & 3

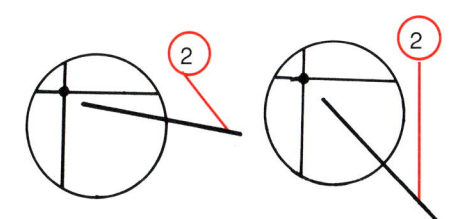

Figure 6.8b Constructing an Asymmetrical Triangle Step 4

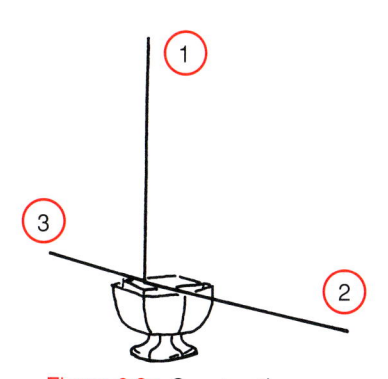

Figure 6.8c Constructing an Asymmetrical Triangle Steps 4 - 6

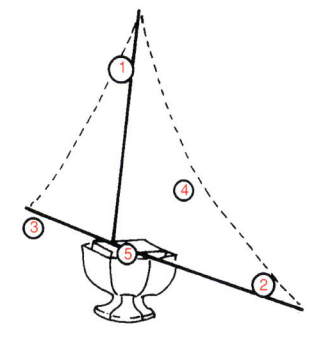

Figure 6.8d Constructing an Asymmetrical Triangle Step 7

front of the container and one two thirds from the right, to establish the vertical axis point of insertion. ***(Figure 6.8a)***

3. Cut the first line flower to a length of 16 inches and insert it 2 inches into the foam at the point of intersection. This flower should be vertical and as straight as possible. ***(Figure 6.8a)***

4. Cut the second flower approximately two-thirds the length of the first. It can be placed in either of two areas for different effects. The line can either angle out in an *L* form or slightly forward in a diagonal direction. ***(Figure 6.8b)*** It should be placed horizontally to the surface of the table on the lip of the container. Diagonal placement is considered more more artistic and is featured here. ***(Figure 6.8c)***

5. Cut the third flower to two-thirds the length of the second. Place the stem directly in front of the first flower, but slant the tip toward the left at a 45-degree angle. ***(Figure 6.8c)***

6. These three flowers complete the structure of the design. If a line connected their tips, the asymmetrical triangle would be seen. ***(Figure 6.8c)***

7. Place all specialty flowers inside the structure, following the same lines established by the first three flowers. Complete the design by filling in holes with greenery. Be sure to cover mechanics. Note: It is very important that the first specialty flower is placed to the left of the first line flower. This assists the viewer in following the flow of the arrangement. ***(Figure 6.8d)***

Pointed Oval - Nosegay or Round Mound

This universal arrangement is compact and free-standing, and its uses are varied and numerous. It is appropriate for placing on a coffee table, office desk, dining table, room divider, or bedside table. Flowers in this design are close to the water source; thus, they will last longer. These designs are easy to carry - a feature which makes them ideal for cash-and-carry specials.

Basic Floral Design

Materials Needed for a Pointed Oval

- Low utility container
- Leatherleaf
- Four stems of daisy pompons with long, lateral stems
- Gypsophila
- Floral foam

Constructing a Pointed Oval *(Figure 6.9)*

1. Secure pre-soaked foam in a container.

2. Score the foam for a free-standing design. *(Figure 6.9a)*

3. Fill the container with leatherleaf. Collar it around the lip with small tips of greenery.

4. Cut a pompon stem to a length of approximately 12 inches, and insert it at the intersection of the scored lines in the center of the container. *(Figure 6.9b)*

5. Cut four pompons to lengths of 8 inches. Place one in each of the quadrants. Be sure that they are opposite each other, that they form an *X*, and that they are on the lip of the container. Visualize a line running from the top of the first flower down to the four flowers at the perimeter. Visualize a second line running around the blossoms at the perimeter. This visualization will assist in achieving the desired roundness of the design. *(Figures 6.9b and 6.9c)*

6. Do not measure the next four flowers. Position them so that their heads are aligned on the imaginary line from the top to the perimeter. *(Figure 6.9d)*

7. The remaining pompons are inserted in empty spaces throughout the arrangement. *(Figure 6.9d)*

8. Add baby's breath, as desired.

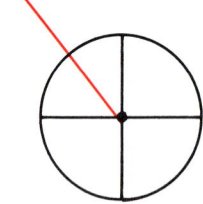

Figure 6.9a Constructing a Pointed Oval Step 2

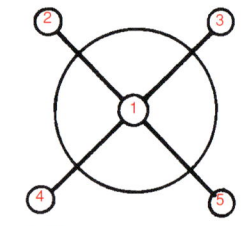

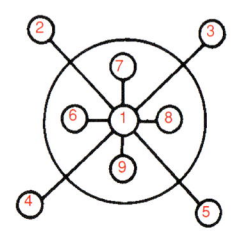

Figure 6.9b Constructing a Pointed Oval Steps 4 & 5 Top View

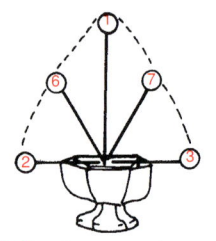

Figure 6.9c Constructing a Pointed Oval Steps 4 & 5 Side View

Figure 6.9d Constructing a Pointed Oval Steps 6 & 7

Designing Basic Arrangements

Vertical Arrangement

Since the vertical line is the strongest line in western floral design, this impressive arrangement makes a bold statement. Artistically, if offers a continuous line of movement that thrusts upward. These tall, slender designs are excellent for hospitals, nursing homes, desks, or any place where space is limited. Cylinder vases are ideal containers for vertical arrangements, because their bases are usually only 6 to 8 inches in diameter.

Materials Needed for a Vertical Arrangement

- A tall cylinder container
- Floral foam
- Strong linear flowers (such as liatris and snapdragons)
- Line foliage (such as long myrtle, flax, and scotch broom)

Constructing a Vertical Arrangement *(Figure 6.10)*

1. Secure foam in a vase. Leave at least 1 inch above the lip.

2. Score the foam using a two-thirds to one-third concept for center line insertion. *(Figure 6.10a)*

3. Insert the first flower. Cut it to a length three or four times the height of the vase. This tallest flower sets the height, balance, and central axis of the arrangement.

4. Place all other materials vertically within the diameter of the vase. Notice that in vertical design, the width lines are severely restricted; they extend only slightly to the right or left of the vase. *(Figure 6.10b)*

5. Use form, mass, or specialty flowers for emphasis in the focal area. *(Figure 6.10b)*

Horizontal Arrangement

The adaptability of horizontal designs makes them an ideal choice for entertaining in homes, hotels, or clubs. They are

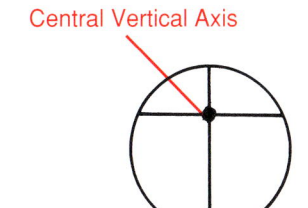

Figure 6.10a Constructing a Vertical Arrangement Step 2

Figure 6.10b Constructing a Vertical Arrangement Steps 4 & 5

usually free-standing and are suitable for display on low tables, where they can be viewed from above. These designs are often used at formal dinners where guests must be able to see each other across tables. In horizontal arrangements, width lines are accentuated, while height lines are restricted.

Materials Needed for a Horizontal Arrangement

- A low bowl or a low, horizontal container
- Wet foam
- Linear flowers and greenery
- Mass or specialty flowers

Constructing a Horizontal Arrangement *(Figure 6.11)*

1. Secure foam in a container. Leave 1 to 2 inches of foam above the lip.

2. Score the foam for a free-standing design. *(Figure 6.11a)*

3. The first flower determines the height of the arrangement. If the arrangement is for a formal dinner, the flower should not be cut to a length longer than 12 to 14 inches, 2 inches of which will be inserted into the foam.

4. If designed for a long table, the arrangement's total length should be about one-third the length of the table. The second and third flowers determine the width of the design. In this instance, they are cut to a length of 10 inches. They are inserted on each side of the arrangement, and they rest on the lip of the container. The structure of the design is long and relatively low - more than 25 inches long and only 10 inches tall.

5. Fill in the structure with the next four long-stemmed flowers. Place them diagonally on each side of the container, but extend them close to its sides. These four insertions are made on the lip of the container and make an elongated *X* across the container. Use additional line material to strengthen these lines.

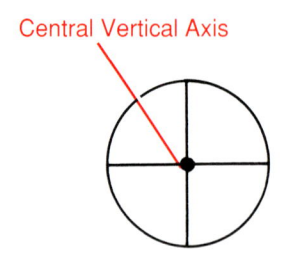

Figure 6.11a Constructing a Horizontal Arrangement Step 2

Designing Basic Arrangements

Figure 6.11b Constructing a Horizontal Arrangement Step 6

6. Insert mass flowers of various sizes and lengths along the lines where the line flowers were inserted. Work toward the center focal area where the larger flowers are inserted. Filler flowers may be added, as desired. Linear and filler greenery may also be added, as desired. *(Figure 6.11b)*

Rose Arrangements

The rose is the official national flower and a favorite of many consumers. Because roses are strongly associated with love and special occasions, they are usually one of the best-selling items in retail flower shops. Roses should always be displayed prominently in floral coolers. Although red roses are the most popular, many other colors are frequently requested and should be made available to consumers. It is important for florists to familiarize themselves with the many types of roses available and to introduce them to their customers.

Roses that are gathered from a personal flower garden or are purchased unarranged are usually placed loosely in a vase in no particular pattern or design. When purchased commercially, however, they are usually formally arranged. Roses in vases are usually arranged as line-mass style designs, specifically, one-sided symmetrical triangles or free-standing ovals. These geometric forms assist in creating the large, showy types of rose arrangements that consumers often prefer.

Mechanics *(Figure 6.12)*

Roses require a large amount of water; thus, preparation of the vase is of the utmost importance. The goal should be to assure the stability of the design and to allow the maximum supply of water to reach the head of the roses. Roses last longer when arranged in water as opposed to floral foam. Small vases are typically used for short-stemmed roses, and tall vases are used for long-stemmed roses. Following are several methods of preparing vases for rose arrangements.

Chicken Wire *(Figure 6.12a)*

1. Select a cylinder container, such as the standard clear or green glass rose vases.

2. Cut a piece of chicken wire from the roll that is twice as long as the height of the vase.

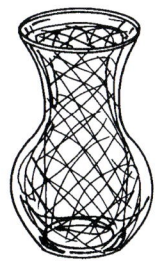

Figure 6.12a Preparing Vases for Rose Arrangements Using Chicken Wire

Basic Floral Design

3. Keeping the smooth sides out, bend the chicken wire in the center, and roll it three turns.

4. Insert the chicken wire into the vase; cut the end off first.

5. With long-nosed shears or another appropriate tool, spread the weave of the wire as evenly as possible to fill the space within the container.

6. Add preservative water.

Grid *(Figure 6.12b)*

Crisscross waterproof tape over the top of a vase to make a grid through which stems may be inserted and held in place. When clear glass is used, clear tape is preferable. Note: The chicken wire method and the grid method may be combined by placing a small roll of wire within the vase prior to making the grid.

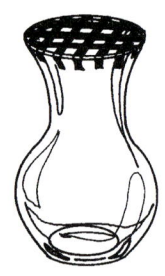

Figure 6.12b Preparing Vases for Rose Arrangements Using a Grid

Floral Foam *(Figure 6.12c)*

1. Fill a vase with preservative water.

2. Cut a piece of floral foam 4 inches thick and wide enough to fit snugly into the opening of the vase. Allow the foam to extend at least an inch above the lip of the container. Additional security may be added by applying waterproof tape.

Shredded Styrofoam *(Figure 6.12d)*

Loosely fill a vase with shredded styrofoam. Place one hand over the top of the vase; spread two fingers apart, and add water to the container. This keeps the styrofoam from floating up and out of the vase.

Figure 6.12c Preparing Vases for Rose Arrangements Using Floral Foam

Arranging One Dozen Roses *(Figure 6.13 on page 159)*

Symmetrical Triangle

1. Prepare a cylinder vase with a foam frog and preservative water.

2. Prepare the roses for insertion by removing the thorns and leaves below the water line. Remove the damaged

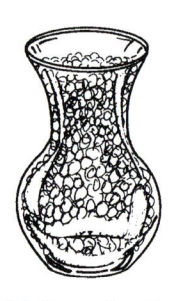

Figure 6.12d Preparing Vases for Rose Arrangements Using Shredded Styrofoam

Designing Basic Arrangements

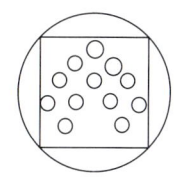

Figure 6.13 One Dozen Roses

leaves and guard petals of the rose above the water line. Be careful not to scrape or damage the stems.

3. Select a long, sturdy, straight rose. Cut it on a slant, and insert it in the back center of the vase. The next six roses should be inserted to the left and right of the center rose. As the six roses are inserted, each one should be cut about 1/2 inch shorter than the one inserted before it. When all seven roses are in place, they should be on the back row, graduating downward into a triangular shape.

4. Bring the roses in the second row forward, and graduate their heights down from the front, as well as, from the sides, while continuing the triangular shape. Place the two remaining roses lower and in front near the lip of the container. Leave space to insert a large bow as a focal point.

5. Following the same triangular line of the design, insert foliage to form a backing. Leatherleaf, eucalyptus, myrtle, and huckleberry are appropriate for use as backing.

6. Filler flowers, such as gypsophila, waxflower, or heather, may be added to increase the value of a design.

Free-standing Oval *(Figure 6.14)*

1. Prepare a large round vase with a foam frog and preservative water.

2. Prepare the roses as described for the symmetrical triangle.

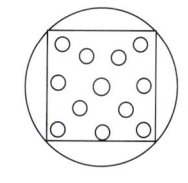

Figure 6.14 Free-standing Oval

3. Select a long, sturdy, straight rose. Cut it on a slant, and insert it in the exact center of the frog. Insert the next three roses around the center rose. The stems of these roses should be 1/2 to 1 inch shorter than the center rose and positioned so that they radiate from the center rose. Insert the next eight roses around the perimeter of the vase. Angle them toward the outside of the design. Note: After the first insertion, all roses graduate downward to create the oval shape.

4. Insert greenery, such as leatherleaf, in the arrangement following the same lines. The greenery should also flow over the lip of the vase.

5. Filler flowers may be added to enhance the arrangement, as desired.

Rose Bowl *(Figure 6.15)*

The rose bowl design is easily transported and requires little space for placement. These factors, along with its clear quality, make it ideal for featuring specialty and short-stemmed flowers. Design time for this piece is very short.

Figure 6.15 Rose Bowl

Materials Needed for a Rose Bowl

- Six- to 8-inch bubble bowl
- One open rose
- Small square of floral foam
- Small fronds of greenery

Constructing a Rose Bowl

1. Cut a piece of pre-soaked floral foam to 1 1/2 by 1 1/2 inches.

2. Collar the foam with leatherleaf fronds by inserting small fronds in a circle like a collar on a shirt. The collar should be no more than 2 inches in diameter.

3. Select a rose that is fully or partially open. Reflex the petals by placing the thumb against the middle of the petal and bending the remaining petal back over the thumb at a 45-degree angle. This technique causes the rose to open to its full extent, displaying the beautiful velvet surface of each petal.

4. Cut the stem of the rose 1 1/2 inches below the blossom.

5. Insert the rose into the pre-soaked foam. Make sure that the stem goes at least 1 1/2 inches into the foam. The rose should rest on the surface of the foam.

Designing Basic Arrangements

6. Drop the foam holding the rose into the bowl. Its own weight will hold it in place. However, for additional security, glue an anchor pin to the bowl and place the foam over it.

7. Add 1 inch of water to the bowl, and mist the face of the flower with water. This will create the effect of dew that has recently fallen. The rose should last approximately 10 days.

8. For variation, encircle the rose with shredded styrofoam after it is placed in the bowl. This is called "a rose in the snow."

Bud Vase *(Figure 6.16)*

Bud vases are excellent cash-and-carry arrangements and should be displayed prominently in the cooler at all times. Bud vases are designed to hold from one to four flowers with greenery *(see Figure 6.16a)*. The individual flowers are showcased; the greenery is merely an accessory. Bud vases are usually simple designs. They may include mixed flowers for a spring look *(see Figure 6.16b)* or twigs and unusual greenery for a creative look. Form flowers, such as anthuriums, may be used to create a tropical look.

Figure 6.16a Bud Vase with One to Four Flowers

Figure 6.16b Bud Vase with Mixed Flowers

Materials Needed for a Bud Vase

- Bud vase
- Greenery
- Roses or carnations
- Ribbon
- Filler

Constructing a Bud Vase

1. Fill a bud vase with preservative water.

2. Cut a rose or carnation to a length of 16 to 18 inches for a standard 8-inch bud vase.

3. Insert the rose into the bud vase so that approximately 10 inches of the rose projects above the mouth of the vase.

4. Place three stems of leatherleaf around the flower. Make sure it cascades over the lip of the vase.

5. Add filler flowers, such as baby's breath, as desired **(Figure 6.16c)**.

6. Add a satin bow and streamers at the mouth of the container, as desired.

Figure 6.16c Bud Vase with a Rose

Designing Profitably

Profitable designing requires conservative use of floral materials and efficient use of designers' time. There are a number of practices that florists can implement to improve efficiency in both of these areas. Following are some effective methods of reducing design costs.

Cost-saving Container Preparation

Stock containers can be pre-filled with floral foam before stacking or storing on display shelves in the design room. Containers that have been pre-filled with dry floral foam will need to be completely submerged to properly saturate the foam before using in designs. Floral foam should never be saturated more than 24 hours prior to the creation of a design. To help increase the length of flower life, foam should be saturated in water that has been treated with floral preservative. Pre-measuring and pre-cutting floral foam prior to saturation can reduce foam waste.

Stock glass containers should be pre-gridded before they are placed on storage shelves. Careful attention must be taken to insure the cleanliness of glass containers after pre-gridding has been completed. Strips of wax paper or cellophane can be cut and placed over the top of the containers on the storage shelf. This will reduce the amount of dust and dirt that is collected on the inside and outside of the containers. Fill glass containers that have been pre-gridded with a long, thin-necked water can. Water that comes in direct contact with the gridding tape can cause the tape to separate from the container lip. All glass containers should be thoroughly cleaned before a grid is placed on them.

Designing Basic Arrangements

Notes

Fresh Flower Waste Management

Fresh flowers that are broken, damaged, or needlessly thrown away can cause florists to lose large amounts of money each year. The best way to start resolving this problem is by checking the garbage can. After a day of heavy designing, empty the trash can onto the floor, and remove all materials that are still usable. Look for various types of foliage and unused floral products, such as wires, buds, or flowers with short, broken stems. In addition to recovering valuable materials, this type of waste inventory will assist in determining if the unnecessary waste is associated with a specific designer. Following is a list of several ways to increase the profitable use of fresh materials in the design work room.

Foliage

The use of greenery needs to be evaluated and decided upon according to the need of the specific design. Use the foliage from all parts of a single stem instead of just the tips. For example, average-sized pieces of leatherleaf can be divided into three or four pieces for design. The first cut on a piece of leatherleaf should be made approximately 4 inches down from the tip of the fern. This cut should be made directly above two fronds, leaving a small piece of stem that can be inserted into the floral foam. The side fronds on the remainder of the stem can then be cut into several more pieces and used in the same design. Leftover pieces of greenery that are too small for arrangements can be stored in plastic zip lock bags and incorporated into corsages or wedding designs at a later date. Other small, unused pieces of foliage should be re-cut and placed in a shallow container of water in a designated area of the cooler. This area could be labelled "flowers looking for a home," or "floral products for creative use."

Fresh Flowers

Multiple-headed flower stems should be treated as if each flower is an individual entity. If the stem is not going to be used as a spray, then each flower can be cut and removed from the stem and used as an individual piece in the design. In some instances, sections of a stem can be cut, leaving two or three flowers in a section that can be used as one unit in a design. Flowers with broken or bent stems can be re-cut and used lower in the arrangement. Flowers that are placed close to the foam or the water source have a longer life expectancy. If a flower has been bent or broken completely off the stem, and there is no stem left to insert into water or foam, it can be saved for use in corsages, used to make potpourri, dried in silica gel or a drying agent, or wired for use at another time. Flowers that are dried may also be glued onto baskets and wreaths.

Efficiency in Design

Efficiency in design does not always refer to the speed of the designer. The number of total insertions affects the efficiency in design. Creating a floral design with as few stem insertions as possible can assist in controlling labor costs. When creating a cost-effective design, keep in mind simplicity, space, and the total number of insertions. The following suggestions will assist in establishing efficient design practices. Establishing three recipes or plans for three specific designs at a major holiday can assist in controlling designers' decision time. Recipe cards should list the style of design, the container to be used, the exact number of flowers, and the amount of foliage that is to be incorporated into the design. On the back side of the card, list three price variations and additional flowers that can be used to increase the value of the arrangement.

When selecting flowers from the cooler, designers should remove only enough flowers to create three designs. These flowers should be kept in a bucket of water on the design table while the designs are being completed. Preparation of flowers for specific needs should be completed before beginning a design. Flowers that require additional wiring and taping for stability should be prepared beforehand. Pre-wiring and pre-taping all ingredients for a corsage or boutonniere will decrease the overall design time required to complete the order.

Assembly Line Designing

When the need to produce mass quantities of arrangements arises, implementing the assembly line process of design will assist in reducing production time and controlling labor costs. An individual designer a or multiple design team can easily be trained to work on an assembly line or to design in quantity.

Individual Designer

An individual designer who establishes and works on an assembly line design system will be required to fulfill all of the steps involved in completing each design. The quickest and most

Notes

Designing Basic Arrangements

Notes

efficient way for an individual designer to work an assembly line is to move down the line from arrangement to arrangement.

Multiple Design Team

Each member of a multiple design team is responsible for completing a portion of a design as it progresses through the assembly line. Members of a multiple design team are best utilized if stationed at a specific spot, with the arrangement rotating from designer to designer. Before the actual designing of arrangements begins, all of the containers or accessories for the design (bows, birds, candles, etc.) should be assembled. These items should be placed at the appropriate station in the assembly line. All fresh floral products should have been processed and hardened off prior to the start of designing. If any product requires wiring or taping for stability or assembly, it should be done before the actual designing begins. Following is the proper progression of steps that will insure efficient assembly line designing.

1. All hardgoods must be purchased and assembled at the design location several days prior to the assembly date.

2. Mechanics for the arrangements should be prepared at least 24 hours in advance. All bows should be pre-tied, containers pre-assembled, floral foam pre-soaked and kept moist, etc.

3. All fresh products should be purchased and pre-conditioned prior to the day of assembly.

4. After securing the mechanics, add moss, greenery, or other materials to cover tape, wire, etc.

5. If adequate space is available in the cooler, containers may be filled with greenery as much as 24 hours prior to the start of design.

NOTE: The remainder of the assembly line process may vary according to the specific type of design being created.

6. Insert all line flowers.

7. Insert all form flowers.

Basic Floral Design

8. Insert all mass flowers.

9. Insert all filler flowers.

10. Insert all accessories: bows, birds, nests, candles, etc.

11. Inspect all arrangements to insure quality control. Visually inspect the arrangement for broken foliage, flowers with bent necks, and flowers that are stressed or aged. Also, inspect the arrangement for visual balance and flower placement. Water should be added to the container at this stage.

Three experienced designers working an assembly line system should be able to complete one hundred arrangements within 3 hours, if all mechanics and assembly of containers is achieved previously. The assembly line method of designing also works well when handling large orders for parties, weddings, holidays, or similar events.

A team captain may be selected to insure that movement of products continues at a smooth pace throughout the line. The captain may also be responsible for bringing additional materials into the design area as they are needed, assisting a designer on a specific portion of the line where a problem has arisen, or filling in for a designer when a break is needed. It is advised that a planning session and meeting of the team be held prior to the day of the actual work. The team should discuss the different needs of the assembly line process. Also, a sample design should be completed and placed in a position that is visible to all members of the line.

The geometric shapes of western style floral design provide many advantages in the daily operation of a retail florist shop. The designs are easily copied and standardized, and assembly line techniques can be used to create them. A blueprint of various arrangements can be shared for study and practice; a training program can be formulated; and flowers and materials can be ordered more efficiently and economically.

The great bulk of floral orders received in retail shops are for standard geometric designs. In time, they can easily be produced by trainees or flower arrangers. Floral designers who have mastered the basics are able to exercise their creativity to a

Notes

Designing Basic Arrangements

<u>Notes</u>

greater degree and to produce high style and other more demanding arrangements that are necessary to operate a successful floral shop.

Flowers have power. They fill our needs and satisfy our emotions. They transmit love, excitement, tenderness, caring, concern, and comfort during times of our greatest joys and greatest sorrows. Professional floral designers should treat every floral design as though it were for someone he or she loves.

Basic Floral Design

Notes, Photographs, Sketches, etc.

Designing Basic Arrangements

Notes, Photographs, Sketches, etc.

Novelty Designs

Chapter 7

Retail florists are frequently asked to design "something different." This request may be made for a special occasion, a child, a sentimental occasion, or a depressed patient. When this request is made, special design techniques must be implemented. Floral design is a sentimental business, and florists are often called upon to design animals, clowns, birthday cakes, etc. For example, friends of a hospital patient may know the patient's devotion to his dog and may want to send a special, personalized gift to the hospital. A dog created with flowers is a special gift that will long be remembered. And what could be more charming than a clown face delivered to a despondent patient, a kitten made of flowers delivered to a child who misses his favorite pet, or a perky poodle resting in a basket with checkered bows perched on his ears?

Novelty arrangements should be suggested to customers to fill special needs. Often florists fail to make creative suggestions and to let customers know that charming novelty arrangements are available. Florists should display novelty designs in their shops to make customers aware that they are available. Likewise, floral presentations made to social, civic, or business organizations should feature novelty designs so that public awareness of them will be increased. Novelty designs provide an excellent way to use flowers with short stems. Therefore, they are profitable. Sales can be increased if novelty designs are recommended by the sales staff.

Popular novelty arrangements include poodles, kittens, clowns, and soda glasses. To insure customer satisfaction, the construction of these novelty designs should be studied and practiced. The construction of novelty design should also be viewed as an opportunity to create imaginative designs. The following instructions can be instrumental in constructing floral novelty designs.

Basic Floral Design

Kitten

A kitten designed with flowers is an easy way to satisfy a pet lover who requests something special. Discriminating customers look for unusual designs to send loved ones. A kitten can be designed with carnations, mums, or other flowers; however, carnations are most frequently used for this purpose. Kitten designs can be placed in baskets or bud vases.

Materials Needed

- #3 ribbon

- Four standard carnations

- Small basket or bud vase

- Three stems of leatherleaf

- Two pink chenille stems

- Two corsage pins

- Pink or blue floral tape

- Floral foam

Constructing the Kitten *(Figure 7.1)*

1. Start with four white carnations. Leave their stems at least 10 inches long.

2. Wire each carnation with a #20 gauge wire. Do this by piercing the base of the calyx of the carnation with at least 1 inch of the wire; then, swirl the wire down the stem of the carnation. The wire will provide control of, and flexibility to, the stem. *(Figure 7.1a)*

3. Place the first flower in the left hand, holding the stem in a vertical position and placing the hand at the base of the carnation. Bend the blossom slightly forward. This flower will become the lower half of the kitten's face. *(Figure 7.1b)*

4. Place a second wired carnation and place this blossom on top of the first carnation, keeping the stems parallel

Figure 7.1a Constructing a Kitten Step 2

Figure 7.1b Constructing a Kitten Step 3

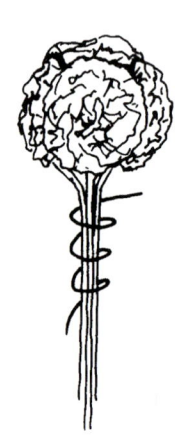

Figure 7.1c Constructing a Kitten Steps 4 - 6

Novelty Designs

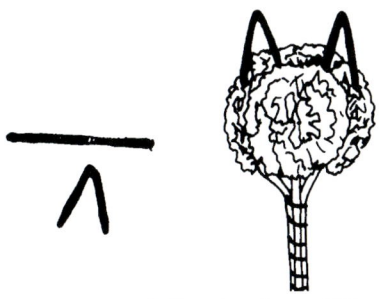

173

Figure 7.1d Constructing a Kitten Step 7

Figure 7.1e Constructing a Kitten Step 8

Figure 7.1f Constructing a Kitten Step 8

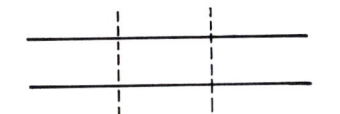

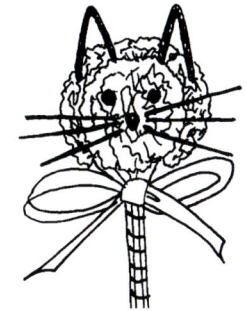

Figure 7.1g Constructing a Kitten Step 9

Figure 7.1h Constructing a Kitten Step 9

to each other. These flowers form the kitten's face. **(Figure 7.1c on page 172)**

5. To form the cheeks, position a third wired carnation against the left side of the face and a fourth wired carnation against the right side of the face. Bend these carnations slightly to the left and to the right as they are placed in position. Keep all four stems parallel to each other. **(Figure 7.1c on page 172)**

6. Bind all four stems together with #24 gauge wire. Cut the stems to lengths of 5 to 6 inches and insert them into a foam-filled basket. **(Figure 7.1c on page 172)**

7. Form a *V*-shape from a 2-inch length of pink chenille stem. Make two of these; they will become the ears. Glue each ear between the cheek and the top carnation. Use pan melt glue or a glue gun. **(Figure 7.1d)**

8. Tape the heads of two corsage pins with pink floral tape for a girl or blue floral tape for a boy. These pins will become the kitten's eyes. A corsage pin can also be used to create the kitten's nose. Insert these pins into the top carnation. **(Figures 7.1e and 7.1f)**

9. Wrap two #24 gauge wires with black floral tape, and cut each into two 1/2-inch strips. Glue six of these strips onto the face for whiskers. Pink chenille stems may also be used as whiskers. **(Figures 7.1g and 7.1h)**

10. Make a bow approximately 5 inches in width with #3 ribbon. Secure this bow with a wrapped #24 gauge wire. Place the bow below the face (under the first carnation), and secure it to the stems of the kitten with the wire.

11. Place pre-soaked floral foam in a small, low basket.

12. Place leatherleaf in the pre-soaked foam, and design a "nest" for the kitten. Keep the design low.

13. Place two or three kittens in the basket for added impact. **(Figure 7.1i on page 174)**

Basic Floral Design

14. A bud vase can be used instead of a basket. Prepare the bud vase by placing a few pieces of greenery into the vase, leaving the greenery no more than 8 inches above the container opening. The stems of the kitten should be long enough to touch the bottom of the vase and to insure that the kitten is properly positioned in the greenery. *(Figure 7.1i)*

Figure 7.1i Constructing a Kitten Step 13

Poodle

Poodle designs are always a favorite of animal lovers. The popularity of the dog is widespread, and since poodles have such varied personalities, it can be fun to create different looks.

Materials Needed

- Two white standard chrysanthemums
- Twenty white cushion pompons
- #3 red velvet ribbon
- Two burgundy plastic grapes or plastic eyes
- Basket
- Three stems of greenery
- Floral foam

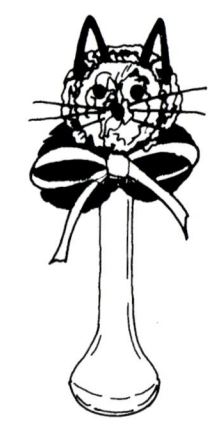

Figure 7.1j Constructing a Kitten Step 14

Constructing the Poodle *(Figure 7.2)*

1. Select two white standard mums. Wire each mum with a #20 gauge wire by piercing the base of the mum and inserting at least 1 inch into the mum. Wrap the wire around the stem in a swirling manner. *(Figure 7.2a)*

2. Bend the first mum slightly forward. This will become the lower half of the face. *(Figure 7.2a)*

3. Add the second mum to the first mum so that its placement is directly on top of the first. This mum should face straight upward. It will become the topknot of the poodle's head. Bind the two mums together with #24 gauge wire. *(Figure 7.2b on page 175)*

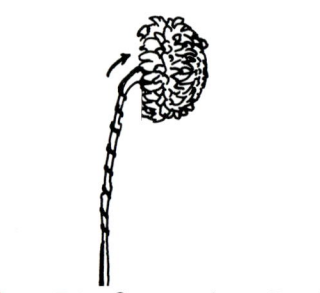

Figure 7.2a Constructing a Poodle Steps 1 & 2

Novelty Designs

175

Figure 7.2b Constructing a Poodle
Step 3

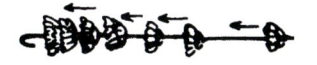

Figure 7.2c Constructing a Poodle
Steps 4 & 5

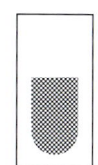

Figure 7.2d Constructing a Poodle
Step 6

Figure 7.2e Constructing a Poodle
Step 8

Figure 7.2f Constructing a Poodle
Steps 10 - 12

4. Glue two burgundy plastic grapes or plastic eyes onto the face where the first and second mum meet. *(Figure 7.2c)*

5. A grape can also be used for the nose. Glue it into place. *(Figure 7.2c)*

6. Cut a small tongue (about the size of a fingernail) out of #3 velvet ribbon, and glue it into place. *(Figure 7.2d)*

7. Make a #3 red velvet ribbon bow and secure it with a #24 gauge wrapped wire.

8. Add the bow to the poodle by placing it under the chin. Secure it by wiring it to the stems of the mums. *(Figure 7.2e)*

9. Make two petite bows of red velvet ribbon, and secure them with #28 gauge wires. These will be added to the ears at a later time.

10. Bend a 1/2-inch hook at one end of a #24 gauge plain wire. Do not wrap the wire with floral tape.

11. Cut the stems off twenty cushion pompons at the base of each blossom.

12. Thread ten cushion pompons one at a time onto the wire. Start at the opposite end of the wire (away from the hook). Insert the wire into the face of the flower, and make sure the wire comes out of the hole that used to be the stem. This completes one ear. *(Figure 7.2f)*

13. To make the second ear, repeat step 12.

14. Add a small velvet bow above the last pompon, and tape the wires from the bow and the pompons together with floral tape. Bend the wire down (in hairpin fashion) and add the ear alongside the topknot of the poodle. Repeat this step on the other side of the poodle's head. *(Figure 7.2g on page 176)*

15. Prepare a basket with a liner. Add pre-soaked floral foam and a base of greenery.

16. Insert the stems of the poodle into the floral foam so that the poodle appears to be resting in the bed of greenery. **(Figure 7.2h)**

Treasure Chest

Materials Needed

- Clear plastic box
- Short-stemmed colorful flowers
- One wooden pick
- #3 ribbon
- Small piece of floral foam
- Small amount of greenery

Constructing the Treasure Chest *(Figure 7.3)*

The treasure chest can be made in a clear corsage box or a clear boutonniere box (for a smaller version). Treasure chests are good cash-and-carry items, because they are easy to design, easy to transport, and use smaller stemmed flowers. Each treasure chest is different, and the variety of designs and combinations of materials is unlimited.

1. Cut a piece of pre-soaked floral foam 2 inches by 3 inches in size. **(Figure 7.3a)**

2. Insert small fronds of leatherleaf in the foam to make a base. Keep the base low. **(Figure 7.3a)**

3. On this base, create a small triangular design that will fit inside the box. Use only small blossoms of florets and keep the design approximately 6 inches long and 6 inches high. The design can be constructed in or outside of the box. **(Figure 7.3b)**

Figure 7.2g Constructing a Poodle Step 14

Figure 7.2h Constructing a Poodle Step 16

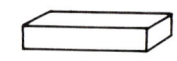

Figure 7.3a Constructing a Treasure Chest Steps 1 - 2

Figure 7.3b Constructing a Treasure Chest Step 3

Novelty Designs

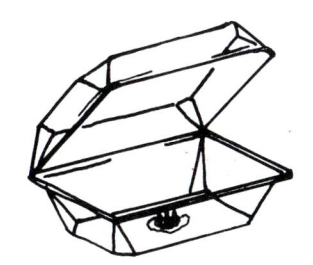

177

Figure 7.3c Constructing a Treasure Chest Step 4

Figure 7.3d Constructing a Treasure Chest Steps 5 - 6

Figure 7.3e Constructing a Treasure Chest Step 8

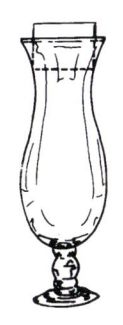

Figure 7.4a Constructing an Ice Cream Soda Step 1

4. Glue an anchor pin with pan melt glue in the center of the box. *(Figure 7.3c)*

5. Place the foam that holds the arrangement on the anchor pin. *(Figure 7.3d)*

6. Insert a 4- to 6-inch pick into the foam about two-thirds of the way back in the arrangement. Be sure that a flower covers the pick. The purpose of the pick is to keep the lid of the box open at least 1 inch. The proper placement of the pick will prevent the lid from closing. *(Figure 7.3d)*

7. Add 1/2 inch of water to the box.

8. Wrap #3 ribbon around the box, and tie a bow that will perch on top. *(Figure 7.3e)*

Ice Cream Soda

Materials Needed

- Soda glass or silver vacu-pac vase
- Shredded foam or pre-soaked floral foam
- Five standard pink carnations
- One standard white carnation
- One artificial cherry or sweetheart rose bud
- Two straws

Constructing the Ice Cream Soda *(Figure 7.4)*

1. Fill the soda glass with shredded styrofoam or pre-soaked floral foam. When using floral foam, it is suggested that shredded iridescent paper be used to surround the foam inside the glass. The foam should extend at least 1 inch above the lip of the container. *(Figure 7.4a)*

2. Cut the stems of five pink carnations to lengths of 4 inches. Insert the stems into the foam to make a mound shape. **(Figure 7.4b)**

3. Cut the stem of the white carnation to a length of 6 inches and insert it in the center of the pink carnations to form a peak. **(Figure 7.4b)**

4. Glue a cherry or a rosebud on top of the white carnation. **(Figure 7.4c)**

5. Add two soda straws at 45-degree angles near the lip of the container. Note: To prevent children from attempting to use the straws, punch a hole in them to make them inoperative. **(Figure 7.4c)**

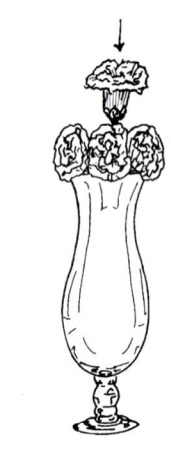

Figure 7.4b Constructing an Ice Cream Soda Steps 2 and 3

Birthday Cake

Birthday cake novelties are a favorite of both children and adults. Regardless of one's age, a birthday cake is always appreciated, especially one that is long lasting. Cakes can be designed in many colors and sizes with a wide assortment of accessories.

Materials Needed

- Floral foam
- Wooden picks
- Low design bowl
- Cushion pompons
- Roses or other flowers for trim

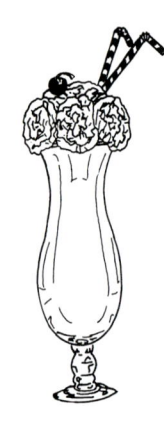

Figure 7.4c Constructing an Ice Cream Soda Steps 4 - 5

Constructing the Birthday Cake *(Figure 7.5)*

1. Cut an 8-inch circle of pre-soaked floral foam. Oversized blocks of foam are available, or several pieces of foam can be pinned together with wooden picks. **(Figure 7.5a)**

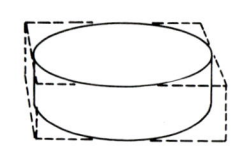

Figure 7.5a Constructing a Birthday Cake Step 1

Novelty Designs

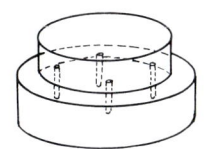

179

Figure 7.5b Constructing a Birthday Cake Step 2

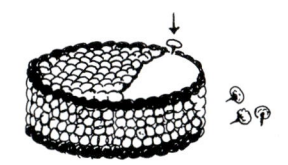

Figure 7.5c Constructing a Birthday Cake Step 3

Figure 7.5d Constructing a Birthday Cake Step 4

2. If a multi-layered cake is desired, cut a 6-inch circle for the second layer and a 4-inch circle for the top layer. Secure the layers together with wooden picks or hyacinth sticks. *(Figure 7.5b)*

3. Cut cushion pompon stems to lengths of 1 1/2 inches. Cover the entire surface of the foam by inserting each stem in the foam so that the flower head rests against it. Flowers should be placed close enough together so that their edges touch and the final look is a flat surface that resembles a cake icing. This technique is called paving. *(Figure 7.5c)*

4. Decorate the cake and sides, as desired. Use roses or other flowers just as a baker would when decorating. The stems of these flowers should be cut to lengths of approximately 3 inches and inserted over the other flowers. Birthday candles may also be added to complete the look. *(Figure 7.5d)*

5. Place the cake in a flat design dish that has several anchor pins glued to the container. These anchor pins, along with the weight of the cake, will hold the cake in place.

NOTE: Styrofoam may be used to create a lightweight birthday cake. In this case, the mums are glued directly to the styrofoam with floral adhesive or pan melt glue.

Love Bug

This inexpensive novelty design is appropriate for children or adults. Short-stemmed flowers and almost any color combination can be used to create an interesting love bug. Red and black can be used to create a charming ladybug.

Materials Needed

- Floral foam
- Pompons
- Two small berries
- Ten chenille stems

Constructing the Love Bug *(Figure 7.6)*

1. Cut pre-soaked floral foam to a length of 6 inches. Carve the top portion to look like a round mound. *(Figure 7.6a)* Place the foam in a flat design bowl. *(Figure 7.6b)*

2. Cut at least a dozen cushion pompons. Leave the stems about 1 1/2 inches long.

3. Cover the round mound with mums. Insert them as far as possible in the foam. Make sure the flowers touch each other and lie flat. This forms the body of the bug. *(Figure 7.6c)*

4. Glue two small berries to the front portion of the bug to form the eyes. The eyes can also be made of chenille stems. *(Figure 7.6d)*

5. Add antennas to the head. These can be made of 6-inch chenille stems or #24 gauge wire that has been wrapped with black tape. *(Figure 7.6d)*

6. Add three legs on each side of the body using black chenille stems. See *Figure 7.6d* for shape and placement.

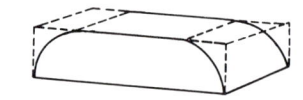

Figure 7.6a Constructing a Love Bug Step 1

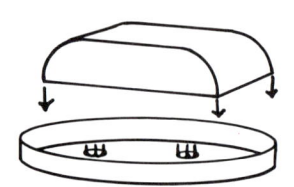

Figure 7.6b Constructing a Love Bug Step 1

Figure 7.6c Constructing a Love Bug Step 3

Figure 7.6d Constructing a Love Bug Steps 4 - 6

Clown

A clown can bring a smile to any face. It is an ideal gift for hospitals, birthdays, and "cheer-up" occasions.

Materials Needed

- One standard chrysanthemum
- Styrofoam cups or construction paper
- One chenille stem
- #40 ribbon
- Cardboard circle

Novelty Designs

Figure 7.7a Constructing a Clown Step 2

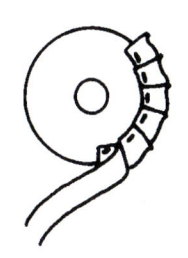

Figure 7.7b Constructing a Clown Step 2

Figure 7.7c Constructing a Clown Step 6

Figure 7.7d Constructing a Clown Step 7

Constructing the Clown *(Figure 7.7)*

1. Remove the cardboard backing from a #40 ribbon bolt, or cut a piece of cardboard into a circle of the same size.

2. Make 1-inch pleats using #40 ribbon. **(Figure 7.7a)** Staple them around the cardboard circle. This will form the clown's collar. **(Figure 7.7b)**

3. Wire a standard chrysanthemum with a #20 gauge wire using the pierce method. Wrap wire around the stem of the flower.

4. Insert the mum through the center of the collar, and place it in the bud vase. Add two or three pieces of foliage. The mum will be the clown's face.

5. Turn a styrofoam cup upside down on a cookie sheet to make the hat. Place it in an oven that has been preheated to 250 degrees. In a few seconds, the cup will shrink and will look like a small hat. Construction paper can also be used to make the hat.

6. Glue a 6-inch taped #24 gauge wire on the side of the hat. A small silk flower can be glued on the wire at the top. **(Figure 7.7c)** Glue the hat to the mum. Position it slightly off-center.

7. Create an eye by making an *X* out of two 1-inch lengths of black chenille. Glue two eyes on the face. **(Figure 7.7d)**

8. Decorate the clown with arms made from chenille stems and other accessories, as desired.

Rabbit

A rabbit is an ideal novelty design for a child in the hospital. Rabbits can be created with a variety of facial expressions and distinct personalities. The rabbit is an excellent add-on item for Easter designs.

Basic Floral Design

Materials Needed

- Polyester cotton (quilt filling)
- Four #18 gauge wires
- Four #22 gauge wires
- One standard mum
- Pink floral paint
- #3 ribbon

Constructing the Rabbit *(Figure 7.8)*

1. Wire a standard mum with a #20 gauge wire. Insert the wire in the base of the mum, and penetrate the mum at least 1 inch. Wrap the remaining wire down the stem. *(Figure 7.8a)*

2. Tape four #18 gauge wires individually with floral tape.

3. Wrap one of the wires with polyester cotton in a swirling manner. The polyester cotton will cling to the floral tape and stay in place. *(Figure 7.8b)*

4. Bend the wire that has been wrapped with polyester batting into a loop, and bind it with a #24 gauge wire, using the clutch method. This will make one ear. *(Figure 7.8c)*

5. Repeat Steps 3 and 4 to make the second ear.

6. Spray the inside of the ear with soft pink floral paint. *(Figure 7.8d)* Add the ears to the face, attaching the wire below the loop to the stem of the face. Bind the stem and the two wires together with #24 gauge wire. Bend one ear forward. The second ear should be left straight.

7. Repeat Steps 3 and 4 to make the arms. Do not spray these. Bind the two arms together with a #22 gauge wire. Use the same wire to attach the arms to the body of the rabbit. *(Figure 7.8e on page 183)* The arms can be bent into different positions.

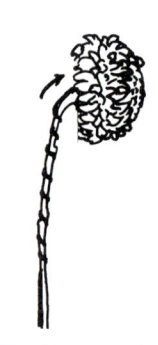

Figure 7.8a Constructing a Rabbit Step 1

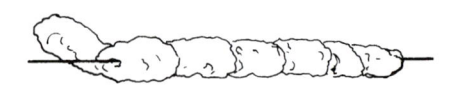

Figure 7.8b Constructing a Rabbit Step 3

Figure 7.8c Constructing a Rabbit Step 4

Novelty Designs

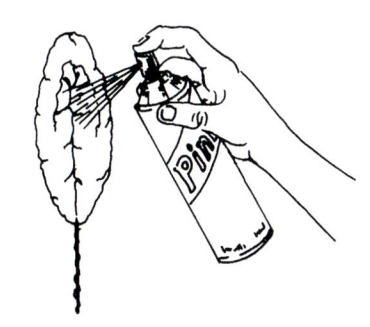

Figure 7.8d Constructing a Rabbit Step 6

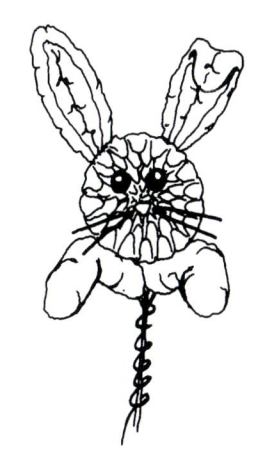

Figure 7.8e Constructing a Rabbit Steps 7 - 9

Figure 7.8f Constructing a Rabbit Step 11

8. Glue either chenille stems or plastic eyes onto the mum to form eyes. *(Figure 7.8e)*

9. Glue a nose into place using a circle of pink chenille stems or pink felt. Make two sets of whiskers by wrapping #24 gauge wires with black floral tape and cutting them to lengths of 2 1/2 inches. Bend the wires in the center, and glue them on the face of the rabbit on each side of the nose. *(Figure 7.8e)*

10. A second mum can be added below the head to create a body. Legs can also be added in the same way.

11. Place the rabbit in a bud vase or a basket that has been prepared with pre-soaked floral foam and greenery. *(Figure 7.8f)*

Bird

Natural materials can be used to create novelty designs, such as birds, snails, bears, and rabbits. Birds can be made in many sizes and are great add-on sales. Birds can be sold individually, or they can be placed in a fresh arrangement, silk design, or dried arrangement.

Materials Needed

- Four-inch styrofoam ball
- Two-inch styrofoam ball
- #24 gauge paddle wire
- Sheet moss or other mosses
- Pliable branches

Constructing the Bird *(Figure 7.9)*

1. Cover a 4-inch styrofoam ball with sheet moss or another type of moss. *(Figure 7.9a)*

2. Secure the moss to the ball with #24 gauge paddle wire that has been wrapped around several times. *(Figure 7.9a)*

3. Choose approximately six pliable branches, such as honeysuckle or deciduous huckleberry. Each branch should be at least 15 inches long.

4. Wrap the branches around the moss-covered styrofoam ball, and pull all of the branches together at the base of the ball to make the body of the bird. Bind the branches together with the paddle wire. **(Figure 7.9b)** Do not cut the branches that extend beyond the binding point; flare them out to form a tail.

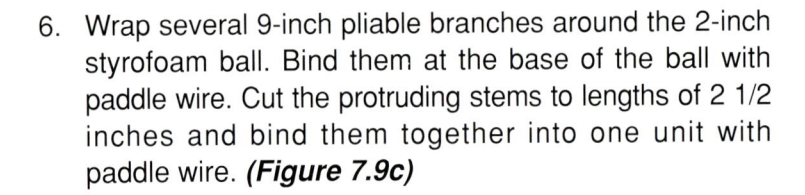

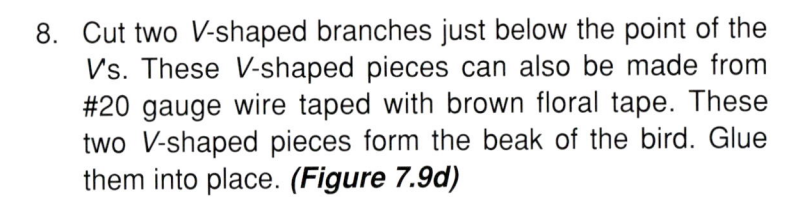

5. Cover a 2-inch styrofoam ball with moss and secure it with paddle wire to make the head.

6. Wrap several 9-inch pliable branches around the 2-inch styrofoam ball. Bind them at the base of the ball with paddle wire. Cut the protruding stems to lengths of 2 1/2 inches and bind them together into one unit with paddle wire. **(Figure 7.9c)**

7. Insert the 2 1/2-inch stems that protrude from the head into the 4-inch styrofoam ball (the body) on the opposite side of the tail. **(Figure 7.9c)**

8. Cut two *V*-shaped branches just below the point of the *V*'s. These *V*-shaped pieces can also be made from #20 gauge wire taped with brown floral tape. These two *V*-shaped pieces form the beak of the bird. Glue them into place. **(Figure 7.9d)**

9. Glue berries in place to create eyes if desired. **(Figure 7.9d)**

10. Insert a wooden pick in the bird to add it to any fresh, silk, or dried arrangement. **(Figure 7.9d)** Add a chenille or wire loop to the top portion of the bird if you wish to suspend it.

Figure 7.9a Constructing a Bird Step 1

Figure 7.9b Constructing a Bird Step 4

Figure 7.9c Constructing a Bird Steps 6 and 7

Figure 7.9d Constructing a Bird Steps 8 through 10

Novelty Designs

Notes

Creating novelty designs requires imagination and ingenuity. These unique arrangements add dollar volume to any retail shop. To maintain a competitive edge, novelties offer a unique difference that customers often look for to fill their needs. These arrangements know no age barriers. Children, teenagers, and adults (both male and female) enjoy receiving unique novelty designs. These money-making arrangements will satisfy customers, excite sales staff, and increase profits.

Basic Floral Design

Notes, Photographs, Sketches, etc.

Novelty Designs

Notes, Photographs, Sketches, etc.

Designing with Permanent Flowers

Chapter 8

Permanent, long lasting, and lifelike are only a few of the descriptive terms used to describe silk and dried floral arrangements. A wide variety of natural-looking permanent flowers is available to the floral industry. The quality and variety of silk and dried products has continually improved, and customers have continued to request permanent flowers, both by the stem and in arrangements. Florists often combine fresh and permanent materials to create unique and lasting designs.

Some florists are hesitant to offer permanent floral designs in their shops, because they are afraid they will not sell. A permanent arrangement that does not sell can be dismantled and redesigned. Likewise, silk and dried materials are often much easier to design with than fresh, because they are not perishable and may be manipulated and mechanically secured without the risk of wilting. This chapter provides a variety of tips and techniques for making permanent flowers easier and more interesting to work with.

Types of Silk Flowers

There are a number of different types of fabric flowers available to floral designers. The term silk is often applied to a wide variety of fabrics used in the construction of fabric flowers. Silk, nylon, cotton, rayon, and blends of each are commonly used to manufacture permanent flowers. Different grades of fabric are used to create silk flowers and foliage of different quality and price levels. When florists are selecting products to be used or displayed together, flowers and foliage manufactured with similar grades of fabric should be used. This helps insure consistency in the overall look of the design. The following types of silk flowers and foliage are readily available to florists.

Basic Floral Design

Molded, Plastic-stemmed Flowers

Fabric flowers with molded, plastic stems are usually made of polyester, which is heat-molded in a die form to create the petal impression or shape of the flower. It is then placed on a stem created with wire that has been covered with a plastic coating. This type of silk flower is normally less expensive than hand-wrapped silks.

Most silk flowers of this type do not have petals and leaves that are individually wired. Therefore, the amount of bending and shaping they will tolerate is limited. Often, these silks are created with multiple flowers and/or flower buds on a single stem. Pre-made silk bushes and bouquets are also frequently made with these types of silk flowers.

Hand-wrapped Silks

Silk flowers with hand-wrapped stems are common items on the permanent flower market. The quality and precise detail of these flowers continues to improve as the variety of colors and types available increases. The petals of hand-wrapped silks are usually stamp-cut before they are formed. Individual petals are attached to wire and positioned to create the floral replica. The flower is then secured to a wire stem which is hand-wrapped with floral tape. To obtain the proper shading, the flower may be hand-painted or hand-dyed.

Many hand-wrapped flowers are so realistic that one cannot tell they are artificial without touching them. Botanically correct lilies with speckled throats and bendable stamens and anthers are an example of the level of quality that hand-wrapped silk manufacturers have achieved. Fantasy flowers are also popular hand-wrapped silks, because they provide flower forms that do not exist in nature. These flowers, which often have unique petal structures, exaggerated flower parts, and unnatural foliage, add character and interest to silk designs. The amount of labor required to produce this type of silk flower is greater than the amount required to produce a molded product. Because of the detail-oriented labor involved, hand-wrapped silk flowers may be expensive and are often sold individually.

Paper Flowers

Paper flowers may be created with a variety of types of paper. Rice paper, parchment, and bark fiber paper are most commonly used to produce this product. Not to be confused with popular

Notes

Designing with Permanent Flowers

Notes

writing paper, these papers are created with a higher fiber content. Rice paper is used to create flowers and foliage with a frosted opaque look. To finish the flower, each petal or leaf created with rice paper is hand-wired and assembled on a main stem that is wrapped with paper tape or floral stem wrap. Parchment flowers are also available in a semi-transparent state. The parchment paper used is thinner than that used for printing. This product is available with or without wired petals and leaves. Like the rice paper flowers, the petals and leaves are formed and attached to a main wire stem and then wrapped with paper or floral tape.

Bark fiber flowers are constructed with paper manufactured from mulberry and ficus trees. For centuries, the inner bark of these two trees has been used to construct heavyweight paper. This paper is easy to mold, and the high fiber content of the bark insures that it will hold its shape. The use of paper flowers eliminates one of the primary problems of using silk flowers - fraying of the edges. Color can be added by pre-dying the product before forming it into the flower shape or by air brushing the product after the flower has been formed and attached to the stem.

Care and Handling of Silk Flowers

Care and handling of silk flowers should begin when the products are purchased. If ordering direct from a manufacturer, florists should find out how the product will be packaged and shipped. If at all possible, silks should be stored in the containers they are shipped in. Following are additional ways to store silk products in flower shops.

1. Cardboard tubing (sono tubes) cut to various lengths and placed upright in a large box or basket can create an individual storage space for specific colors or types of silk flowers. Head crushing and stem tangling can also be eliminated with this process.

   Cardboard tubing of this type is usually available from yardage or fabric stores, carpet stores, or concrete construction firms. Yardage cardboard tubing is available in widths ranging from 3 inches to 5 inches and lengths from 32 inches to 60 inches. Carpet tubing is available in widths ranging from 3 inches to 6 inches and from 45 inches to 12 feet. Cardboard tubing from concrete construction firms is available in widths ranging from 6 inches to 4 feet and a length of 12 feet. All of these tubes may be cut to size, as needed.

2. Shipping boxes can be used for flat storage. To eliminate product crushing, shallow boxes are best for this type of storage. Boxes used by the garment industry to ship clothing to retailers are the best type to use for flat storage.

3. Silk products can be stored or displayed in the flower shop in ceramic or heavy glass vases. This type of storage allows for high visibility of the product and adds color interest to the shop. It is suggested that flowers be placed in vases according to color and flower type.

Notes

Restoring Old Silk Flowers

If after storing or excessive handling, silk flowers become faded or slightly frayed on the edges, they may be restored in the following ways.

1. Trim the edges of the flowers with sharp fabric scissors.

2. Sear frayed flowers by passing the edges quickly over an open flame from a candle or lighter.

3. Restore color to a faded silk flower by lightly spraying with floral paint. To check for color change, absorption, and drying time, it is advisable to test the paint on a corner of the silk flower before applying it.

Cleaning Silk and Paper Flowers

After being stored or displayed for an extended period of time, silks, due to static electricity, will attract dust and dirt to their surfaces. When cleaning silk flowers, it is important to consider their fabric content, as well as, the manner in which they were colored. Some fabrics do not hold dye well. If water is used to clean such silks, it can cause colors to separate or to run onto the

Designing with Permanent Flowers

Notes

surface of the flowers. Before using any cleaning method, test a small surface of a leaf or petal before processing the entire flower. Following are suggested methods for cleaning silk and paper flowers.

1. Cold Water Laundry Detergent. Cold water laundry detergents, such as Woolite®, designed for use on delicate fabrics also work well on polyester flowers. The solution should be mixed in water according to the instructions on the package. The flower should be totally submerged in the solution and moved from side to side; the flower should be rinsed and suspended on a line to drip dry. This is not recommended for high quality or hand-wrapped silk flowers.

2. Aerosol Sprays. Aerosol silk spray cleaners are available from many wholesalers. These sprays should be used according to the directions on the label. It is a good idea to test the spray on a small piece of the silk before applying it to the overall surface of the flower or arrangement. Again, test a small piece of the product before utilizing this cleaning method.

3. Damp-dusting. In cases where total immersion and aerosol sprays are not possible due to color separation, dirt can usually be safely removed from the surface of a leaf or petal with a sponge that has been lightly dipped in cool water.

4. Paper Flowers. None of the methods discussed above are suggested for use with paper flowers. Paper flowers are not affected by static electricity and very seldom attract or hold dust and dirt. If this does happen, however, a hair dryer may be used to blow dust or dirt off the surface of the flowers.

Preparing Silk Flowers

One of the most important steps in creating a lifelike silk arrangement is the preparation of the flowers. To make a silk flower look more realistic, the petals, leaves, and stem usually need to be bent into soft curves to eliminate the typical rigid wired appearance. Most silks are meant to be replicas of fresh flowers and may need only a slight manipulation of the petals or leaves to resemble their counterparts. Fresh flowers have a natural progression of aging. Older flowers open fully, while younger flowers progress at a different rate from bud form. Often, flowers of all ages can be found on the same stem. Silk flowers with wired petals and stems are best prepared in this manner.

If the petals on a silk flower are hand-wired, they can be moved, rolled, or bent slightly to create a natural look. If the silk is molded, the main stem may have to be manipulated to achieve a more gentle line. When preparing a silk flower, take into consideration the way its natural counterpart grows. Not all petals should be perfectly placed.

When working with a multiple-flowered stem, a stem with one or two main flowers and one or two small buds, place the flowers in the natural progression of growth and age. Flowers at the base of the stem should appear more mature in age. *(Figure 8.1)* Flowers in the middle of the stem should be closed. Flowers at the top of the stem should be budding.

Paper flowers require a different type of preparation. If a paper flower is crushed, often it may be reshaped by lightly steaming and re-shaping by hand. However, caution should be used when steaming the flowers. Too much moisture can result in a color change. Crepe paper flowers can be hand-shaped without steam by slightly pulling and rolling the flower petal in the desired direction.

Figure 8.1 Positioning Silk Flowers in Natural Progression

Types of Dried and Preserved Flowers

Dried and preserved flowers are often used when fresh flowers are not available. Several methods of preservation have been developed, and almost any flower or foliage can be preserved. As a result, florists have access to a wide variety of natural materials. Dried and preserved flowers are available from several commercial sources, particularly wholesale distributors and suppliers. Some retailer florists, however, may choose to preserve floral products themselves. The following drying and preserving methods are most commonly used.

Glycerine

Glycerine is used to preserve certain types of flowers and foliage. Miniature oak, maple, and magnolia leaves, baby's breath,

Designing with Permanent Flowers

Notes

and eucalyptus are materials that are commonly preserved with glycerine. This preserving method is completed by mixing three parts water to one part glycerine. The flowers or foliage are placed in the solution and allowed to absorb it. As the glycerine is absorbed through the tissue of the plant material, it acts an an embalming agent, leaving the product supple to the touch.

Air-drying

Many types of fresh flowers and foliage may be suspended upside down in a warm, dry area to allow the moisture in each flower's cell structure to dissipate. Frequently, this method is done in an attic, basement, or another area that is warm and dry. The flowers should be prepared in bundles, and secured with rubber bands or another binding material that can be adjusted as the bundle shrinks during the drying process. If wire, string, or ribbon is used, it will need to be tightened as the drying process progresses.

The amount of drying time needed depends on the type of flower being preserved and the atmosphere in which they are placed to dry. Generally, most flowers and foliage dry in 1 to 3 weeks using the air-dry method. Once dry, it is best to leave bundles hanging until they are needed for designs. If necessary, they may be loosely packed in large cardboard boxes. The following flowers and foliage dry well using the air-dry method.

Bells of Ireland	Monk's Hood
Delphinium	Roses
Eucalyptus	Statice
Gypsophila	Yarrow
Larkspur	

Freeze-drying

Freeze-drying was initially developed for the food industry, but has been utilized in the floral industry. Freeze-dried floral products have had all the moisture mechanically removed from their cell structures. However, the product retains its shape perfectly with a percentage of suppleness to its texture.

Freeze-dried flowers are available from select manufacturers and wholesalers. Although the specially-designed equipment necessary for freeze-drying is expensive and often cost prohibitive for retail shops, some florists have decided to preserve wedding bouquets as a way of maximizing the expenditure of this piece of equipment.

Desiccant-drying

Desiccant drying utilizes a substance that will absorb at least 50 percent of its own weight in water to surround flowers and extract their moisture. The agents most commonly used for this drying method are sand, silica gel, cornmeal, borax, kitty litter, or a mixture of any of these products. Multi-petaled flowers are often used in this process, because their petal structures require the support provided by the drying agent. Flowers dried using this method are fragile and must be handled with the utmost care.

To use the desiccant-drying method, place flowers on a bed of the selected agent. Then, cover the flowers completely with more of the desiccant by gently supporting the petals and working the substance into and between the folds of the flowers. Seal the container to prevent the desiccant from absorbing moisture from the atmosphere. Experimentation is suggested for determining the best desiccant or mixture for various types of flowers. The length of time a flower needs to be covered with the desiccant varies. Normally, 2 to 6 weeks are required for complete drying. When flowers have dried completely, they should be removed carefully from the container and brushed with a small paint brush to remove particles from between the layers of the flowers. Flowers that have been dried with a desiccant are extremely fragile. Therefore, they may be difficult to use in ordinary arrangements. These flowers are probably best used to accent bowls or boxes of potpourri.

A microwave oven may be used to speed up the desiccant-drying method. Flowers should be placed in a microwave safe container and gently covered with a desiccant until no petals are exposed. Kitty litter works best for this method. Do not cover the container. The oven should be set to a medium heating temperature. The flowers are then cooled for a few seconds or as long as 2 minutes, depending on the type of flowers being dried. Experimentation is required to determine the optimum heating time for various flower types. Heating for more than 2 minutes may cause complete deterioration of the flowers. During the drying process, all standard rules for using the microwave should be followed. Therefore, no metal or wire can be inserted into the flowers prior to being placed in the microwave. After the flower has been dried, the desiccant can be removed from around the flower by gently brushing it with a paint brush. The flower can then be wired or secured to a stem.

Dried Flower Identification

Using drying techniques effectively requires practice and experimentation. Although any of the preservation techniques

Notes

Designing with Permanent Flowers

Notes

listed above may be used by retail florists, most florists prefer to purchase dried materials from commercial sources. However, the infinite varieties of dried and preserved flowers and foliage available can be rather confusing. They are sometimes packaged without labels which identify the flower type. Distributors often attach different names to the same product, thus, giving that item a brand name. Dried materials that are grown locally are sold in wholesale outlets with no packaging whatsoever. To maintain communication when purchasing and selling dried materials, it is important to know the names of the materials most commonly used. Following is a list of dried and preserved materials that have been divided into several categories. The illustrations in Appendix B provide examples of various dried and preserved materials.

Care and Handling of Preserved Flowers

Preserved flowers and foliage are often more fragile and require more delicate handling than silks. Dried materials may be brittle and easily damaged if not stored or handled properly. Preserved materials may be stored using any of the methods described for silk flowers. Additionally, many dried materials may be bundled and suspended overhead for short-term storage. Several examples of dried and preserved materials are illustrated in Appendix B.

Environmental Conditions

Temperature and humidity are the key environmental factors which affect the life span of preserved materials. Use and storage of these flowers and foliage is dependent upon the geographical location of the shop. The following effects of various environmental conditions should be considered when working with preserved materials.

High Humidity

High humidity causes problems for glycerine-treated materials and freeze-dried materials. Glycerine-treated material may tend to weep or lose color in high humidity situations or areas. Storing glycerine-treated material in boxes with a small bag of silica gel will help absorb some of the excess moisture. Freeze-dried materials become limp and almost lifeless in high humidity. This problem can be eliminated by spraying the freeze-dried product with a light coat of sealing spray, such as a dry sealer or super surface sealer recommended for floral products. Be sure to cover all exposed surface areas of the freeze-dried item when spraying.

For shops located in high humidity areas, it is advisable to test a small quantity of glycerine or freeze-dried product before investing in a large amount of inventory.

Medium Humidity

Most preserved and dried products hold up well in medium humidity situations. Freeze-dried materials are the only products which may prove problematic. These products should be tested in all areas of the shop before selecting a storage place.

Dry or Very Low Humidity

In dry climates, it may be necessary to keep products that have been treated with glycerine in the cooler. Air-dried, freeze-dried and desiccant-dried materials do not usually require any special handling or storage conditions.

Cleaning Dried Materials

Unlike silk flowers, dried floral materials should not be cleaned with water. Submerging most dried flowers in water will destroy them, and even a light misting of water can be damaging. Instead, materials should be cleaned by feather dusting, blowing with a hair dryer on the lowest speed and coolest temperature, or spraying with a commercial aerosol cleaning product. As with silk flowers, it is recommended that each cleaning method be tested on a small portion of the product before proceeding.

Preparing Preserved Materials

Dried materials need little, if any, preparation before being used in a design. They may require fluffing, separating into small clusters, or dividing into single stems before being used in arrangements. Following are tips for preparing preserved materials.

- Materials that have been air-dried or preserved with glycerine may be misted with water and allowed to stand for 30 minutes to retrieve their suppleness in texture and to make them easier to work with.

- Preserved German statice may be stored in the cooler. This will allow suppleness to return to the product prior to its being used in designs.

Notes

Designing with Permanent Flowers

- Dried roses may be lightly steamed immediately before being placed in designs. This expands the flower head and allows the designer to shape the petals with his fingers.

- Freeze-dried materials should not come in contact with water. They should be sealed with a super surface sealer or a finishing spray designed specifically for floral products.

- Materials that have been freeze-dried, air-dried, or preserved with glycerine or a desiccant may require additional stem length to be inserted in a design. Wood picks, wire, or tape may be used for this purpose.

- Filler materials with small stems may need to be bundled in single units before being used in designs. A pick machine is ideal for this purpose. Chapter 3 provides more information about the mechanics of designing.

Purchasing Permanent Flowers

A large selection of both botanically correct and fantasy flowers is available from manufacturers and wholesalers of silk floral products. An abundance of unique and exotic dried floral materials are also available to florists. With such a wide variety to choose from, it is important to remember the principles and elements of floral design. Since the flowers that are purchased will eventually be transformed into arrangements, a well-balanced mixture of line, mass, form, and filler materials should be selected *(see Figures 8.2a through 8.2d, pages 199 through 200)*. To enhance textural variation, different types of materials should be combined, such as hand-wrapped silks, parchment flowers, and dried filler flowers.

Color selection is also particularly important when buying silk and dried materials. Since most permanent arrangements are used for months or years, they are often designed to match specific interiors. Color trends for home furnishings should be used as a guide for purchasing silk flowers. When selecting materials for custom orders, a simple rule of thumb will help determine the best color choice. For rooms with monochromatic color schemes (tints, tones, and shades of a single hue), an

Figure 8.2a Flower Types - Line

Figure 8.2b Flower Types - Mass

Basic Floral Design

arrangement in complementary colors will stand out. For a room decorated in several different colors, a monochromatic arrangement in an accent color will make the strongest statement.

Permanent flowers may be purchased from a variety of sources. Regardless of the source, florists should shop with a list of flower types, colors, and quantities. This will help prevent random buying and purchasing to satisfy personal tastes and preferences. Following is a list of permanent floral suppliers.

- Manufacturers. Some manufacturers sell directly, but most prefer to sell products through a distributor. Often, a minimum dollar amount is imposed when purchasing in this manner. For example, a manufacturer might require a $250.00 order to establish an account for first time buyers and a $100.00 minimum thereafter.

- Wholesalers or Jobbers. Wholesalers and jobbers usually have showrooms where a large variety of floral products are displayed. An abundance of silk, dried, and other permanent flowers is normally available. Often, no minimum order is required to purchase from wholesalers or jobbers; however, a resale license may be required, depending on the geographical location of a flower shop.

- Gift Shows and Trade Fairs. Gift shows and trade fairs are held in major cities throughout the United States. They may take place only once or twice per year or on a regular monthly basis. Gift shows and trade fairs provide an excellent opportunity for florists to examine several products at the same time. Manufacturers, importers, exporters, and wholesalers of permanent floral products are often found at these types of shows.

Designing Permanent Arrangements

Designing with permanent materials is similar to designing with fresh materials. A fresh floral arrangement is governed by specific design rules known as the principles and elements of design. These rules do not change when the flowers are silk or dried. In some respects, permanent products allow more creativity in design due to the availability of a wide variety of colors and flowers that are not found in nature.

Figure 8.2c   Flower Types - Form

Figure 8.2d   Flower Types - Filler

Designing with Permanent Flowers

Notes

Combining Silk Types

When designing, plastic-stemmed and hand-wrapped silks can be combined to control the cost of the end product. When choosing silks to combine, plastic-stemmed silks with flowers of similar quality to the hand-wrapped silks should be selected. To provide a variety of flower types, the major flower placements or focal flowers should be the hand-wrapped silks with the plastic-stemmed silks used as filler.

Combining Silk and Dried Materials

Silk and dried materials can be combined to create designs that are cost effective and visually appealing. Adding baby's breath to a silk arrangement can have a softening effect on the design. Dried star flowers or German statice added to an arrangement can add texture and color. Lines can be created by using preserved eucalyptus, dried larkspur, or dried bird of paradise leaves. These are only a few of the ways in which silk and dried materials can be combined to provide optimum variety of color, texture, and form.

Combining Fresh and Permanent Flowers

The addition of silk or dried materials to a fresh design adds interest and can create a change in texture, color, and the overall feeling of a design. Using sponge mushrooms at the base of an arrangement can create a woodland effect. Likewise, silk orchids added to a bridal bouquet make an ideal keepsake and add extra interest to the design.

Specialty Design Mechanics

Some designs created with silk and dried materials may require special mechanical techniques. Since the longevity of an arrangement depends upon the quality of the mechanics, it is imperative that sound mechanical techniques be used. Taking shortcuts can lead to dissatisfied customers and a reputation for poor quality. The following mechanical techniques are recommended for best results when designing with silk and dried materials.

Increasing Stem Length

Wood picks, hyacinth stakes, or #18 gauge wires may be used to extend stem lengths on silk or dried materials. Whichever mechanism is used, it should overlap the stem of the flower at least halfway to insure that the stem is balanced in the design. A light-gauge wire (#26 gauge to #28 gauge) may be used to secure the flower stem to the extension stem. The entire stem is then taped to disguise the mechanics and create a uniform appearance. Lightweight flowers with narrow stems may be lengthened by simply taping them to the extension stems. If additional length is needed, a second extension stem may be added by overlapping it halfway with the first extender and then securing it. Usually, no more than two extensions should be added to a stem to maintain stability in the design.

Reducing Stem Bulk

Some silks are created with a layer of cotton padding wrapped around the wire before it is taped. This gives a more realistic look to thick-stemmed flowers, such as calla lilies. When designing, thick stems can be difficult to insert in floral foam and often have a tendency to wobble after insertion. The following technique may be used to eliminate stem bulk before inserting in a design.

1. Determine the point at which the stem should be cut. Approximately 1/2 inch above the cutting point, use a pencil to make a line around the stem.

2. Use a sharp knife or scissors to cut along the line through the cotton and fabric covering. Cut all the way around the stem. To prevent dulling, avoid touching the blade of the knife or scissors to the wire.

3. Strip the cotton cover from the wire.

4. Use wire cutters to cut the bare portion of the wire to the desired length.

Adding Bulk to Stems

Not all silk flowers are designed botanically correct. Some silks achieve a more realistic appearance when bulk is added to their stems. Padding a stem can be accomplished quickly and efficiently by using cotton or tissue paper. The following steps for adding stem bulk provide professional results.

1. Cut the flower stem to the desired length for the design.

Notes

Designing with Permanent Flowers

Notes

2. Working from the top of the flower downward, wrap the stem with a thin layer of cotton or tissue paper. Finish wrapping about 1/2 to 1 inch before the end of the stem.

3. Secure the padding to the stem with floral tape. For lengthy stems, this padding should be applied and taped on one small section at a time. Floral adhesive glue may also be used to hold the padding to the wire before taping. For additional bulk, repeat the process. Apply a second layer of padding over the first.

Coloring Dried or Silk Material

Color on silk or dried materials can be changed by using spray paint designed specifically for the floral industry. This technique can be used to change color, accent color, or improve faded color. The following methods are effective ways of painting silk and dried materials. It is recommended that paints be tested on a small portion of any product before it is spray painted.

1. A light coating of spray paint may be applied directly to silk or dried materials. To prevent the paint from running or coating too heavily, hold the paint can 20 to 24 inches away from the flower, and spray in short, quick bursts.

2. To create special effects, spray floral paint into a pie tin and brush it onto the surface of the silk flowers or dried materials. This technique might be used to apply specks to the throat of a lily or to add a variegated look to leaves.

3. A coat of primer may need to be added to the surfaces of dried materials with porous surfaces prior to the application of color. Silver floral spray paint may be used for this purpose. Once the primer has dried, the dried material may be sprayed normally with the desired color. Repeated coats of paint may be required on dried materials to cover the surface. Dried materials may not absorb the paint as quickly as silk flowers. To prevent running, ample drying time should be allowed between the application of each coat of paint.

Basic Floral Design

Design Tips for Permanent Arrangements

Although the same principles of floral design apply to the construction of silk and dried arrangements and fresh arrangements, a few special considerations for working with artificial materials are important to remember. The following tips will assist in designing permanent arrangements efficiently with respect to time and cost.

- **Multiple-Flowering Stems (Figure 8.3)** - Multiple-flowering stems may include buds, fully developed flowers, and mature flowers on a single stem. They may also include several branched sections with all of these flower types on each branch. These types of stems are often better utilized by cutting them into several individual stems. Stem length may be added mechanically, as needed. This allows a single stem to be used in several different places in the design. It also reduces the fullness of the stem and creates an open, airy look.

- **Flowering and Foliage Silk Bushes (Figure 8.4)** - Designing with silk bushes can be very cost effective. One silk flowering bush can have as many as twelve or more major flowers that can be utilized in design. One foliage bush can provide enough greenery for one or more arrangements. Cutting these bushes into individual stems enhances design flexibility and provides the materials with a more natural look.

- **Pre-formed Silk Bouquets (Figure 8.5)** - Pre-formed silk bouquets consists of three or more flowers of different types on the same stem. This type of silk bouquet should be cut apart and combined with other materials (silk and/or dried) to create a more pleasing variety of textures, colors, and forms in the design.

- **Greenery** - Most silks are manufactured with greenery attached to the stem. This greenery is often discarded as stems are cut off during design. Incorporating greenery into the arrangement or saving it for a future design is more cost effective. Some silk flowers have lush foliage that may overwhelm an arrangement.

Figure 8.3 Multiple Flowering Stems

Figure 8.4 Flowering Silk Bush

Figure 8.5 Pre-formed Silk Bouquet

Designing with Permanent Flowers

Excess leaves can be clipped from the stems in advance or after insertion, but should be saved for future use. Wooden picks or pick machines may be used to add stems to these leaves, as needed.

- Gluing for Permanency - Permanent flower arrangements are usually meant to last indefinitely. To help insure the longevity of a design, stem insertions may be glued in place as the design is constructed. Dipping stem ends in pan melt glue before inserting them is probably the easiest method. Other glues, such as Oasis® Floral Adhesive, Elmer's Glue All™, or hot glue, are also effective. However, these methods are more time-consuming and take longer to set and dry.

- Mossing Containers - Fresh arrangements are usually constructed by covering the mechanics with greenery before adding flowers. Because fresh foliage is inexpensive compared to flowers, this procedure is cost effective. In contrast, silk foliage, in the form of bushes, plants, or individual leaves, is often as expensive as the flowers. To cover the mechanics in a silk design without using costly foliage, a layer of dry sheet moss or Spanish moss can be laid over the foam. Stems can easily be inserted through the moss, and a minimal amount of foliage can be added, as needed. This results in a design that is more cost effective.

Designing Wreaths

Wreaths are a common form of permanent design. Different sizes and shapes of wreaths, made of grapevine, birch, willow, wire, straw, and styrofoam, are generally available. Specialty wreaths created out of unusual materials, such as cork, corn husks, and cinnamon sticks, are also available from select sources. Silk and/or dried decorations can be added to these wreaths in a variety of ways. Depending on the type of wreath, flowers, and foliage may be directly attached with greening pins, glue, waxed string, or raffia. The following mechanical techniques are recommended for the types of wreaths listed.

- Grapevine, Birch, and Willow Wreaths **(Figure 8.6a)**. Wreaths made from vines and branches often have a somewhat open weave. This allows floral materials to

Figure 8.6a Grapevine Wreath

be attached with glue. Pan melt glue is the quickest and easiest, but a glue gun can also be used with good results. With this technique, stem ends are covered with glue and inserted into the weave of the wreath. The glue, combined with the network of the stems and branches, holds the floral materials in place.

- Straw and Styrofoam Wreaths **(Figure 8.6b and 8.6c)**. The composition of straw and styrofoam wreaths is usually quite dense. This allows floral materials to be attached with greening pins. A heavy wire (#20 gauge to #22 gauge) cut into 2-inch pieces and bent in half can be used as a substitute for greening pins if necessary. The ability to secure materials with pins in these types of wreaths makes it easy to cover them with mosses, lichens, or ribbons to create a special effect.

- Wire Wreaths **(Figure 8.6d)**. Inexpensive wire wreaths, which are intended to be used as frames, are available. These frames must be camouflaged so that they are not visible in the finished design. This can be done by laying a light coating of Spanish moss around the top of the frame. Some wire wreaths are rounded instead of flat. The rounded side of these wreaths is the top. Waxed string or raffia is then tied to the frame and loosely wrapped around the moss to hold it in place.

Small bundles of flowers or foliage may be added to cover the wreath frame and provide fullness. These bundles are added by laying them one at a time on the frame and wrapping them two or three times around the stems. The second bundle is positioned with the tips overlapping the first bundle approximately halfway. This process of binding bundles to the frame is continued all the way around the wreath until the last bundle added connects with the first bundle. The end of the binding material is then tied to the frame. The wreath is then ready for use, or it can be enhanced with ribbons, tulle, or floral accents.

Dry floral foam may be used instead of the mechanical techniques described above. This foam can be attached to any

Figure 8.6b Straw Wreath

Figure 8.6c Foam Wreath

Figure 8.6d Wire Wreath

Designing with Permanent Flowers

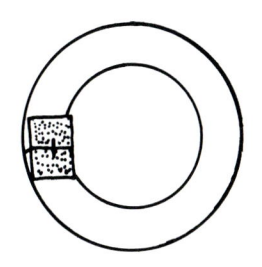

Figure 8.7a Wreath Mechanics

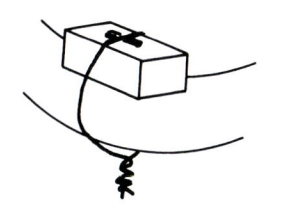

Figure 8.7b Wreath Mechanics

type of wreath to make designing easier. The following steps describe the proper method of attaching floral foam to wreaths. *(Figures 8.7a and 8.7b)*

1. Cut a block of dry foam to the required size. A block that is approximately 20 percent the size of the finished design will be sufficient.

2. Apply hot glue to the base of the foam using a hot glue gun or pan melt glue.

3. Press the foam against the wreath in the location of the planned focal point. After the foam has been glued to the wreath, secure it in place with a chenille stem or taped wire. To prevent the wire or chenille stem from cutting through the foam, place a small wooden pick between the wire and foam.

There are unlimited possibilities for designing wreaths. The type and placement of floral materials used influence the personality of a design. The wreath form itself often dictates the type and placement of floral decorations. Following are several options for designing a variety of wreaths.

Wreath-making Tips

- When constructing a wreath with a cluster or crescent accent, it is best to start the design in the center and gradually work outward in each direction to the tips.

- For wreaths covered completely with flowers, start at one point and work around the wreath in one direction until reaching the starting point again.

- Place the wreath on a wall or easel during design to insure that the arrangement is constructed from the proper perspective.

- When designing permanent wreath accents in dry foam, dip each flower stem in pan melt glue before insertion to insure the security of individual flower placements.

- For a wreath designed with the floral accent off center, physical balance can be maintained by positioning the hanger off center.

Trimming Baskets

Trimming the outside of a basket with silk flowers and foliage is an easy way to enhance an ordinary basket and to increase its value. To maintain cost effectiveness, leftover silk florets and leaves can be used for this purpose. The finished baskets are ideal for use as gift items and specialty containers for fresh designs. A variety of looks, ranging from feminine to earthy or natural, can be achieved by using this technique. The selection of materials for these designs is probably the most important step in creating these baskets. In most cases, all of the materials may be glued directly to the basket with a glue gun or pan melt glue. This helps reduce the amount of construction time needed for each basket. The following tips will assist florists in creating basket trims with precision. *(Figure 8.8)*

Figure 8.8 Trimming a Basket with Silks

- If lace is to be used in the design, it is suggested that pre-gathered lace be purchased from a yardage store. Pre-gathered lace can be glued directly around the edge of a basket or over a handle of a basket to achieve a full look.

- After the lace has been glued to the surface of the basket, a thin strip of satin tubing or ribbon can be glued on the top edge of the lace to hide the glue.

- If the handle of the basket is to be wrapped with lace or ribbon, it should be done in the early stages of design. The handle can be wrapped with lace or ribbon, starting from one edge of the basket, working up and over to the other edge of the basket, and gluing both ends securely with a hot glue gun or pan melt glue.

- Using specialty or decorator ribbons on decorative baskets is recommended. Since the detail in these baskets is so precise, a small piece of expensive ribbon can be used to increase the sight value of the product.

- Instead of a bow, small, individual loops of ribbon can be glued on the basket.

- Bows can be used at the top of the handle, on either side of the handle where it connects to the basket, or

Designing with Permanent Flowers

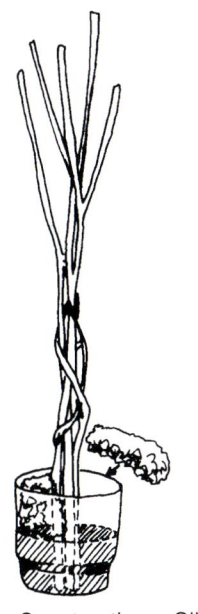

Figure 8.9a Constructing a Silk Tree Steps 2 & 3

Figure 8.9b Constructing a Silk Tree Step 4

Figure 8.9c Constructing a Silk Tree Step 4

lower on the side of the basket, depending upon the desired appearance of the overall design.

Making Silk Trees *(Figure 8.9)*

Silk trees are ideal for homes and offices where live plants have difficulty growing. Silk trees purchased commercially are usually expensive and are available in a limited number of shapes, sizes, and colors. Florists can construct green or flowering trees using materials that are readily available.

1. Select a type of branch, such as birch, willow, or aspen. The trunk of the branch selected should be at least 2 1/2 inches to 4 2/3 inches in diameter. A clump-type tree can be constructed using several smaller branches.

2. Place the trunk in a heavy container, such as a ceramic pot, and fill the container two thirds of the way with plaster of Paris. Support the trunk in the desired position, and hold it in place until the plaster is hard. *(Figure 8.9a)*

3. After the plaster of Paris has dried completely, cover it with moss. *(Figure 8.9a)*

4. If green or flowering silk branches are to be used *(Figures 8.9b and 8.9c)*, drilling will be required. Select a drill bit that is approximately the same size as the stems of the silks to be inserted in the tree trunk.

5. Starting at the top of the branch, drilling in a vertical direction, drill several holes. Insert the silk stems in the holes created; add more branches for fullness if needed. (*Figure 8.9d on page 210*)

6. After creating the top of the tree with silks placed in a vertical direction, drill holes down the sides of the branch at varied angles. *(Figure 8.9d on page 210)*

7. Prepare the leaves and stems of the silks to give them a natural look. Insert the silk stems in all of the holes. Work from the top of the tree downward. Each silk stem should be cut to an appropriate length and

dipped in glue before being inserted in the holes. As a general rule, stems placed at the top of the tree should be shorter than those at the base. **(Figure 8.9d)**

8. After inserting ten to twelve stems, evaluate the overall form and shape. At this point, minor adjustments may need to be made in the placement of branches. If necessary, additional holes may be drilled for more branches, or some holes which have already been drilled can be left empty. **(Figure 8.9e)**

Dish Gardens

Producing a silk dish garden is no different from producing a dish garden made with fresh green plants. Silk dish gardens can be created in a ceramic containers, plastic containers, or baskets. The key difference in assembly is in the preparation of the container. Selecting plants for a silk dish garden is vitally important. A variety of plant heights, sizes, and colors should be combined to create interest and realism in the design. The following steps can be used to make a lifelike silk dish garden **(see Figure 8.10 on page 211)**.

1. The container may be prepared in one of the following ways.

   - An anchor pin may be secured to the inside base of the container with floral clay. The floral foam may then be secured to the anchor pin.

   - The floral foam may be glued directly to the base of the container, using a glue gun or pan melt glue.

   - A liner may be utilized if an expensive container is used. This also insures that the container can be easily cleaned. Foam can be taped to the liner, or it may be glued for permanency.

2. Cover the mechanics of the container with a light layer of moss.

3. Visually divide the container into four equal quadrants. Starting with the back, left hand quadrant, create visual

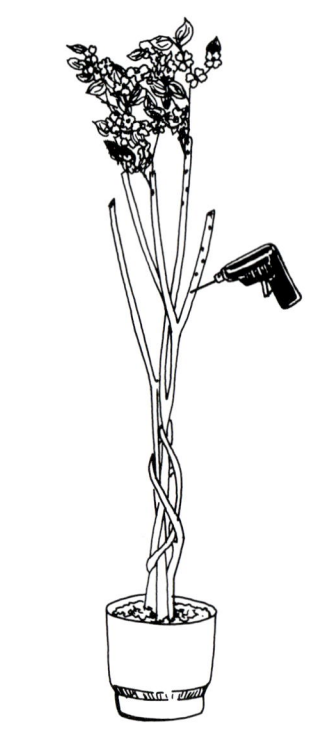

Figure 8.9d Constructing a Silk Tree Steps 5 - 7

Figure 8.9e Constructing a Silk Tree Step 8

Designing with Permanent Flowers

Figure 8.10 Constructing a Silk Dish Garden

height. This can be done with one or two silk plants that are at least one and one half times the height of the container.

4. Moving to the back, right hand quadrant, add one or two plants which are at least two thirds the height of the first plants inserted.

5. Add two or three plants which are about half the height of the plant material directly behind them in the front, left hand quadrant.

6. Add one or two low plants directly against the foam in the last remaining quadrant of the container. African violets or low spredding vines are ideal in this position.

7. Create interest at the lip of the container by using a mixture of mosses, mushrooms, pods, birds, etc.

Custom Designing Permanent Arrangements

Since silk and dried arrangements are permanent designs, customers often order custom-made pieces that will enhance a specific decor. Typically, when a customer places a custom order, she has already established a visual image of the desired arrangement. Florists must extract that image from the customer. Sometimes the design style desired by the customer is not appropriate for the situation. Professional florists guide customers to appropriate choices whenever possible. To insure customer satisfaction, the following considerations should be discussed when accepting a custom order.

Color

Color is a vitally important factor in any custom-made floral design. Usually, the customer has already determined where the design will be placed, so the colors in that area must be considered when selecting the silk and dried materials to be used. It is difficult to discuss color without looking at color samples. Often, individuals do not agree on the identification specific colors. For this reason, it is helpful to look at samples of the wall covering, upholstery fabric, and carpeting that a design must complement. If samples are not available, the customer might be asked to provide paint sample chips that are representative of the colors in the room. If absolutely necessary, florists may visit the customer's home before selecting colors. Although this requires additional time, it is often worth the effort.

Size

Customers often relate the desired size of an arrangement with their hands. Many times this results in a design that is either too large or too small. Specific measurements of the area of placement are helpful in achieving a properly-sized arrangement. Measurements might include the size of the table top, height of the table, and distance between the table top and the bottom of a chandelier.

It is important to keep scale in mind when creating a design for a specific area. For example, large rooms usually require large arrangements if the flowers are to be noticed. Other items that will be placed near a design in the area of display must also be kept in mind. For example, a bedroom end table may have a lamp and picture frame on it in addition to the silk arrangement.

Style

The style or mood of a room usually dictates the appropriate style of design. An oriental style dining room would not be enhanced by a traditional mass arrangement. Likewise, a rustic, dried mass design would enhance a country style family room better than a contemporary one. By asking questions about furniture styles, wall coverings, and window dressings, florists can familiarize themselves with the look of a particular room.

Placement

The location where a design will be placed in the customer's home will greatly influence the style of design created. If the design will be seen from both sides, an all-around style should be used. If the design will be placed on the left or right side of a mantel or table, the overall line of the design should be shifted accordingly. If the design will be one of two designs that will be placed opposite each other, a pair of mirror-image designs will probably be desired.

Containers

The container selected for a custom-made floral design should be consistent with the color, size, style, and placement of the arrangement. A design for a country French living room might be

Notes

Designing with Permanent Flowers

Notes

designed in a basket, terra cotta pot, or ceramic bowl decorated with country accents. A design for a room with contemporary decor might be placed in a metallic, crystal, or sculpted ceramic container. Customers often provide containers in which designs are to be created. If florists are going to store several customers' containers before using them in designs, it is wise to verify that the shop's insurance policy covers any loss or damage which might occur.

    The use of silk and dried materials in basic design can expand the selection of products a flower shop offers its customers. Silk designs are often profitable, decorative pieces which add color and fullness to the display area of the shop. Displaying different types of silk and dried arrangements, trees, dish gardens, wreaths, and gift items will alert customers to the versatility of the designers in the shop. Permanent flowers are useful on a day-to-day basis and for special occasions, such as weddings and holidays. Customer interest in silk and dried designs will be generated if designs are created with quality products and if attention is paid to detail and botanical representation. The skills needed to design successfully with permanent flowers can only be gained with practice. However, florists who are motivated and persistent will become experts at designing and selling this special type of design in a relatively short period of time.

Basic Floral Design

Notes, Photographs, Sketches, etc.

Designing with Permanent Flowers

Notes, Photographs, Sketches, etc.

Glossary

Advancing Colors - Red, orange, and yellow are called advancing colors because of their intensity. They are considered warm colors.

Aerosol - A pressurized gas container used to dispense or spray various liquids, such as those sprayed on flowers to seal pores and minimize water loss.

Air-brushing - The art of spraying paint from a pressurized container nozzle. It is often referred to as color controlling.

Air-drying - A method of drying fresh flowers by hanging the plant material upside down so that moisture in the cell structure dissipates.

Analogous Color Harmony - A color combination consisting of one primary color and its adjacent colors within a ninety degree angle on the color wheel.

Anchor Pins - Round plastic holders (about the size of a quarter) with four prongs. They are glued inside the bottom of a design bowl to hold floral foam stable.

Anti-transpirants - Liquid sprays or dips used to coat flowers or foliage to minimize water loss.

Asymmetrical Arrangement - An arrangement in which the physical or visual weight on each side of the central vertical axis is unequal. It is usually triangular in shape.

Balance - The equal distribution of weight, whether visual or physical, in floral design. Balance brings the various components of a floral design into harmonious proportion. The

Glossary

placement of materials in the arrangement will determine whether it is of symmetrical or asymmetrical balance.

Banking Pins - Straight silver pins, 1 to 2 inches long, used to pleat ribbon, pin flowers on styrofoam backings, etc. The term comes from the early use of such pins for wrapping currency in banks.

Baroque Period - Refers to 17th and 18th century France. During that time, flowers were arranged in a tight, semi-ovoid (egg-like) shape with each flower placed separately so that it could be viewed individually.

Beauty Clips - Plastic *U*-shaped gripping devices used to fasten chicken wire to the edge and around the perimeter of a floral container.

Blueprint - The predetermined drawing of a design specifying height, width, and placement.

Bowl Tape - Waterproof tape used primarily to hold floral foam in place.

Bracts - A modified leaf, usually small and scale-like, sometimes large and colorful, growing at the base of a flower or its stalk.

Calyx - The outermost part of a flower; it surrounds the petals and is usually green and leaf-like.

Central Vertical Axis - The point in an arrangement from which all plant material appears to radiate outward.

Chain of Life - A special program developed to promote the proper care and handling of flowers.

Chenille Stems - A 12-inch wire covered with fuzzy chenille fibers. It is similar to a pipe cleaner.

Chicken Wire - A pliable fencing wire rolled in 12-inch widths with 1-inch openings. In floral design, it is used as a mechanical aid for holding flowers.

Chroma - The purity of a color determined by its degree of freedom from white and gray. It refers to the strength or weakness of a color.

Glossary

Citric Acid - A naturally-occuring chemical found in citrus fruit that influences (lowers) pH. It is used to prevent water stress problems (like rose bent neck) by maximizing water uptake.

Clear Bowl Tape - A transparent, sticky tape used to create a grid over the opening of a vase to make designing easier.

Clutch Wiring - A wiring method used to secure clusters of flower stems. Cluth wiring is also referred to as the wrap-around or extension method.

Cold Melt Glue - Specially prepared glue that has a lower melting temperature than does Hot Melt Glue.

Collaring - Refers to foliage placed in foam along the lip of the container. The greenery encircles the container like a collar on a shirt.

Color Harmony - The emotional effect of two or more colors on each other or on the viewer. A reaction to viewing color may be pleasant or discordant.

Color Wheel - A color circle which divides colors into primary, secondary, and tertiary colors, including tints, tones, and shades of those colors.

Complementary Colors - Two colors which are directly opposite from each other on the color wheel.

Compote - A vase attached to a pedestal.

Continental Design - Traditional European design employing many varieties, sizes, and colors of flowers. It is referred to as mass design.

Curvilinear Line - A transitional line between the vertical and horizontal lines.

Depth - The distance from the top downward, from the surface inward, or from the front to the back in an arrangement.

Desiccants - Materials used to remove moisture from flowers and foliage to preserve them as dried plant material.

Glossary

Dip Dye - The tinting of fresh flowers by directly dipping flower heads into color solution. These dyes are semi-transparent.

Dixon Pins - Two 1/2-inch wooden picks attached on opposite ends of a flexible metal strip. They are used as a mechanical aid in floral work, often sympathy work.

Dominance - One outstanding or prevailing characteristic. It is achieved in an arrangement through the use of repetition, contrast, or change.

Dry Foam - A semi-dense, water-repellent floral foam used with silk and dried arrangements.

Elements of Design - The physical characteristics of plant material; they are line, form, pattern, texture, and color.

Equilateral Triangle - A triangle with three equal sides.

Ethylene Damage - Damage which results from exposure to ethylene, an ordorless, colorless gas produced by all plants, flowers, and fruits. It is called the aging hormone because it stimulates the aging process in flowers and plants, causing petals to drop, leaves to fall off, and fruits to ripen.

Families - Broad groups of Genera having similar traits.

Feathering (Frenching) - The technique of dividing a full carnation into smaller parts to make miniature florets, usually for corsage work.

Ferning Pins (Greening Pins) - Metal, staple-like pins used to secure flowers, plants, vines, mosses, etc. in foam.

Filler Flowers - Small blooms used to fill space between major flowers in an arrangement and to add color or volume. Baby's breath, statice, acacia, and feverfew are examples of filler flowers.

Flat-back Arrangement - A one-sided design created to be viewed from the front, as opposed to an all-around design; it is usually placed next to a wall or against a flat surface.

Floral Adhesive - A glue-like, sticky substance used to secure fresh flowers or mechanical aids.

Glossary

Floral Clay - A fine-grained, plastic material used to anchor and stabilize the securing devices in floral arranging.

Floral Mechanics - A wide assortment of methods, aids, and devices used to facilitate production of floral designs and to stabilize plant materials in a design. By definition, mechanics are the things not seen in an arrangement; i.e., foam and tape hidden by greenery.

Focal Area - The part of an arrangement that has the strongest visual weight, largest blossoms, and greatest concentration of materials. It is usually located at the base of the main stem near the lip of the container.

Form - A three-dimensional shape. In western style (line-mass) design, the forms take geometric shape.

Form Flowers - Flowers which have a distinctive shape, such as cattleya orchids, irises, and anthuriums.

Free-standing Design - A design that can be viewed from all sides, often referred to as an all-around arrangement.

Freeze Drying - A method of removing moisture from the cell structure of flowers by mechanical means. The flower retains its shape and suppleness.

Frog - Any device used to hold flowers or foliage securely in place.

Genus - A group of similar, genetically-related species that have major characteristics in common.

Glitter Glue - A thin, spray glue that is used to adhere glitter to fresh flowers and foliage.

Glycerine Treatment - A solution of one part glycerine to three parts water which, when absorbed by flowers, acts as a preservative.

Growth Regulators - Special solutions used by growers to prevent problems, such as leaf yellowing.

Hand-tied Bouquets - A bouquet of flowers arranged in the hand and secured by binding or tying with string or raffia.

Hardening Off (Conditioning) - The process of preparing flowers for shipping, storage, or arranging by cutting stems and allowing the uptake of a conditioning solution.

Hogarth Curve - A design style in a lazy *S* shape, created by William Hogarth, an eighteenth century English painter.

Hot Melt Glue - Rounded glue sticks, 6 to 15 inches in length, which are inserted into a glue gun, heated, and used to secure objects in place.

Hue - A specific color regardless of the quantity of black, white, or gray it contains. Color that is distinguished by degrees of intensity of hues.

Hyacinth Stakes - Wooden sticks of various lengths used to support plants, lengthen stems, or secure accessories in arrangements.

Hydration - The uptake of liquid, often referred to as "giving the flowers a drink." Flowers need to hydrate with preservative solution to replace moisture that is lost during shipping and handling.

Ikebana - A Japanese word that means "flower arranging." It is an artistic statement of Oriental philosophy.

Intensity - The brightness or dullness of a color.

Isosceles Triangle - A triangle with only two equal sides.

Jardinere - An ornamental bowl or pot for plants or flowers.

Kenzan - The Japanese word for a heavy metal pin holder used to secure flower stems.

Lacing - A technique of weaving greenery in eight opposing directions to form a grid-like frog in a vase.

Line - The visual movement between two points.

Line-mass Design - Western style design; a combination of Oriental and European Continental design.

Glossary

Line Flowers - Flowers whose individual blossoms or florets are arranged in a single line. For example, gladioli are line flowers.

Mass Flowers - A mass flower is any full, round flower.

Monochromatic Color Harmony - A color combination that includes all of the tints, tones, and shades of one hue (color).

Mylar - A lightweight polyester material made in thin sheets.

Nosegay - A round bouquet style with flowers placed closely together. It is also called a colonial bouquet.

Paddle Wire - Wire that has been continuously wrapped around a small length of wood.

Pan Melt Glue - Small pellets of glue which are melted down in an electric skillet and used to secure mechanical aids in design.

Papier-maché - A container that has a waterproof lining and is made of pressed paper.

Parallelism - A design in which all flowers are positioned parallel to each other. There is no radiation in this design. Space is left between the stems, and basing is important to the completion of the design.

Pattern - The physical characteristics of plant material.

Pigment - Any coloring matter in the cells of plants and flowers.

Pistil - The female, seed-bearing part of a flower.

Point of Centralization - An area at the base of the central vertical axis from which all stems radiate, or appear to radiate.

Poly Foil - Aluminum foil that has been strengthened with a layer of translucent plastic bonded to one side. It is usually available in rolls in a variety of embossed patterns and colors.

Psychology of Color - The emotional reaction of humans to color and the way they perceive it as it exists in plant materials.

Glossary

Preservative - A mixture of ingredients that keep flowers alive longer by supplying an energy source in the form of sugar, lowering pH (acidity), keeping the water and food conducting system working, and reducing the stem contamination caused by bacteria and fungi. It may also be called floral preservative, cut flower food, or fresh flower food.

Pre-treatment (Supplements) - Treatments that prevent flower problems and greatly extend the vase life of fresh flowers.

Primary Colors - Red, yellow, and blue.

Proportion - A pleasing relationship between the height and width of an arrangement or between the size and shape of both plant material and container. Proportion is a conjunctive of balance, size, and shape.

Radiation - The appearance of movement from a central point, such as from the base of the central vertical axis.

Receding Colors - The colors on the cool side of the color wheel; they are blue, green, and violet.

Reflex - To fold back the petals of a flower to create additional interest. Reflexing a rose which is centered in an arrangement is an example.

Repetition - The repeated use of a flower or color; it provides unity in a design.

Rhythm - A continuous line that flows through a design without interruption. Rhythm is visual movement.

Secondary Colors - The colors created by combining two primary colors. They are orange, green, and violet.

Shade - Any color that has had black added to it.

Spathe - A large, leaf-like part of a flower that encloses a flower cluster or a spadix, i.e. anthurium.

Species - A group of plants that have definite, constant characteristics in common.

Glossary

Split Complement - A color harmony achieved by combining one hue with the two colors on either side of its direct complement on the color wheel.

Spray Tints - Translucent colors that allow some part of the underlying (base) color to show through.

Stamen - The collective term for the pollen-bearing, male part of a flower. It is made up of filament and the anther.

Stem Dying - A process of coloring a flower by allowing it to drink from dye-treated water.

Styrofoam - A dense, hard foam material which comes in various widths and lengths.

Symmetrical Triangle Arrangement - A formal arrangement that has an equal distribution of weight on each side of the central vertical axis.

Texture - The surface quality or tissue structure of plant material

Tint - Any color that has had white added to it.

Tone - Any color that has had gray added to it.

Topiary - A shrub or tree which has been trimmed or trained to an unnatural shape or an arrangement designed to create this appearance.

Transition - Refers to easy visual movement. An orderly movement in plant material from small to large; gradual degrees of change.

Triadic - A color harmony that uses three hues equally spaced on the color wheel.

Unity - An arrangement of materials that will produce a single, harmonious design or effect in a flower arrangement.

Value - The llightness or darkness of a color; the amount of white, gray, or black that has been added to a pure hue.

Vase Life - The useful life of a cut flower after harvest; may also be referred to as longevity, lasting quality, or keeping quality.

Glossary

Waterproof Tape - Plastic tape with both a smooth and sticky side; used in securing mechanics.

White Glue - A slow-drying glue used primarily for attaching wood to wood or paper to paper.

Wilt-sensitive Flowers - Flowers that wilt quickly and become limp when shipped or held out of water. These flowers should be unpacked and processed first when a shipment arrives and should only be stored for minimal time periods.

Wire Gauge - The measurement used to determine the thickness of a wire.

Wooden Picks - Small, thin, pointed sticks used to secure flowers and foliage in an arrangement.

Appendix A - Care and Handling Charts and Checklists

Tools, Equipment, and Chemicals Checklist	231
Flower Longevity	232
Flower Sensitivity	233
Flower Storage Potential	234
Chilling Sensitive Flowers	235

Tools, Equipment, and Chemicals Checklist

Tools

___ **Plastic display and storage buckets**

___ **Processing tools:**

___   **Hand held:**

     ___ Wire cutters

     ___ Floral knife

     ___ Stem cutters

___   **Automated:**

     ___ Counter mounted stem cutter

     ___ Portable underwater cutter

___ Floral Foam Soaking Bin

___ Brushes, sponges, and spray bottles for cleaning

___ Pump or proportioner for liquid floral preservative

___ Measuring spoons

___ Measuring containers with cup, quart, and gallon markings

___ Measuring cup with once markings

___ Finishing sprays and dips

___ Floral wrapping paper

Equipment

___ Floral cooler(s)

Chemicals

___ Flower preservative

___ **Special supplements:**

     ___ Ethylene Reduction Treatment (like STS)

     ___ Citric acid (or hydrating) solution

     ___ Stem sanitizing solution

___ Floral cleaning agent

Flower Longevity

MINIMAL (1-2 days)	FAIR (3-5 days)	GOOD (5-7 days)	EXCELLENT (7-14 days)	SUPERIOR (14 days or more)
Camellia	Cornflower	Anemone	Agapanthus	Anthurium
Gardenia	Daffodil	Bouvardia*	Alstroemeria	Carnation
	Iris*	Calla*	Aster 'Monte Casino'	Miniature Carnation
	Lilac	Delphinium*	Bells of Ireland	Spray Chrysanthemums
	Peony	Freesia	Standard Chrysanthemum	Star of Bethlehem
	Phlox	Gerbera*	Gladiola	Statice
	Queen Anne's Lace	Gloriosa Lily	Heather	
	Stephanotis	Gypsophila*	Liatrus	
	Tulip	Marguerite Daisy	Asiatic (hybrid) Lily	
		Rose	Oriental (Rubrum) Lily	
		Snapdragon	Lily-of-the-Valley	
		Stock	Nerine	
		Zinnia	Cymbidium Orchid	
			Dendrobium Orchid	
			Sweet William	
			Tuberose	
			Wax Flower	
			Yarrow	

* Vase life is variable, depending on source, variety, and treatment.

• Vase life varies widely for gingers (few days to 2 weeks or more), heliconias (few days to 3 weeks), and proteas (few days to few weeks), so they are not categorized.

• Common names are used on this chart.

Flower Sensitivity

Wilt Sensitive Flowers

Anemone

Bouvardia

Cornflower

Delphinium

Gardenia

Gerbera

Iris

Marguerite Daisy

Peony

Phlox

Queen Anne's Lace

Rose

Snapdragon

Tulip

Special Care Tips:

- Remove wilt-sensitive flowers first from box of mixed cut flowers that comes from the wholesaler.
- Cut underwater.
- Use stem-sanitizing dip or solution on flowers that will not be treated with STS.
- Keep buckets and solution clean (change every couple of days).
- Re-cut stem ends every couple of days.

Ethylene Sensitive Flowers

Agapanthus

Alstroemeria

Anemone

Babies Breath

Bouvardia

Carnation

Miniature Carnation

Cornflower

Delphinium

Freesia

Lily

Phlox

Snapdragon

Sweet William

Special Care Tips:

- Order products that have been pre-treated with an ethylene-reduction solution (like STS).
- Do not leave flowers in tightly closed boxes.
- Treat with ethylene-reduction solution (like STS) if they have not already been treated.
- Keep away from ethylene sources, such as dead or dying flowers, fruit, engine exhaust, and kerosene heaters.

Flower Storage Potential

Minimal (1-2 days)	**Fair** (3-4 days)	**Good** (5-7 days)	**Excellent** (7-14 days)
Anemone	Anthurium	Agapanthus	Carnation
Babies Breath	Aster 'Monte Casino'	Alstroemeria	Miniature Carnation
Bouvardia	Cornflower	Bells of Ireland	
Camellia	Freesia	Bird of Paradise	Chrysanthemum (standard or spray)
Daffodil	Ginger	Calla	
Delphinium	Asiatic and Oriental Lilies	Gerbera	Star of Bethlehem
Garenia		Liatrus	
Heather	Nerine	Lily-of-the-Valley	Statice
Heliconias	Snapdragon	Cymbidium Orchid	
Iris	Solidaster	Dendrobium Orchid	Wax Flower
Lilac	Stock	Cattleya Orchid	
Marguerite Daisy		Peony	
Phlox		Stephanotis	
Queen Anne's Lace		Rose	
Tulip (in water)		Tuberose	
Zinnia			

Chilling Sensitive Flowers

Do not put the following flowers in a cooler or open-air merchanidiser. Do not expose them to temperatures below 55 fahrenheit.

- Anthurium
- Bird of Paradise
- Ginger
- Heliconia
- Protea
- Poinsettia (cut or potted)
- Orchids (some orchids, such as cymbidium, can tolerate short exposure to lower temperatures, but it is best to provide special protection to all to prevent confusion)

Appendix B - Dried and Preserved Materials

Branches and Line Materials	239
Filler Flowers	241
Foliages	244
Mass Flowers	245
Pods and Cones	246

Branches and Line Materials

Assagi

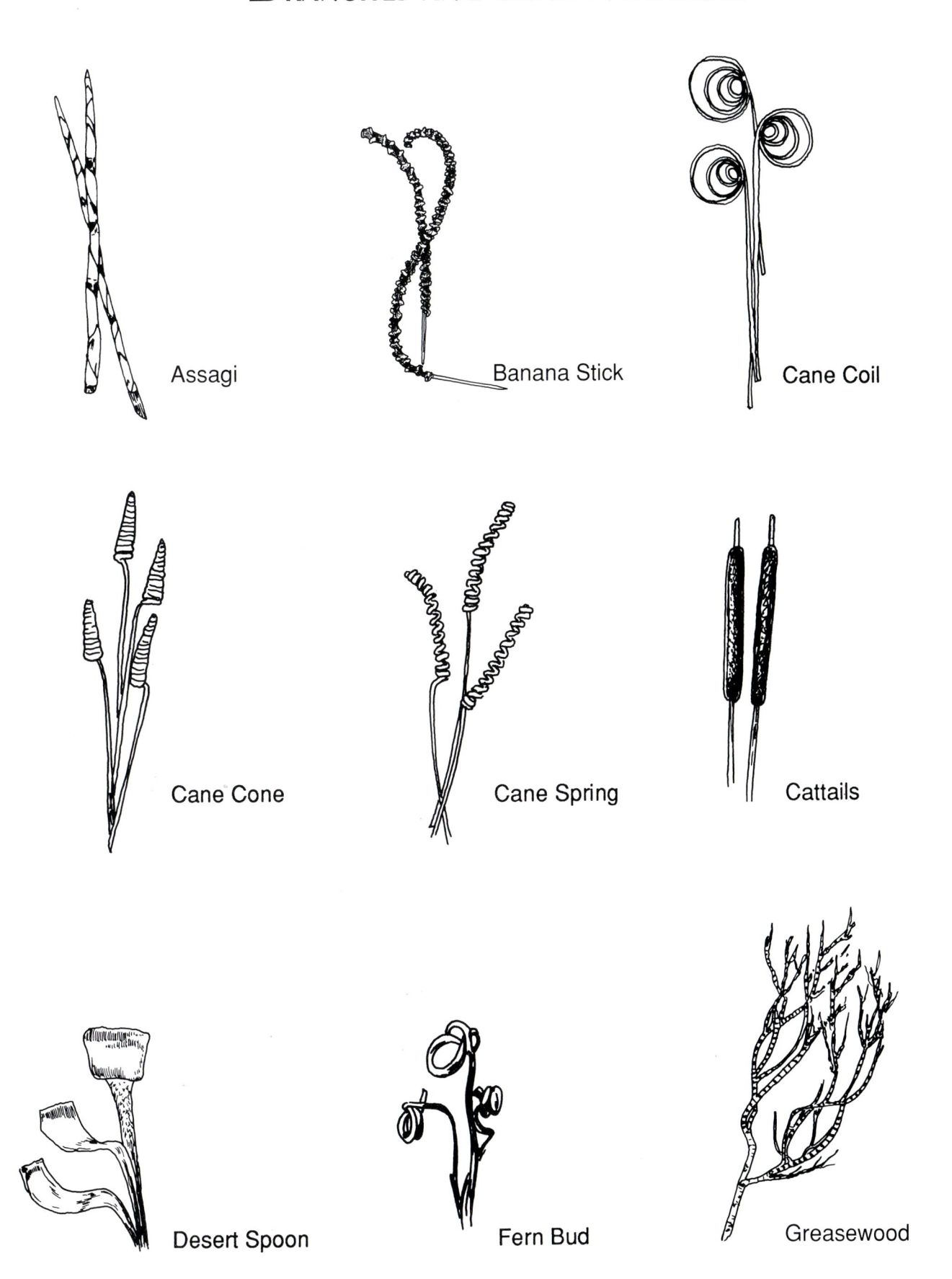

Banana Stick

Cane Coil

Cane Cone

Cane Spring

Cattails

Desert Spoon

Fern Bud

Greasewood

Branches and Line Materials

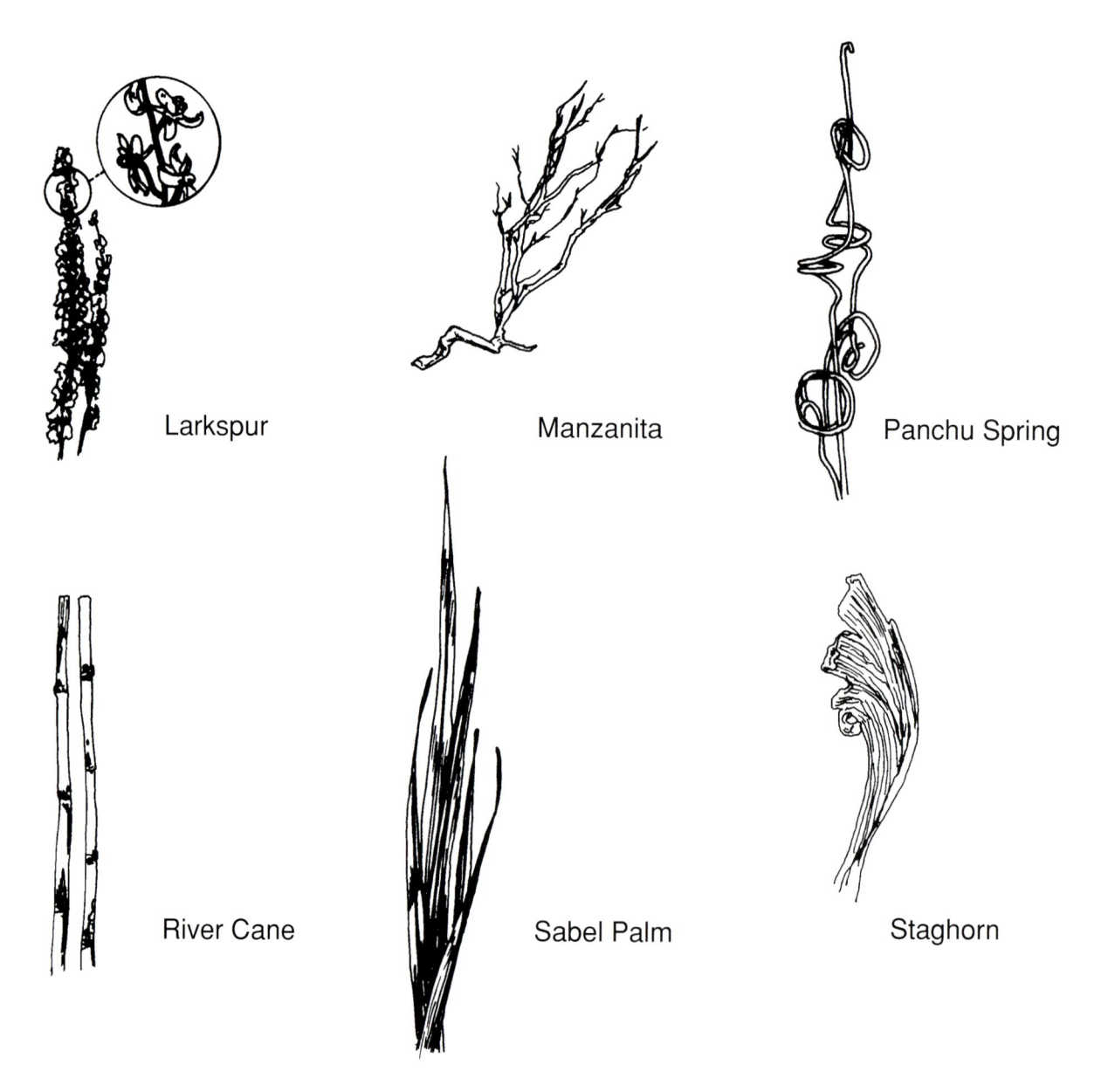

Larkspur

Manzanita

Panchu Spring

River Cane

Sabel Palm

Staghorn

Ting Ting

Filler Flowers

Amaranthus

Artemisia

Broom Bloom

Bruneia

Bunny Tails

Canella Berry

Caspia

Eryngium

German Statice

Filler Flowers

Globe Amaranth

Globe Thistle

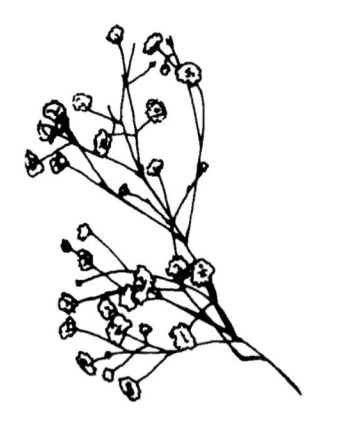

Gypsophila

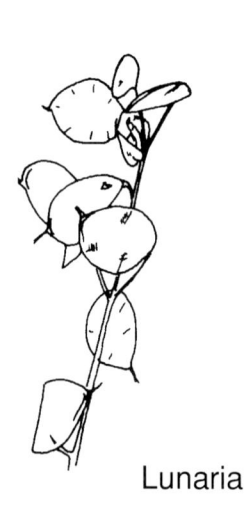

Hill Flower

Lavender

Lunaria

Nigella

Phlaris

Queen Anne's Lace

Filler Flowers

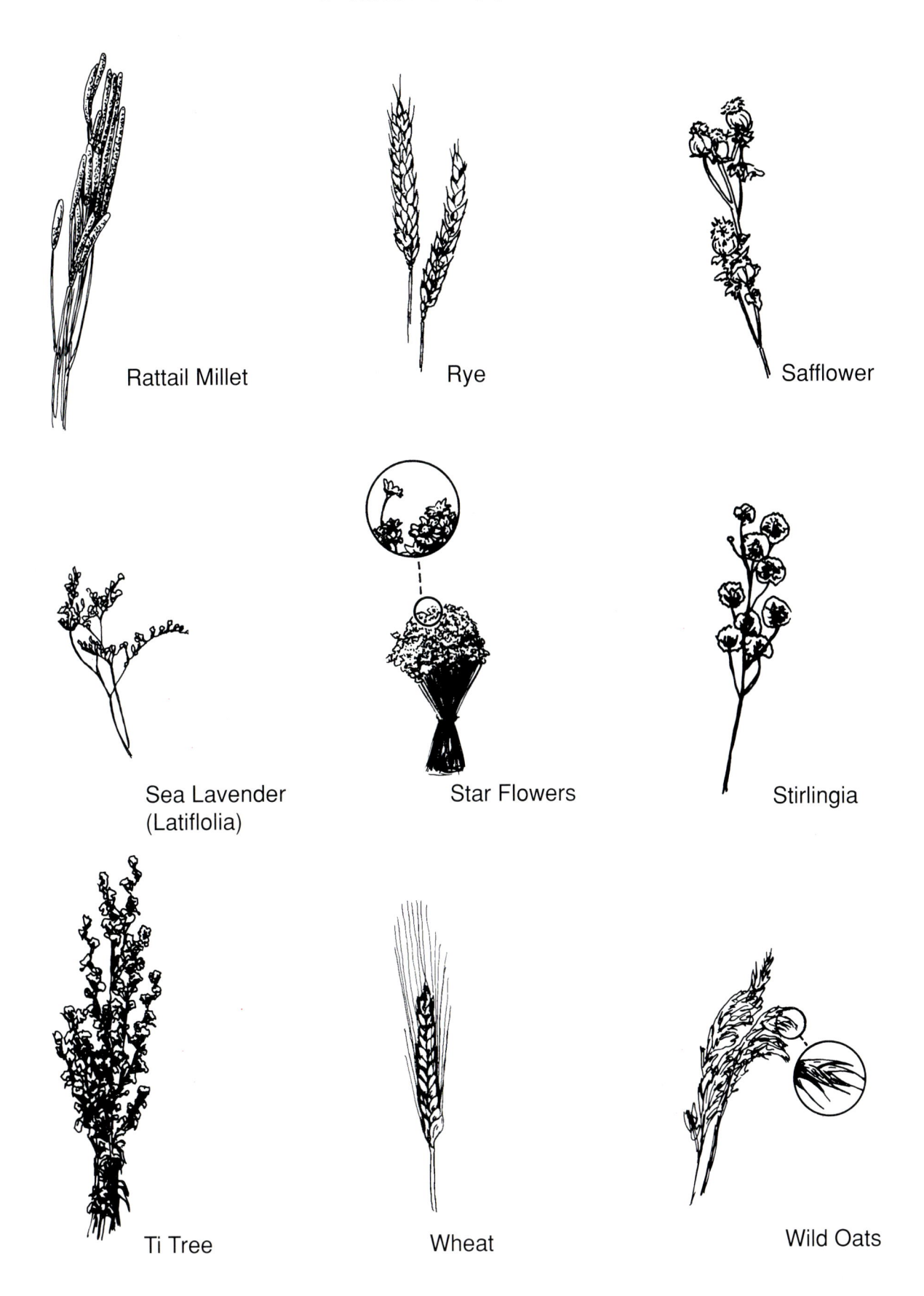

Rattail Millet

Rye

Safflower

Sea Lavender
(Latiflolia)

Star Flowers

Stirlingia

Ti Tree

Wheat

Wild Oats

Foliages

Cedar	Eucalyptus	Leatherleaf
Magnolia Leaves	Oak	Oregonia
Palmetto	Plumosa	Scotch Broom

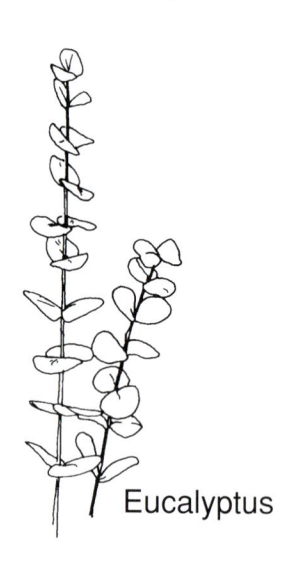

Foliages

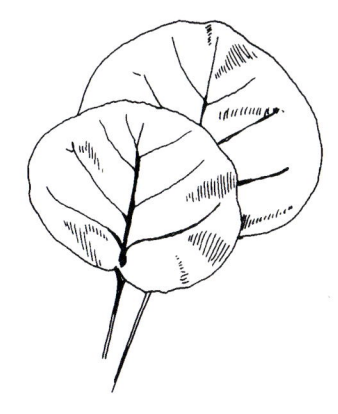

Sea Grape Leaves

Sprengeri

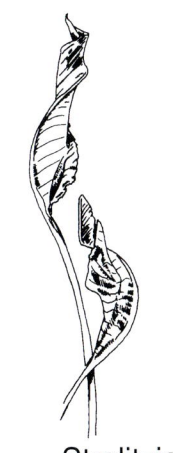

Strelitzia

Mass Flowers

Chinese Lantern

Drumstick Allium

Roses

Sugar Star

Yarrow

Pods and Cones

Adam Cone	Bell Cups	Artichoke
Decorum Cone	Golden Mushroom	Jinga Pod
Lotus Pods	Mallee Pears	Mahogany Pods

Pods and Cones

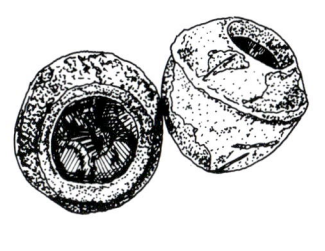

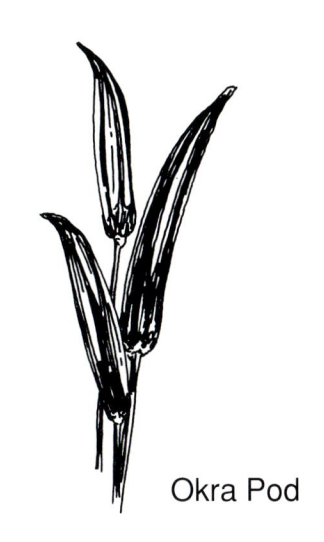

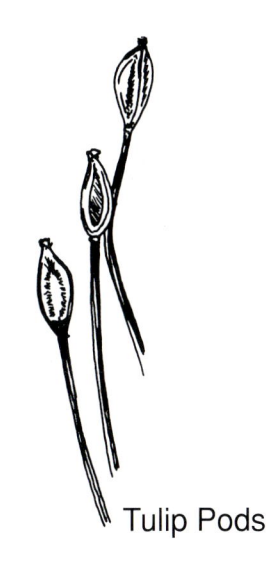

Menzeii Cone

Monkey Pod

Okra Pod

Poppy Pods

Salignum

Spidergum

Sponge Mushroom

Star Cone

Tulip Pods

Bibliography

Alexander, T., R. Will Burnett, and Harbert S. Zim. 1970. <u>Botany</u>. New York: Golden Press.

Arlt, Bob. 1982. "The Theory of Paper Production for Art Use." Los Angeles, California: Presented at the Gutenburg Seminar.

Ascher, Amalie Adler. 1974. <u>The Complete Flower Arranger</u>. New York: Simon and Schuster.

Floralife, Inc. 1989. <u>Dew-y's FloraCare Manual</u>. Alexandria, Virginia: Society of American Florists.

Friese, Robert. 1990. "Designing Novelty Birds." Houston, Texas: Presented to the Shelton School of Floral Design.

Gibbons, Bob. 1984. <u>How Flowers Work</u>. New York: Sterling Publishing Co., Inc.

Holstead, Christy. 1985. Care and Handling of Flowers and Plants. Alexandria, Virginia: Society of American Florists.

John Henry Company. 1979. <u>Tips and Techniques for Wedding Design</u>. The John Henry Company.

M. Gurbacher. 1974. "The Color Compass." New York: M. Grumbacher, Inc.

McDaniel, Gary L. 1980. <u>Floral Design and Arrangement</u>. Reston, Virginia: Reston Publishing Co., Inc.

Paul Ecke Ranch. "Fresh Cut Poinsettia Care Instructions." Care tag information for poinsettia flowers. Encentias, California.

Bibliography

Saxtan, John H. 1986. <u>Fresh Flower Book</u>. Lansing, Michigan: The John Henry Company.

Taylor, Jane. 1981. <u>Plants and Flowers for Lasting Decorations</u>. New York: Larousse and Co., Inc.

Vaughan, Mary Jane. 1988. <u>The Complete Book of Cut Flower Care</u>. Portland, Oregon: Timber Press.

Wilkins, Harold. Dec. 1986. "Alcohol Pretreatments of Cut Poinsettia Flowers." Article in the North-Central Florist Association Newsletter. Minnesota: p. 10.

Index

A

Accessories, mechanics for *72-73*
Adhesives *27-29*
    floral *28*
    florist clay *28-29*
    glue gun *28*
    glue sticks *28*
    pan glue *27-28*
Aerosol sprays *29*
Analogous colors *17*
Anchor pins *31*
Anther *79*
Artificial flowers
    See silk flowers.
    See dried flowers.
Assembly line designing *164-166*
    individual designer *164-165*
    multiple design team *165-166*
Asymmetrical triangle arrangement *13, 141*
    construction of *152-153*
    scoring foam for *145*

B

Balance *7*
    asymmetrical *7*
    physical *7*
    symmetrical *7*
    visual *7*
Balloons, mechanics for *72*
Baskets, trimming *208-209*
Boutonnieres *110-112, 123-124, 132-134, 136*
    construction tips *133-134*

Boutonnieres *(continued)*
    flowers and foliage for *110*
    garden style *112*
    nestled *123-124*
    single flower *111*
    stem finishes *132-133*
    three flower *111-112*
    wearing *136*
Bows, construction of *65-69*
    with center loop *66-67*
    without center look *67*
    double loop tuck-in *68*
    single loop tuck-in *68-69*
    tails *69*
    three loop tuck-in *67-68*
    tips *65-66*
Bracts *80*

C

Calyx *55, 80*
Candles, mechanics for *31, 74-75*
    in fresh arrangements *74*
    pillar *75*
    in silk/dried arrangements *74*
    stakes *31*
    taper *75*
Care and handling, fresh flowers *85-103*
    purchasing considerations *85-87*
    steps *87-102*
        clean stems *91*
        conditioning techniques *95*
        during design *101-102*
        floral preservative *91*

Index

Care and handling, fresh flowers, steps *(continued)*
    overview *87-89*
        packaging *100*
        43-cutting stems *90*
        sanitation/ethylene prevention *97-99*
        storage and display *95-97*
        supplements and pre-treatments *93-94*
        warm water storage *90-91*
    tips *103*
Chain of Life *79*
Chenille stems *27*
Chilling sensitive flowers *Appendix A*
Chroma *15*
Color *15-18*
    cool *15*
    harmonies *16-17*
        analogous *17*
        complementary *17*
        monochromatic *16*
        split complement *17*
        triadic *17*
    physics *18*
    psychology *17-18*
    vocabulary *15-16*
        chroma *15*
        hue *15*
        intensity *16*
        shade *16*
        tint *16*
        tone *16*
        value *16*
Complementary colors *17*
Conditioning, fresh flowers
    to wear *109-110*
    poinsettias, cut *122*
    See care and handling.
Containers *34-36, 162*
    composition of *35-36*
    liners for *36*
    preparation *102*
    styles of *35*
Continental design *5-6*
Corolla tube *55*
Corsages *113-128, 132-136*
    accessories for *134-135*

Corsages *(continued)*
    construction tips *133-134*
    crescent *116-117*
    double flower *114-115*
    double spray *117-118*
    flowers and foliage for *113*
    football mum *126-128*
        accessories for *127-128*
        collars *128*
    glamellia *119-122*
    mechanics for *53-69*
        bow construction *56-59*
        taping *58*
        wiring *54-65*
    nose gay *119*
    over-the-shoulder *118*
    packaging *135-136*
    poinsettia *122-123*
    single flower *114*
    stem finishes *132-133*
    triangular *116*
    triple flower *115*
    wearing *136*
    wrist *124-125*
Crescent arrangement *13, 141*
Cultivar *81-82*

D

Date coding fresh flowers *103*
Depth *7-8*
Dominance *8*
Dried flowers *194-205, 211-213*
    care and handling *197-199*
        humidity *197-198*
    cleaning *198*
    custom designing *211-213*
    designing with *200-205*
        coloring *203*
        combining with fresh flowers *201*
        combining with silk flowers *201*
        mechanics *201-203*
        tips *204-205*
    identification *Appendix B*
    preparing *190-199*

Index

Dried flowers *(continued)*
    types of *194-96*
        air-drying *195*
        dessicant-drying *106*
        freeze-drying *195*
        glycerine *194-195*
Dry storage of fresh flowers *96*
Dye, floral *70-72*
    dip *71-72*
    stem *70-71*

E

Elements of design *11-18*
    color *15-18*
    form *12-14*
    line *11-12*
    texture *14*
Ethylene
    prevention program *97-99*
    reduction treatments *94*
    sensitive flowers *Appendix A*
European mass design *5-6*

F

Family, plant *81*
Feathering flowers *63-64*
Filament *79*
Filler flowers *144*
Finishing sprays and dips *101-102*
    for flowers to wear *135*
Floral sprays *29*
Flower deterioration
    causes of *84*
Flower growth patterns *144-145*
Flower longevity *Appendix A*
Flower needs, basic *82-83*
    failure to meet *83-84*
    meeting *84-85*
Flower storage potential *Appendix A*
Flower structures *79-80*
Foam, floral
    cutting *42-43*
    disguising *53*

Floral foam *(continued)*
    dry *30*
    fresh *30*
        specialty sizes *30*
    securing *43-48*
        in baskets *45-46*
        in clear glass *47-48*
        gluing *44*
        in non-glazed pottery *46-47*
        pinning *44-45*
    taping *43-44*
        soaking *41*
        styrofoam *30-31*
            shredded *31*
Focal area (also focal point, point of interest, Emphasis) *8*
Foil *32*
Form *12-14*
    asymmetrical triangle *13*
    crescent *13*
    Hogarth curve *14*
    oval *14*
    symmetrical triangle *13*
    vertical *13*
Form flowers *144-145*
Fresh flower waste management *163-164*
Frog, floral *31, 143*

G

Gelatin sealer *102*
Genus, plant *81*
Geometric designs *141*
Glue
    See adhesives.
Grids *48-50*
    chicken wire *49*
    lacing greens for *49-50*
    tape *48-49*
Growth regulator treatment *94*

H

Hair flowers *129-132*
    accessories for *134-135*

Index

Hair flowers *(continued)*
    barrette hairpiece *130*
    cluster hairpiece *129*
    construction tips *133-134*
    floral wreaths and headbands *131*
    hair comb hairpiece *130*
    profile hairpieces *131-132*
    single flower headpiece *129*
    wearing *136-137*
Hand-held flowers *125-126*
    miniature nosegay *126*
    single rose *125-126*
Harmony *10*
Hogarth curve *14, 141*
Horizontal arrangement *13-14, 141*
    construction of *155-156*
Hue *15*
Hyacinth stakes *27*
Hydrating solutions *94*

I

Ikebana *5-6*
Intensity, color *16*

J

Japanese Ikebana *5-6*

L

Line *11-12*
    curvilinear *12*
    diagonal *12*
    horizontal *11*
    vertical *11*
    zigzag *12*
Line flowers *144*
Line-mass design *0*
Linnaeus *80*

M

Mass flowers *144*
Monochromatic colors *16*
Morphology, flower *80*

N

Needlepoint holder *143*
Nomenclature *80-82*
    common name *82*
    cultivar *81-82*
    family *81*
    genus *81*
    specific epithet *81*
    variety *81-82*
Nosegay, miniature *126*
Novelties, mechanics for *72-73*
Novelty designs *171-185*
    bird *183-184*
    birthday cake *178-179*
    clown *180-181*
    ice cream soda *177-178*
    kitten *172-174*
    love bug *179-180*
    poodle *174-176*
    rabbit *181-183*
    treasure chest *176-177*

O

Oval *14, 141*
    See pointed oval.
Ovary *79*

P

Packaging
    for protection *100*
        body flowers *100*
        bouquets *100*
        wilt sensitive flowers *100*
    supplies *31-33*
    boxes *33*
    clear bags *32*
    foils *32*
    outer wrap *32*
    plant sleeves *32*
    tissue paper *32*
Paint, floral *29*
    techniques *69-70*
Papier-maché *36*

Index

Perianth *80*
Permanent flowers
    See silk flowers.
    See dried flowers.
Picks *26-27*
    hyacinth stakes *27*
    steel, machines *27*
    wooden *26*
Pin holders *31*
Pins *26*
    bank *26*
    boutonniere *26*
    corsage *26*
    dixon *26*
    greening (also philly pins, fern pins) *26*
Pistil *55-79*
Plush animals
    mechanics for *73-74*
Pointed oval *153*
    construction of *154*
Pre-design considerations *142-143*
Preservatives, floral *29, 91-93*
    benefits *91*
    contents *91*
    mixing for bud opening *92*
    tips for use *92-93*
Preserved flowers
    See dried flowers.
Principles of design *6-11, 142*
    balance *7*
    depth *7-8*
    focal area *8*
    harmony *10*
    proportion *9-10*
    repetition *6-7*
    rhythm *8*
    transition *8-9*
    unity *10-11*
Profitability in design *162-166*
    assembly line *164-166*
    container preparation *162*
    efficiency *164*
    waste management *163-164*
Proportion *9-10*
    color *10*

R

Radiation *6*
Refrigerator containers *29*
Repetition *6*
Rhythm *8*
Ribbon *34*
    uses in body flowers *134-135*
Rose arrangements *157-162*
    construction of *158-162*
        bud vase *161-162*
        free-standing oval *159-160*
        rose bowl *160-161*
        symmetrical triangle *158-159*
    mechanics *157-158*
        chicken wire *157-158*
        floral foam *158*
        grid *158*
        shredded styrofoam *158*
Round mound arrangement *153-154*

S

Sepals *80*
Shade, color *16*
Silk flowers
    care and handling *191-192*
    cleaning *192-193*
    custom designing *211-213*
    designing with *200, 211*
        constructing dish gardens *210-211*
        constructing trees *209-210*
        mechanics *201-211*
            coloring *203*
            cutting foam *51-53*
            securing foam *51-52*
            weighting containers *52-53*
    preparing *193-194*
    restoring *192*
    types of *189-191*
        combining *201*
        hand-wrapped *190*
        molded, plastic stemmed *190*
        paper *190-191*
    wiring for corsages *64-65*

Index

Spathe *80*
Specific epithet *81*
Stamen *55-79*
Stationery *33*
    care tags *33*
    enclosure cards *33*
Stem finishes, body flower *132-133*
    curled *132*
    garden *132*
    ribbon-wrapped *132-133*
Stigma *79*
Storage containers *29*
Storage potential, fresh flower *97*
Style (flower part) *79*
Symmetrical triangle arrangement *13, 141*
    construction of *146-151*
    scoring for *146*

T

Tape *24-25*
    aisle runner *25*
    floral *24-25*
    waterproof *25*
Taping *58-59*
    wired stems *50*
    wireless *58-59*
Texture *14*
Throat, flower *55*
Tint *16*
Tone *16*
Tools *23-24*
    checklist *Appendix A*
    knives *24*
    scissors *24*
    wire cutters *24*
Transition *8-9*
    color *9*

U

Unity *10-11*

V

Value, color *16*
Variety, plant *81-82*

Vertical arrangement *13, 141*
    construction of *155*

W

Western style design *6*
Wilt sensitive flowers *Appendix A*
Wire *25, 54*
    chicken *25*
    florist *25*
    gauges *54*
    paddle *25*
Wiring techniques *54-65*
    hairpin *56*
    hook *56*
    insertion *55-56*
    pierce *55*
    specialty *59-65*
        carnations, feathering *63-64*
        camellia *62*
        cattleya, cymbidium, and japhet orchids *59*
        delicate blossoms *62-63*
            gelatin *63*
            gluing *62-63*
        dendrobium and cypripedium orchids *59-60*
        gardenias *61-62*
        phalaenopsis orchids *60-61*
        silks *64-65*
    stitch *56-57*
    wrap-around (also clutch) *56*
Wreaths *205-207*
    design tips *207*
    mechanics *206-207*
    types *205-205*
Wristlets *124-125, 136*
    attaching *124*
    constructing *124-125*
    wearing *136*

Wiring Chart

Flowers

Flower Type	Wiring Method	Wire Gauge	Comments
Alstroemeria	pierce	26	fragile
Aster	insertion	22-24	weak neck
Astilbe	wrap-around	24	
Bouvardia	wrap-around	26	cotton base recommended
Carnation-mini	pierce	24-26	
-standard	cross-pierce	26	
Cornflower	pierce	26	
Daffodil	pierce	24-26	cotton base recommended
Chrysanthemum-standard	hook	20-22	shatters easily
Pompon	hook or insertion	22-24	
Daisy	hook	24	
Fuji	hook	22	
Delphinium-stem	wrap-around or hairpin	26	except large hybrid varieties
-floret	hook	28	very fragile, wilt-senstive
Freesia-stem	wrap-around	26	
-floret	pierce	26-28	
Gardenia	pierce or specialty	24	fragile; cotton base recommended
Gerbera	hook	24	
Gladiolus floret	cross-pierce	24-26	cotton base recommended
Gypsophila/Baby's Breath	wrap-around or hairpin	26-28	see Lily of the Valley
Heather	wrap-around	24-26	
Hyacinth-stem	wrap-around	22	
-floret	hook	28	
Iris	pierce	24-26	
Liatris	wrap-around	22	cotton base recommended
Lilac	wrap-around	22	
Lily	pierce	24	cotton base recommended
Lily of the Valley	specialty	28	remove pollen from stamen
Nerine Lily-floret	pierce	26-28	
Orchids:			remove pollen from stamen
Cattleya	pierce or specialty	24	
Cymbidium	pierce or specialty	24	
Cypripedium/Paphiopedilum	specialty	24	
Dendrobium-blossom	specialty	26	
-stem	wrap-around	22	
Japhet	pierce or specialty	24	
Phalaenopsis	specialty	26-28	
Ranunculus	hook	26	
Rose-standard	pierce	24-26	fragile
-sweetheart	pierce	24-26	
-spray	wrap-around	26	
Star of Bethlehem-stem	wrap-around	24	
-floret	hook	26-28	
Stephanotis	specialty	26	fragile
Statice	wrap-around or hairpin	24-26	
Tulip	pierce	24-26	
Yarrow	wrap-around	24-26	cotton base recommended
Waxflower	wrap-around	26-28	

Foliage

Foliage	Wiring Method	Wire Gauge	Comments
Bear Grass	wrap-around	24-26	
Camellia	stitch	26	
Eucalyptus	wrap-around	24	
Fern	hairpin	26-28	
Galax	stitch	26	
Italian Ruscus	wrap-around	26	
Ivy	wrap-around or stitch	26-28	

The Color Wheel

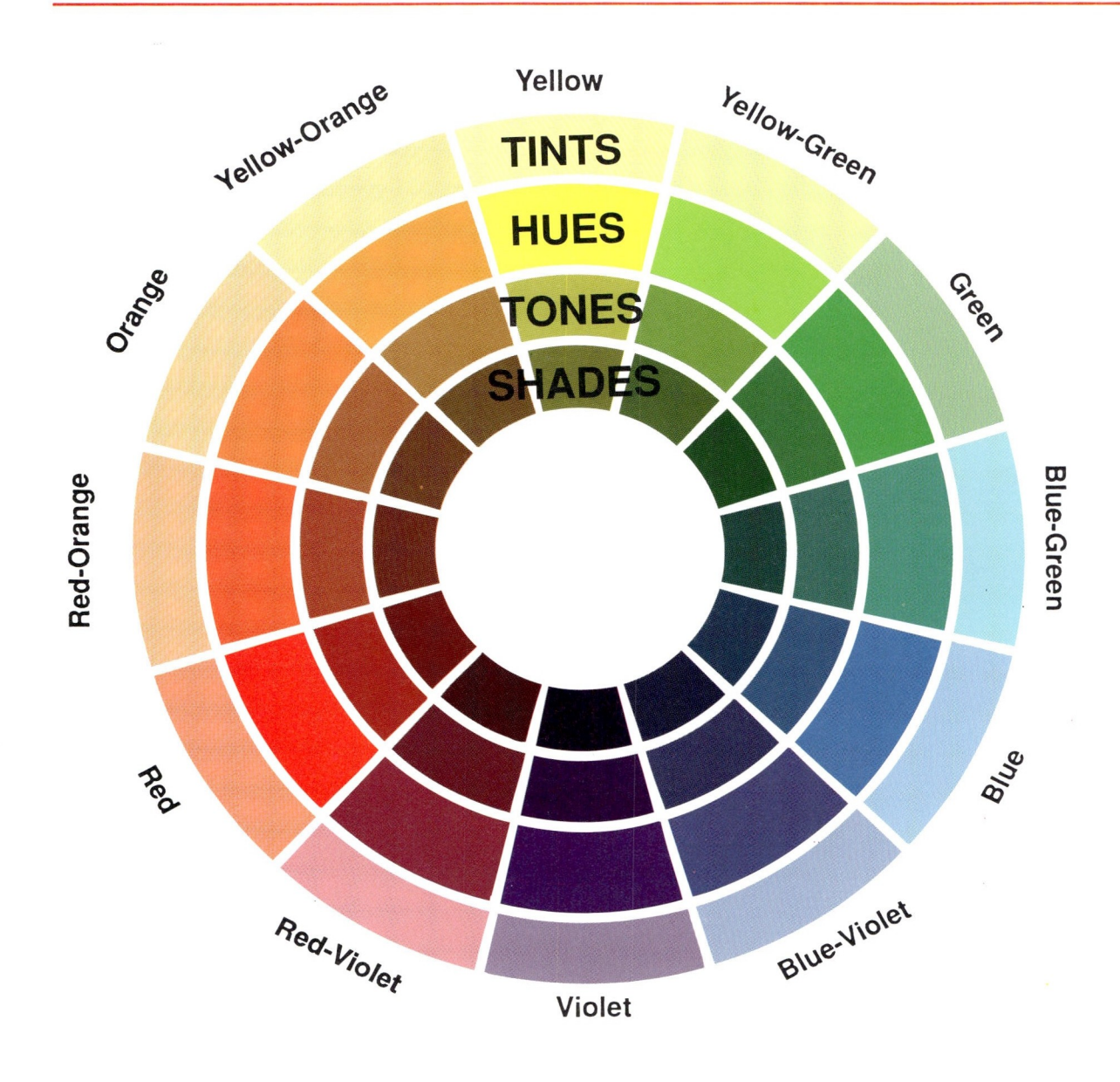

TINTS
HUES
TONES
SHADES

Yellow, Yellow-Green, Green, Blue-Green, Blue, Blue-Violet, Violet, Red-Violet, Red, Red-Orange, Orange, Yellow-Orange

Split-Compliment

Analagous

Mono-Chromatic

Hue - Full intensity of color

Tint - Hue lightened with white

Tone - Hue mixed with gray

Shade - Hue darkened with black

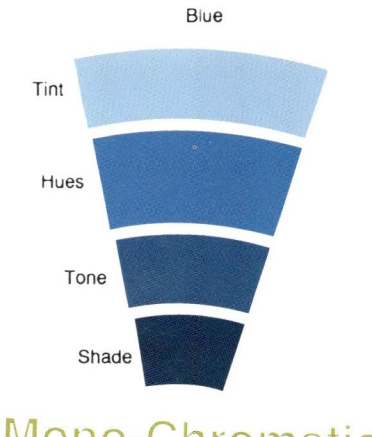

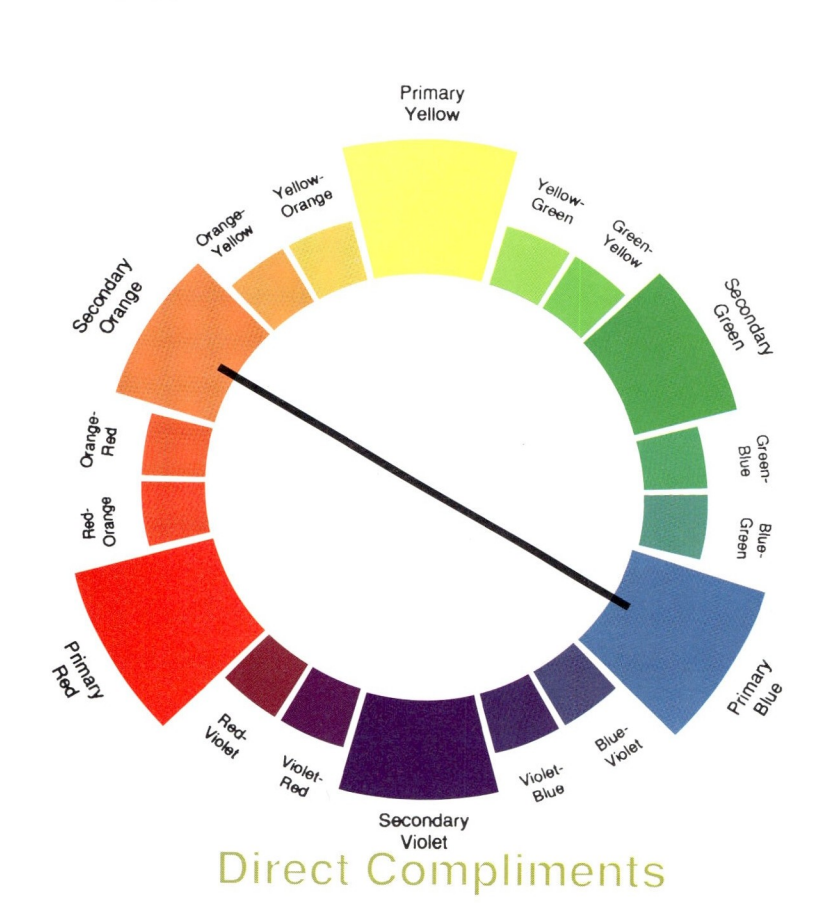

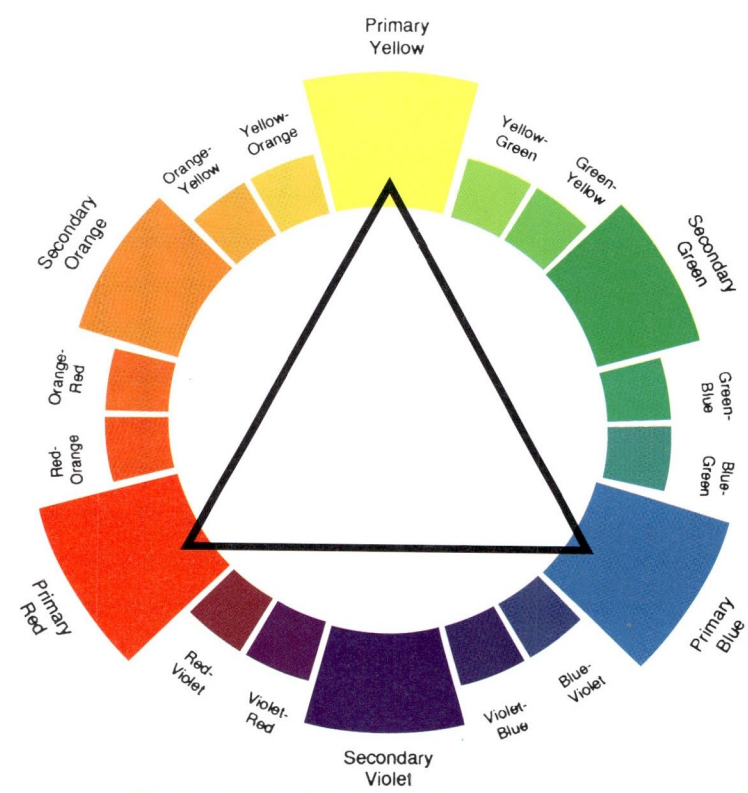

Direct Compliments

Triadic Color Harmony

© 1991 Redbook "Basic Floral Design"